Affirmative Psychotherapy with Bisexual Women and Bisexual Men

Ronald C. Fox, PhD
Editor

Affirmative Psychotherapy with Bisexual Women and Bisexual Men has been co-published simultaneously as *Journal of Bisexuality*, Volume 6, Numbers 1/2 2006.

HPP

Harrington Park Press®
An Imprint of The Haworth Press, Inc.

New York • London • Victoria (AU)
www.HaworthPress.com

Published by

Harrington Park Press®, 10 Alice Street, Binghamton, NY 13904-1580 USA

Harrington Park Press is an imprint of The Haworth Press, Inc., 10 Alice Street, Binghamton, NY 13904-1580 USA

Affirmative Psychotherapy with Bisexual Women and Bisexual Men has been co-published simultaneously as *Journal of Bisexuality*, Volume 6, Numbers 1/2 2006.

The development, preparation, and publication of this work has been undertaken with great care. However, the publisher, employees, editors, and agents of The Haworth Press and all imprints of The Haworth Press, Inc., including The Haworth Medical Press® and Pharmaceutical Products Press®, are not responsible for any errors contained herein or for consequences that may ensue from use of materials or information contained in this work. With regard to case studies, identities and circumstances of individuals discussed herein have been changed to protect confidentiality. Any resemblance to actual persons, living or dead, is entirely coincidental.

The Haworth Press is committed to the dissemination of ideas and information according to the highest standards of intellectual freedom and the free exchange of ideas. Statements made and opinions expressed in this publication do not necessarily reflect the views of the Publisher, Directors, management, or staff of The Haworth Press, Inc., or an endorsement by them.

Cover design by Kerry E. Mack

Library of Congress Cataloging-in-Publication Data

Affirmative psychotherapy with bisexual women and bisexual men / Ronald C. Fox, editor.
     p. cm.
    "Co-published simultaneously as Journal of bisexuality, Volume 6, Numbers 1/2 2006."
    Includes bibliographical references and index.
    ISBN-13: 978-1-56023-298-8 (hard cover : alk. paper)
    ISBN-10: 1-56023-298-6 (hard cover : alk. paper)
    ISBN-13: 978-1-56023-299-5 (soft cover : alk. paper)
    ISBN-10: 1-56023-299-4 (soft cover : alk. paper)
    1. Bisexuals–Mental health. 2. Bisexuals–Counseling of. 3. Psychotherapy. I. Fox, Ronald C. II. Journal of bisexuality.
RC451.4.B57A44 2006
616.89′1408663–dc22
                           2005037033

Indexing, Abstracting & Website/Internet Coverage

This section provides you with a list of major indexing & abstracting services and other tools for bibliographic access. That is to say, each service began covering this periodical during the year noted in the right column. Most Websites which are listed below have indicated that they will either post, disseminate, compile, archive, cite or alert their own Website users with research-based content from this work. (This list is as current as the copyright date of this publication.)

(continued)

- *Ulrich's Periodicals Directory: International Periodicals Information Since 1932 (Bibliographic Access)* <http://www.Bowkerlink.com> 2006

- *zetoc (The British Library)* <http://www.bl.uk/> 2004

Special Bibliographic Notes related to special journal issues (separates) and indexing/abstracting:

- indexing/abstracting services in this list will also cover material in any "separate" that is co-published simultaneously with Haworth's special thematic journal issue or DocuSerial. Indexing/abstracting usually covers material at the article/chapter level.
- monographic co-editions are intended for either non-subscribers or libraries which intend to purchase a second copy for their circulating collections.
- monographic co-editions are reported to all jobbers/wholesalers/approval plans. The source journal is listed as the "series" to assist the prevention of duplicate purchasing in the same manner utilized for books-in-series.
- to facilitate user/access services all indexing/abstracting services are encouraged to utilize the co-indexing entry note indicated at the bottom of the first page of each article/chapter/contribution.
- this is intended to assist a library user of any reference tool (whether print, electronic, online, or CD-ROM) to locate the monographic version if the library has purchased this version but not a subscription to the source journal.
- individual articles/chapters in any Haworth publication are also available through the Haworth Document Delivery Service (HDDS).

Affirmative Psychotherapy with Bisexual Women and Bisexual Men

CONTENTS

About the Contributors

Mary Bradford, PhD, is a clinical psychologist in private practice in Berkeley, California, and is a faculty member of the Pacific Center for Human Growth in Berkeley and the Women's Therapy Center in El Cerrito.

Amity Pierce Buxton, PhD, is a researcher, educator, and author. Her writings include the book *The Other Side of the Closet: The Coming-Out Crisis for Straight Spouses and Families*, as well as the articles "The Best Interest of Children of Gay and Lesbian Parents," in *The Scientific Basis of Child Custody Decisions*, "Writing Our Own Script," in *Bisexuality in the Lives of Men: Facts and Fictions*, "Works in Progress," in *Current Research on Bisexuality*, and "Paths and Pitfalls," in the *Journal of GLBT Family Studies*. Executive Director of the international Straight Spouse Network, she counsels spouses in mixed-orientation marriages and lectures across the country and abroad. She served on the board of the Family Pride Coalition and has led a spouse support group in the San Francisco Bay Area for the past fourteen years.

Julie Ebin, MEd, is the Program Manager for BiHealth and the Safer Sex Education Program at Fenway Community Health in Boston. She received her MEd from Harvard Graduate School of Education's Risk and Prevention program. Julie's educational work and learning include building bisexual cultural competency among providers, bisexual health organizing, issues of sexual communication, and working toward a sexually empowered society.

Nick Embaye, PhD, is a psychiatric crisis clinician, a diversity consultant and, occasionally, a therapist. He is co-chair of the Committee on Transgender Issues and Gender Variance of Division 44 of the American Psychological Association. He works and lives in Massachusetts.

Leo Goetstouwers, Drs, is a psychotherapist in private practice in Amsterdam. He has been active in the Dutch Bi movement for many years. He served as Chair of the Amsterdam BiGroup, in which capacity he organized lectures on bisexuality, social activities, and self-help groups. Leo was also an advisor for the First European Bisexual Conference, held in Rotterdam in 2001. He has appeared on several Dutch television and radio talk shows and has been involved in a documentary film about bisexuality. Leo recently started organising and facilitating coming out workshops for bisexual women and men. He is also currently working at Parnassia Psycho-Medisch Centrum in The Hague.

Bobbi Keppel, MSW, ACSW, LCSW, is a social worker, educator, author, activist, and well-respected elder and mentor in the bisexual community. She frequently provides training for counselors, therapists, and the general public on the topics of sexual orientation, bisexuality and aging, and safer sex for seniors of all identities. She works with the Safer Sex Outreach Educator Program at Fenway Community Health in Boston, MA. Bobbi, with Alan Hamilton, developed the Sexual and Affectional Orientation and Identity Scales (SAOIS) as a model for understanding sexual orientations and identities.

Raymond L. Scott, PhD, is Associate Professor of Psychology at the University of La Verne. He received his PhD in Clinical Psychology in 1996 from the University of Tulsa. His areas of clinical concentration and research interests include diversity and multicultural competence, HIV disease and health disparities, spirituality and psychotherapy, and gender, sexuality and critical theory. He is also a Health Disparities Scholar for the National Institutes of Health. His research areas are published by Columbia University Press and Sage Publications.

Aimee Van Wagenen is a PhD candidate in Sociology at Boston College. In her dissertation, she investigates identity, public health and power in the science and practice of HIV prevention and education. Aimee's research and teaching is particularly inspired by her interest in and passion for contemporary social theory.

Geri Weitzman, PhD, is an openly bisexual and polyamorous psychologist whose practice is based in the San Francisco Bay Area. She provides clinical training on working with bisexual and polyamorous clients to other therapists, and she has presented on this topic at numerous conferences including the 2003 North American Conference on Bisexuality. She is the moderator of the psych-polyamory mailing list (*http://groups.yahoo. com/group/psych-polyamory*), dedicated to the discussion of psychological themes within polyamory. She also maintains the Bisexuality-Aware Professionals Directory (*http://bizone.org/bap/*), which lists therapists and other professionals who are savvy about bi concerns.

ABOUT THE EDITOR

Ronald C. Fox, PhD, is a San Francisco based psychotherapist, researcher, author, and educator. He has provided psychotherapy services to bisexual clients for the past twenty years. He has also presented clinical supervision, in-service trainings, and workshops on working with bisexual clients at professional conferences, graduate schools, and community agencies, as well as at U.S. and international conferences on bisexuality. He conducted the first large-scale study of bisexual identity development and has contributed several chapters on bisexuality and bisexual issues to LGBT psychology books. Ron was the guest editor of a recent special issue of the *Journal of Bisexuality* on current research on bisexuality. He was also a member of the Task Force that wrote the recently adopted American Psychological Association Guidelines for Psychotherapy with LGB Clients. He is Co-Chair of the Committee on Bisexual Issues in Psychology of APA Division 44 (Society for the Psychological Study of LGB Issues).

Affirmative Psychotherapy with Bisexual Women and Bisexual Men: An Introduction

Ronald C. Fox

Available online at http://www.haworthpress.com/web/JB
© 2006 by The Haworth Press, Inc. All rights reserved.
doi:10.1300/J159v06n01_01

Both homosexuality and bisexuality have been the focus of theory, research, and clinical interest throughout the history of psychology. There have been three conceptual shifts in perspective that have resulted in significant changes regarding homosexuality and bisexuality in the field of psychology and in terms of clinical work with lesbian, gay, and bisexual clients (Firestein, 1996; Fox, 1996). These are: (1) the shift from an emphasis on the illness model and etiology to a focus on the lived experiences of lesbian and gay people; (2) the shift from a dichotomous model of sexuality to a multidimensional approach that includes bisexuality as a related but distinct sexual orientation and sexual identity; and (3) the shift in gender and sexuality studies from an exclusive emphasis on lesbian and gay issues to the acknowledgment of the interrelatedness of lesbian, gay, and bisexual issues, and an emerging and ongoing integration of these areas theoretically, as well as in terms of research and approaches to clinical work.

BEYOND THE ILLNESS MODEL: AFFIRMATIVE APPROACHES TO HOMOSEXUALITY

From the 1890s through the early 1970s, the illness model approach toward homosexuality was embedded in psychological theory and psychotherapist training and was therefore broadly reflected in clinical practice (Fox, 1996). Through the lens of the illness model, adult homosexuality and bisexuality were seen as indicative of psychopathology, arrested psycho-sexual development, and dysfunctional relationships in the family of origin. The sexual orientation of the client was seen as problematic, regardless of the client's presenting issues, and therapists often aspired toward exclusive heterosexuality as their treatment goal for gay, lesbian, and bisexual therapy clients. This approach to clinical practice was not universally accepted, however, and the American Psychiatric Association decided in 1973 to eliminate homosexuality as a mental illness and clinical diagnostic category (Bayer, 1981).

In the period of time immediately following this action, gay/lesbian affirmative models of identity development emerged, important research on the lives of lesbians and gay men was published, and clinical approaches to working with this population based on affirmative models and research began to be disseminated through education, training, and the professional organizations in the mental health field (Fox, 1996). During this time period, Blumstein and Schwartz (1976a, 1976b, 1978) published findings from their research on bisexual women and bisexual men. Two books were published that also approached bisexuality from an affirmative perspective: *The Bisexual Option* (Klein, 1978) and *Bisexuality: A Study* (Wolf, 1979). The authors were psychiatrists and experienced clinicians who discussed relevant theoretical issues, presented findings from their research, and addressed common issues faced by both bisexual clients and therapists who work with them.

BEYOND THE DICHOTOMOUS MODEL: MULTIDIMENSIONAL APPROACHES TO SEXUAL ORIENTATION

The general shift in the 1970s within psychology that encouraged the development of affirmative theory and research on homosexuality also encouraged the articulation of affirmative clinical approaches to working with lesbians and gay men. There was not generally a corresponding shift within psychology, however, regarding attitudes toward bisexuality or clinical work with bisexual women and bisexual men (Firestein, 1996; Fox, 1996). This was partly related to the long-standing belief that sexual orientation is dichotomous, an either/or heterosexual/homosexual proposition. This was also due the persistence of negative attitudes specifically regarding bisexual people. Some of these attitudes were historically part of the illness model approach to homosexuality, while others were reformulations of stereotypes about lesbians and gay men. These include: bisexuality does not exist; bisexuals are really heterosexuals with a pathological case of developmental arrest; bisexuals are really lesbians and gay men who are in denial and have not yet come out all the way; bisexuals are promiscuous, untrustworthy, and incapable of normal healthy monogamous relationships; and, more recently, bisexuals are a bridge spreading AIDS to the heterosexual population. To the degree that these stereotypes and attitudes have been embedded historically in psychological theory and therapists' training and practice, providers have not had sufficient access to accurate information on bisexuality and have been at a disadvantage in terms of providing knowledge-based, affirmative mental health services to bisexual clients.

In the 1980s, there was a gradual but important shift in psychology from a polarized view of sexual orientation to a multidimensional model that viewed sexual orientation and sexual identity as a combination of factors along a continuum that for many people may change significantly over time (Coleman, 1987; Klein, Sepekoff & Wolf, 1985;

Shively & De Cecco, 1977; Shively, Jones, & De Cecco, 1983/1984; Storms, 1980). This more accurate and comprehensive approach to sexual orientation and sexual identity acknowledges bisexuality as a sexual orientation and identity. The Klein Sexual Orientation Grid (1985), for example, includes a range of factors that are involved in sexual orientation and sexual identity, including not only sexual attraction and behavior, but also sexual fantasy, emotional preference, social preference, lifestyle, and self-identification, and self-ratings based on past, present, and ideal time frames.

The multidimensional model of sexual orientation also laid the groundwork for the emergence since the 1980s of theory, research, and clinical perspectives that more accurately portray the lives and experiences of bisexual women and bisexual men, and a corresponding gradual shift in attitudes in psychology regarding bisexuality (Firestein, 1996; Fox, 1996). This is reflected not only in terms of theory and research, but also in the emergence of a clinical literature specifically focused on working with bisexual clients (Bradford, 2004; Butt & Guldner, 1993; Deacon, Retake, & Viers, 1996; Dworkin, 1996; 2001; Guidry, 1999; Hayes & Hagedon, 2001; Horowitz & Newcomb, 1999; Lourea, 1985; Markowitz, 1995; 2000; Mascher, 2003; Matteson, 1996; Nichols, 1988; 1994; Oxley & Lucius, 2000; Smiley, 1997; Weasel, 1996; Wolf, 1987a, 1987b, 1992).

BEYOND POLARIZATION: INCLUSIVE APPROACHES TO LESBIAN, GAY, AND BISEXUAL ISSUES IN PSYCHOLOGY

Paralleling the shift from the illness model of homosexuality and bisexuality to an affirmative model, and the shift from a dichotomous model of sexual orientation to a multidimensional perspective, there has been a corresponding shift in theory, research, and clinical writing from an exclusive focus on lesbian and gay issues in to a more inclusive focus on lesbian, gay, *and* bisexual issues (Cabaj & Stein, 1996; D'Augelli & Patterson, 1995; Garnets & Kimmel, 2003; Greene & Croom, 2000; Perez, Debord, & Bieschke, 2000). There is a further shift in process that also acknowledges the interrelatedness of transgender issues in an even more inclusive lesbian, gay, bisexual, and transgender psychology.

This is reflected within professional psychology in several very significant ways. Within the American Psychological Association's Public

Interest Directorate, in 1995, the committee devoted to sexual minority issues expanded its focus to include bisexual issues, becoming the Committee on Lesbian, Gay, and Bisexual Concerns. In 1997, the membership of Division 44 of the American Psychological Association voted overwhelmingly to change its name and expand its mission statement to include bisexual issues, becoming the Society for the Psychological Study of Lesbian, Gay, and Bisexual Issues. The Division created a standing Committee on Bisexual Issues which has been charged with maintaining awareness of and education about bisexual issues within the Division.

Another important event occurred in 2001, when the American Psychological Association voted to approve their *Guidelines for Psychotherapy with Lesbian, Gay, and Bisexual Clients*. This document goes much further than any previous professional organization in its focus on competent clinical practice and training on lesbian, gay, *and* bisexual issues. The Guidelines achieve a significant first in formally acknowledging bisexuality as a valid sexual orientation and in formally taking the position that bisexuality is not a mental illness (American Psychological Association, 2001). It further goes on in a separate section to acknowledge and address the impact that negative stereotypes and attitudes about bisexuality in society and within psychology have had on bisexual women and bisexual men. The Guidelines strongly recommend that therapists proactively learn about bisexual issues and bisexual community resources to be able to provide more competent and effective mental health services to this population. This is in accord with the finding of research conducted by Page (2004) on the psychotherapy experiences of bisexual women and bisexual men. She found that these views of bisexuality do in fact affect bisexual clients in terms of their experiences of both psychotherapy and psychotherapists, with an overwhelming proportion of her research participants advocating for greater therapist knowledge and education about bisexuality and bisexual issues.

AFFIRMATIVE PSYCHOTHERAPY WITH BISEXUAL WOMEN AND BISEXUAL MEN

The contributions to this volume add to the already existing literature that provides therapists with practical tools to provide more culturally competent mental health services to their bisexual clients. The contributors use their extensive experience in working with bisexual women and bisexual men to provide overviews on affirmative psychotherapy with bisexual women and bisexual men, as well as information that is essential to working with bisexual transgender people, African American bisexuals, and older bisexuals. Also included is equally important information on counseling heterosexual spouses of bisexual women and men and bisexual-heterosexual couples, on psychotherapy with clients who are bisexual and polyamorous, and on providing sexual health and support services for bisexuals in the context of a community health center.

Mary Bradford, in "Affirmative Psychotherapy with Bisexual Women," presents an overview of important factors involved in working with bisexual women in psychotherapy. She emphasizes that although the experiences of bisexual women are similar in some ways to those of lesbian and heterosexual women, in fact significant diversity exists among bisexual women. She also discusses the role that the common polarization of sexual orientation has in invalidating the life experiences of bisexual women in their daily lives, and the role that the therapist can take in helping to counter the effects of external and internalized biphobia within the therapeutic relationship. Her model of bisexual identity development and the case examples that she offers provide a deeper understanding of the typical issues that bisexual women bring to therapy and a practical framework for affirmative and effective treatment.

In "Affirmative Psychotherapy with Bisexual Men," Leo Goetstouwers points out that bisexual men experience and understand their sexual orientation in a variety of ways, and that they seek out psychotherapy for many of the same more general psychological reasons that most individuals seek therapy, often having nothing to do with their bisexuality. He also focuses on the issues that bisexual men typically present when they do seek psychotherapy for sexual orientation related reasons, including identity, coming out, disclosure, relationships, and HIV related questions. He discusses the importance of cultural context in the experiences of men who are both bisexual and members of non-dominant racial, ethnic, and cultural groups. He also examines the advantages and disadvantages of a range of therapeutic approaches in working with bisexual men.

Nick Embaye, in "Affirmative Psychotherapy with Bisexual Transgender People," presents an overview of the typical issues that individuals who are both bisexual and transgender bring to psychotherapy. Through case studies and a discussion of the experiences of bisexual transgender individuals, he provides essential information and guidance in working effectively with this population in an affirmative way.

In "Promoting Well-Being: An Ecology of Intervening with African American Bisexual Clients," Raymond Scott provides a comprehensive overview of the contextual issues involved in the experiences of African American bisexual women and men. He emphasizes the impact on the well-being of bisexual individuals of sexism and heterosexism on the part of the dominant culture and from within the African American community. He also provides specific guidance and direction for psychotherapists in working affirmatively with this population.

Bobbi Keppel, in "Affirmative Psychotherapy with Older Bisexual Women and Men," examines typical issues that individuals who are older and bisexual experience in their daily lives and that they are likely to bring to psychotherapy. She points out how traditionally less accepting attitudes about homosexuality have a significantly negative impact on older bisexuals in terms of their access to a range of elder services. She also emphasizes the generally positive effect that therapist awareness and knowledge about bisexuality can have in providing services to this population.

In "Counseling Heterosexual Spouses of Bisexual Men and Women and Bisexual-Heterosexual Couples: Affirmative Approaches," Amity Buxton provides a comprehensive overview of the experiences and issues of heterosexual spouses of bisexual married women and men. She presents a in-depth description of the characteristic stages that couples in bisexual-heterosexual relationships undergo following the bisexual partner's disclosure of sexual orientation. She also provides very helpful guidance for therapists on how to work with this population in an respectful and affirmative way.

Geri Weitzman, in "Therapy with Clients Who Are Bisexual and Polyamorous,'" presents an overview of the typical issues that individuals who are both bisexual and polyamorous bring to therapy. She gives an introduction to polyamory, and uses examples from her own research to provide therapists with specific guidance on working effectively with bisexual polyamorous people.

In "Developing Successful Sexual Health and Support Services for Bisexual People: Lessons learned from the BiHealth Program," Julie Ebin and Aimee Van Wagenen provide an in-depth look at the BiHealth program, located at the Fenway Community Health Clinic in Boston. BiHealth is a unique and effective program that focuses specifically on providing medical and mental health services to bisexual people in a supportive LGBT community context. The program that these authors describe can be seen as a model for offering community based services to bisexual people.

Taken together, the articles in this volume make a significant contribution to our understanding of how mental health service providers can provide affirmative mental health services to bisexual people.

REFERENCES

Auerback, S., & Moser, C. (1987). Groups for the wives of gay and bisexual men. *Social Work, 32*(4), 321-25.

Bayer, R. (1981). *Homosexuality and American psychiatry: The politics of diagnosis.* New York: Basic Books.

Blumstein, P., & Schwartz, P. (1976a). Bisexuality in men. *Urban Life, 5*(3), 339-358.

Blumstein, P. W., & Schwartz, P. (1976b). Bisexuality in women. *Archives of Sexual Behavior, 5*(2), 171-181.

Blumstein, P. W., & Schwartz, P. (1977). Bisexuality: Some social psychological issues. *Journal of Social Issues, 33*(2), 30-45.

Bradford, M. (2004). Bisexual issues in same-sex couples therapy. *Journal of Couple and Relationship Therapy,* 3(3/4), 43-52.

Butt, J. A., & Guldner, C. A. (1993). Counselling bisexuals: Therapists' attitudes towards bisexuality and application in clinical practice. *Canadian Journal of Human Sexuality, 2*(2), 61-70.

Cabaj, R. P., & Stein, T. S. (Eds.). (1996). *Textbook of homosexuality and mental health.* Washington, DC: American Psychiatric Press.

Coleman, E. (1987). Assessment of sexual orientation. *Journal of Homosexuality, 14*(1/2), 9-24.

D'Augelli, A. R., & Patterson, C. J. (Eds.). (1995). *Lesbian, gay, and bisexual identities over the lifespan: Psychological approaches.*

Deacon, S. A., Retake, L., & Viers, D. (1996). Cognitive-behavioral therapy for bisexual couples: Expanding the realms of therapy: *The American Journal of Family Therapy, 24,* 242-258.

Dworkin, S. H. (1996). From personal therapy to professional life: Observations of a Jewish, bisexual lesbian therapist and academic. In N. D. Davis, & E. Cole (Eds.), *Lesbian therapists and their therapy: From both sides of the couch* (pp. 37-46). New York: Harrington Park Press.

Dworkin, S. H. (2001). Treating the bisexual client. *Journal of Clinical Psychology, 57*(5), 671-80.

Firestein, B. A. (1996). Bisexuality as paradigm shift: Transforming our disciplines. In B. A. Firestein (Ed.), *Bisexuality: The psychology & politics of an invisible minority* (pp. 261-291). Thousand Oaks, CA: Sage.

Fox, R. C. (1996). Bisexuality in perspective: A review of theory & research. In B. A. Firestein (Ed.), *Bisexuality: The psychology & politics of an invisible minority* (pp. 3-50). Thousand Oaks, CA: Sage.

Garnets, L. D., & Kimmel, D. C. (Eds.). (2003). *Psychological perspectives on lesbian, gay, and bisexual experiences.* New York: Columbia University Press.

Greene, B., & Croom, G. L. (Eds.). (2000). *Education, research, and practice in lesbian, gay, bisexual, and transgendered psychology: A resource manual.* Thousand Oaks, CA: Sage.

Guidry, L. L. (1999). Clinical intervention with bisexuals: A contextualized understanding. *Professional Psychology: Research and Practice, 30*(1), 22-26.

Hayes, B. G. & Hagedon, W. B. (2001). Working with the bisexual client: How far have we progressed? *Journal of Humanistic Counseling & Development, 40*(1), 11-20.

Horne, S., Shulman, J., & Levitt, H. M. (2003). To pass or not to pass: Exploration of conflict splits for bisexual-identified clients. In J. S. Whitman & C. J. Boyd (Eds.). *The therapist's notebook for lesbian, gay, and bisexual clients* (pp. 32-26). New York: Haworth.

Horowitz, J. L., & Newcomb, M. D. (1999). Bisexuality, not homosexuality: Counseling issues and treatment approaches. *Journal of College Counseling, 2*(2), 148-163.

Klein, F., Sepekoff, B., & Wolf, T. J. (1985). Sexual orientation: A multi-variable dynamic process. *Journal of Homosexuality, 11*(1/2), 35-50.

Lourea, D. (1985). Psycho-social issues related to counseling bisexuals. *Journal of Homosexuality, 11*(1/2), 51-62.

Markowitz, L. M. (1995). Bisexuality: Challenging our either/or thinking. *In the Family: A Magazine for Lesbians, Gays, Bisexuals & Their Relations,* 1(1), 6-11, 23.

Markowitz, L. M. (2000). Therapy with bisexuals: An interview with Ron Fox. *In The Family, 6*(2), 6-9, 21.

Mascher, J. (2003). Overcoming biphobia. In J. S. Whitman & C. J. Boyd (Eds.). (2003). In J. S. Whitman & C. J. Boyd (Eds.). (2003). *The therapist's notebook for lesbian, gay, and bisexual clients* (pp. 78-83). New York: Haworth.

Matteson, D. R. (1987). Counseling bisexual men. In M. Scher (Ed.), *The handbook of counseling and psychotherapy with men* (pp. 232-249). Beverly Hills, CA: Sage.

Matteson, D. R. (1996). Counseling & psychotherapy with bisexual & exploring clients. In B. A. Firestein (Ed.), *Bisexuality: The psychology & politics of an invisible minority* (pp. 185-213). Thousand Oaks, CA: Sage.

Matteson, D. R. (1996). Psychotherapy with bisexual individuals. In R. P. Cabaj & T. S. Stein (Eds.), *Textbook of homosexuality and mental health* (pp. 433-450). Washington, DC: American Psychiatric Press.

Matteson, D. R. (1999). Intimate bisexual couples. In J. Carlson & L. Sperry (Eds.), *The intimate couple* (pp. 439-459). Philadelphia: Brunner/Mazel.

Nichols, M. (1988). Bisexuality in women: Myths, realities, & implications for therapy. In E. Cole & E. Rothblum (Eds.), *Women & sex therapy: Closing the circle* (pp. 235-252). New York: Harrington Park Press.

Nichols, M. (1994). Therapy with bisexual women: Working on the edge of emerging cultural and personal identities. In M. P. Mirkin (Ed.), *Women in context: Toward a feminist reconstruction of psychotherapy* (pp. 149-169). New York: Guilford.

Oxley, E., & Lucius, C. A. (2000). Looking both ways: Bisexuality and therapy. In C. Neal & D. Davies (Eds.), *Issues in therapy with lesbian, gay, bisexual and transgender clients* (pp. 115-127). Buckingham, England, United Kingdom.

Page, E. (2004). Mental health services for bisexual women and bisexual men: An empirical study. *Journal of Bisexuality, 4*(1/2), 137-160.

Perez, R. M., DeBord, K. A., & Bieschke, K. J. (Eds.). (2000). *Handbook of counseling and psychotherapy with lesbian, gay, and bisexual clients*. Washington, DC: American Psychological Association.

Rust, P. C. R. (Ed.). (2000). *Bisexuality in the United States: A Social science reader*. New York: Columbia University Press.

Shively, M. G., & De Cecco, J. P. (1977). Components of sexual identity. *Journal of Homosexuality*, *3*(1), 41-48.

Shively, M. G., Jones, C., & De Cecco, J. P. (1983-1984). Research on sexual orientation: Definitions and methods. *Journal of Homosexuality*, *9*(2/3), 127-136.

Smiley, E. B. (1997). Counseling bisexual clients. *Journal of Mental Health Counseling*, *19*(4), 373-382.

Storms, M. D. (1980). Theories of sexual orientation. *Journal of Personality and Social Psychology*, *38*(5), 783-792.

Weasel, L. H. (1996). Seeing between the lines: Bisexual women & therapy. *Women & Therapy*, *19*(2), 5-16.

Wolf, T. J. (1987). Group counseling for bisexual men. *Journal of Homosexuality*, *14*(1/2), 162-165.

Wolf, T. J. (1987). Group psychotherapy for bisexual men & their wives. *Journal of Homosexuality*, *14*(1/2), 191-199.

Wolf, T. J. (1992). Bisexuality: A counseling perspective. In S. H. Dworkin, & F. J. Gutierrez (Eds.), *Counseling gay men and lesbians: Journey to the end of the rainbow* (pp. 175-187). Alexandria, VA: American Association for Counseling and Development.

Affirmative Psychotherapy with Bisexual Women

Mary Bradford

Available online at http://www.haworthpress.com/web/JB
© 2006 by The Haworth Press, Inc. All rights reserved.
doi:10.1300/J159v06n01_02

SUMMARY. While bisexual women may bring issues to psychotherapy that are similar to those of other women, and they share many common experiences with lesbians, there is also considerable diversity within this population. In addition, bisexual women face special challenges due to the absence of visibility and validation of bisexuality, the social pressure to dichotomize sexual identity, and biphobia. Providing therapy for bisexual women entails assessment of their stage of identity development and awareness of the challenges that may result in distress. Case examples are provided, as well as recommendations for therapists working with bisexual women. *[Article copies available for a fee from The Haworth Document Delivery Service: 1-800-HAWORTH. E-mail address: <docdelivery@haworthpress.com> Website: <http://www.HaworthPress.com> © 2006 by The Haworth Press, Inc. All rights reserved.]*

KEYWORDS. Bisexuality, bisexual women, bisexual identity, sexual identity, biphobia, psychotherapy

Bisexual women have all the common experiences of being women in this culture, and they share many of the experiences of lesbian women, but they also have some unique experiences due to their sexual and relational cross-cultural status. Affirmative psychotherapy for bisexual women relies on an understanding of the impact of these overlapping conditions.

INTRODUCTION

It is difficult to generalize about bisexual women due to the diversity of the population. For many women, being bisexual is not problematic; it is an integrated, accepted part of their identity and lifestyle that has enriched their lives and relationships. For these women, it is likely that their bisexuality will be incidental to the issues they bring to therapy. It may come up only in the mention of the gender of a prior partner that is different from that of a current one.

For some women, the process of forming a bisexual identity is difficult. They may need help sorting out their feelings, experiences, and attractions and making sense of it all, and coming to terms with the personal and social meaning of a bisexual identity.

Some women are in transition from one identity or lifestyle to another. Having lived as lesbian previously and now relating intimately to men, or coming out of a long term marriage to a man and falling in love with a woman for the first time, a woman may be experiencing confusion or anxiety over the shift in her sense of sexual identity. Some women are clear about their bisexual identity but are experiencing problems resulting from homophobic or biphobic reactions and rejection by family, partners, friends, and community, causing loss and grief.

Those women who discover or allow themselves to acknowledge their bisexuality for the first time only after entering into committed monogamous relationships may struggle with the meaning of this experience for themselves and their partners and must consider the consequences of acting on their desires or not. There may be fallout from having had an affair to further complicate the issue. Thus, there are many different ways that issues related to bisexuality can be presented by bisexual women in therapy.

ASSESSING DEVELOPMENTAL STAGE

When bisexuality *is* presented as an issue for a woman in therapy, it is important to begin by assessing her stage of bisexual identity development. A helpful paradigm for conceptualizing the formation of bisexual identity includes questioning reality, inventing identity, maintaining identity, and transforming adversity (Bradford, 2004).

Questioning Reality

A woman may be having her first awareness of dual attractions, questioning the reality of her attractions, and experiencing confusion due to living in a culture that dichotomizes sexuality and allows only two options: straight or lesbian. If so, she will need a safe place to explore her feelings without pressure to fit into a binary system that does not reflect her experience.

Inventing Identity

Having accepted the truth of her capacity for attractions to both sexes, a woman may be questioning the meaning of these attractions and searching for language and models that reflect her experience. If so, she will be faced with inventing an identity for herself that is not mirrored in the culture. A therapist can be most helpful by providing information, resources, access to role models, support, and validation of bisexuality.

Maintaining Identity

A client who has established her identity and found a way of conceptualizing it for herself–a label, or language that fits–may now find herself continually challenged with maintaining that identity, a life-long stage for bisexual people. This is where the trajectory of sexual identity formation differs for bisexual people from that of gay men and lesbian women. A gay or lesbian identity tends to be confirmed with the visible choice of partners, involvement in the gay and lesbian community, and coming out to a wider group of family and friends. A bisexual identity can be less apparent to others the longer one is in a monogamous relationship, does not have the support of a visible bisexual community, and is often denied or ignored by those to whom it is disclosed. Under continual pressure by the dominant dichotomous view of sexual orientation to deny her sexual identity, a bisexual woman is constantly threatened with invisibility and isolation. She will need continued validation and recognition as bisexual, affirmation of the legitimacy and reality of her identity.

These stages of sexual identity development can be complicated by geographical location, the age and developmental stage of life at coming out, and other-minority status. For instance, the degree of visibility of bisexual, lesbian, gay, or queer peers, the availability of support groups, and the level of homophobia and biphobia in a location affect the pace at which a woman traverses the stages of sexual identity development, her choice of language to describe her experience, and the stability of her identity.

An adolescent girl may struggle more with the need for belonging to her peer group, which might propel her to choose a lesbian identity over a bisexual one so as to have a supportive subculture. For young women, especially those of college age, sexual identity may be connected to feminist issues of autonomy and self-determination. They may grapple with anxiety over gender roles and issues of intimacy and differentiation as they are experienced differently in relationships with males and females. Older women who formed their identities in more closeted times may be less comfortable seeking resources, talking about their sexual orientation, and exposing themselves.

Women coming out of long-term marriages to men and having their first relationships with women in middle age may be frightened by the loss of security and heterosexual privilege; they are likely to be having their first experiences of being on the receiving end of homophobia and biphobia. Some women who have already dealt with being marginalized due to race, gender variance, size, or disability, may have acquired a measure of ego strength and self-sufficiency from the experience of being outsiders, while others may be less resilient, more conflicted, and in need of more support for carrying the burden of multiple oppressions.

SPECIAL CHALLENGES

While many of the issues bisexual women bring to psychotherapy are the same as those of any other women–issues of relationship, life transitions, loss and grief, depression, anxiety, trauma–there are special challenges bisexual women face that may become problems for which therapy can be helpful. These challenges include: establishing identity, coming out, coping with biphobic discrimination, forming relationships, and developing community and support.

Identity

Forming a bisexual identity can be problematic due to the pressure of dichotomous thinking, the pathologization of bisexuality, the absence of models, and its general invisibility in the culture. It is difficult to confirm an identity without a visible option, and it is confusing when that identity is denied. Relational theory tells us that the self develops in relationship, by the ways we are reflected by others, as well as the ways we contribute to relationships. When our sense of self is not reflected back to us, when we have to keep our true self out of relationship, we are subject to shame, disconnection, and isolation. The therapy relationship, then, offers an opportunity for relational healing by mirroring the true self.

Coming Out

A woman who discloses her bisexuality may be met with discomfort, confusion, fear, condemnation, invalidation, or outright denial of the existence of bisexuality. Bisexual women are faced with a difficult decision each time they contemplate coming out, having to choose between remaining hidden or risking reactions that require educating others, defending themselves, or suffering rejection. The lack of visible bisexual community makes coming out doubly difficult; people in general have little idea what bisexuality actually means, and bisexual people may see no community into which to come out.

Many women feel relief at first coming out as bisexual. They are glad to be able to put words to their experience and claim their rightful identity. For others, coming out can be full of grief and loss–of the security, privilege, and acceptance that accompany a straight identity; or of lesbian subculture, community, and belonging. Bisexual women struggling with these challenges of disclosure can use the safety of therapy to contemplate decisions about how, when, and to whom to reveal their bisexuality, and to process the feelings that accompany coming out.

Discrimination

The absence of positive images of bisexuality in the culture allows negative stereotypes to flourish. Bisexual people are seen, variously, as oversexed or sexually perverted, promiscuous, irresponsible, confused, undecided, too cowardly to "come all the way out" as gay or lesbian, and carriers of HIV. Bisexual women confront homophobia in the straight community, and, if they are in long term relationships with men, their sexual identity is often ignored or discounted. In the lesbian/gay community they are met with biphobia, and–particularly painful for bisexual women–they may face the hostility of their lesbian sisters for "opting for heterosexual privilege," "sleeping with the enemy," and betraying lesbian solidarity. The therapist can be a valuable ally and support for building self-esteem and developing the personal empowerment needed to withstand such discriminatory blows to one's sense of self.

Relationships

The first relationship issue facing a bisexual woman is when to disclose her bisexuality: in a singles ad? on first acquaintance with a potential date? on the first date? at the time of sexual attraction? before or after becoming sexually involved? when contemplating a long-term commitment? Weighing the risks of early or delayed self-revelation and having to prepare oneself for a potential negative reaction can be stressful.

Once in a relationship, a bisexual woman and her partner need to communicate clearly regarding the woman's own definition of her bisexuality, preferences for monogamy or polyamory, and issues of safer sex. Special issues will arise for the partners of bisexual women, as well, as they are met with stereotypes and myths of bisexuality and the biphobic reactions of others. All of this can be more difficult when there is an absence of observable models for bisexual relationships.

Of course, the issues will be very different in a same-sex relationship than in an other-sex one. Many bisexual women in same-sex relationships are pressured to identify as lesbian–by friends in the lesbian community, by family (who may find "lesbian" more comprehensible and acceptable than "bisexual"), or even by their partners. In same-sex relationships, bisexual women face all the same homophobic responses as lesbians: from rejection, to lack of legal rights, to outright danger. In other-sex relationships they face the lack of validation that accompanies their invisibility as queer, potential absence of affiliation with and support from queer community, and pressure from community, family, or partners to identify as straight.

One of the most difficult challenges for bisexual women in relationships comes when they first discover or acknowledge their bisexuality within the context of a committed relationship, perhaps because of an attraction to someone else. When this occurs, a woman may enter therapy with her relationship in crisis and needing to consider the danger to the relationship if she acts on her desires, and the consequences for her and her partner if she does not. Of course, the threat of sex outside the relationship would present a crisis for any monogamous couple, but the issue of bisexuality complicates the matter. The bisexual woman is confronted with the risk of wounding or losing her partner, or the sacrifice of forgoing the exploration and experience of a vital part of her sexual and relational self.

Community

Finding a support system is important for bisexual women, who often feel relegated to a marginalized status and need affiliation with others with shared experience but have no available bisexual community. Often they are dealing with losses of support of family, friends, or lesbian/gay community. Although sources of support are now available through the Internet, it has been common for bisexual women to have no contact with others like them. If it exists at all, their known bisexual network is small. There are no areas of town, no bookstores, cafes, or bars where they can go and depend on finding bisexuals. So the struggle to form new community for themselves can be a slow and difficult one. Usually, the community they do form is made up of a mix of bisexual, gay, lesbian, and straight people with shared values and openness. It is very helpful for therapists to be able to provide resources in the form of books, Internet sites, and support groups to assist in this process, as well as to be empathic to the particular emotional needs for affiliation of bisexual women and the obstacles in their path.

CASE EXAMPLES

1. A young college student, whose intimate relationships historically were with men, was already in therapy working through childhood wounds when she entered into her first relationship with a woman and assumed a lesbian identity. She joined the campus gay and lesbian student alliance, became active in gay/lesbian politics, and came out to her parents. When that relationship ended after six months, after a period of grieving the breakup, she found herself interested in dating a man again. This threw her into confusion about her sexual identity and anxiety over the potential loss of her recently formed lesbian community. She felt she had no one to talk to outside of therapy, as her family had reacted with homophobia, and her friends were invested in her lesbian identity. She did not at first have a concept of bisexuality as an option and, on being introduced to the idea, rejected it out of identification with negative stereotypes associated with it and fear of the invisibility and invalidation it portended.

Therapy provided her with the safety, acceptance, and permission to explore the personal, social, and political meanings of her attractions and choices in relationships without pressure to conform to any rigid definitions of gender or sexuality. In time, she moved from trying to fit a dichotomous model that did not reflect her experience, to accepting a more flexible view of her sexuality and adopting language ("queer") that suited her. Though resentful of having to assert her rights and educate others at a time when she felt vulnerable, she was able, gradually, to find allies and friends who supported her.

2. A 36-year-old woman who had identified as bisexual since her early 20s was married to a man and had two children. She came into therapy after falling in love with a woman with whom she worked. She felt pulled between her love for her husband and wish to maintain her family, on the one hand, and her desire to follow her attraction to the

woman on the other. She stated that the two relationships stimulated and satisfied different parts of her and that she did not want to have to choose between them, but neither did she wish to cause either person pain. She spent her time in therapy looking at her own unmet needs, exploring her feelings for all those she cared about, and considering her options and choices. She was in the turmoil that anyone might be who loves two people, who feels guilt and is faced with difficult choices and potential loss. But there was the additional factor of sexual identity in her case and the questions it raised for her and for her partners.

Therapy for this woman involved couple work with her husband, allowing them both to express their feelings, empathize with each other's positions, and adjust to the shift that had occurred in their relationship with the emergence of her same-sex desires. They were able to reinforce the closeness of their bond and their mutual commitment, and then explore the possibility of restructuring their relationship to allow for a trial of polyamory. While some women in this position decide to recommit to monogamy with their husbands and forgo sexual intimacy with a woman, and some leave their families for a female lover, this client and her husband chose to open their relationship and embark on a journey of responsible nonmonogamy, which then included the involvement of the other woman in the therapy. The therapy entailed ongoing negotiations typical of structuring a polyamorous relationship, addressing such issues as jealousy, trust, limits, management of time, and safer sex.

3. A woman in her 50s had come out as lesbian in college, had lived in a women's community for several years, and was then in a long-term monogamous relationship with a woman. She sought the support of a therapist for help with the depression that she experienced when that relationship ended. Working through that life transition, she adjusted to being single, became involved in GLBT political activism, and began casually dating women again. She had reduced her therapy sessions to bi-monthly, with the intent of gradually terminating, when she was surprised to find herself strongly attracted to a man she met volunteering in a hospice program. She entered into a sexual adventure (her first with a man) that soon advanced to deep intimacy.

Her involvement in this relationship presented a challenge. She experienced sorrow over the loss of her long-held lesbian identity that had sustained her in her formative years. She felt guilt at finding herself the recipient of heterosexual privilege and shock over the condemnation by her lesbian friends, which hurt her deeply. She felt cut off from her roots and shared values at the same time as she was entering an unfamiliar culture which she had previously rejected. Her therapy was revived as a place in which to sort through her reactions, recount and integrate her history, and grieve her loss. It was also a safe and accepting place to savor and appreciate all the discoveries of her new relationship. She was able to formulate an identity for herself as a bisexual woman, still affiliated with queer community, but traversing the divide between the dominant culture and the lesbian/gay subculture as a bi-cultural person.

RECOMMENDATIONS FOR THERAPISTS

There are a few important considerations that I think are helpful for therapists to hold in mind when working with bisexual women.

Acknowledge Our Own Homophobia and Biphobia

Like racism and sexism, homophobia and biphobia are endemic in our culture, and we have all absorbed them in some ways. It is essential that we do our own work and examine our own fears, prejudices, and stereotypes before working with this or any oppressed population. The more comfortable, open, and humble we are with these issues, the more helpful we can be for others.

Make No Assumptions About Sexual Identity

In other words, do not assume that you know a person's sexual identity by the gender of her partner, her appearance, or her history in relationships. Such assumptions are silencing and marginalizing and serve to further the invisibility of bisexuality and bisexual people. Instead, ask how a person identifies and allow her to define herself. It is important, as well, not to make assumptions about a client's definition of bisexuality, but to ask what it means for her. There is healing in the acknowledgement, reflection, and affirmation of one's experience.

Recognize That the Problems Are Culturally Conferred

There is no inherent problem in being bisexual (or lesbian or gay). The problems arise from homophobia and biphobia, from prejudice and discrimination. There are, indeed, effects when the self is devalued or hidden, including internal conflicts and negative coping strategies. But these effects are not indications of inherent pathology; they are expected outcomes of social intolerance and isolation. By always holding in mind the social context for our clients, we give them perspective that can be liberating and empowering, and help them counteract the psychological effects of oppression.

Take an Affirmative Approach

By taking an affirmative approach to bisexuality, the therapist can counteract the shame and isolation that result from marginalization. It is important to recognize that resiliency develops from overcoming obstacles. Value the strength, courage, and endurance necessary for the journey to bisexual identity, and acknowledge the enrichment gained from variety of experience.

Be Familiar with Resources

Locate books, films, support groups, and bisexual resources where clients can find information, models, and support for themselves and their partners. Since much of what is challenging for bisexual women is culturally or community conferred, psychotherapy alone may not meet all their needs. The problems of isolation and alienation call for community support.

CONCLUSION

Because bisexual women have issues that overlap with other people, it is easy to underestimate the uniqueness of this population. For some women, their bisexuality is not a primary reason for entering psychotherapy, while for others, concerns regarding their sexual orientation and identity are more central to why they are seeking out the support and understanding of a psychotherapist. Having an awareness and sensitivity to the potential complexity of the challenges that bisexual women clients may face allows the therapist to address needs that may not be met elsewhere and makes working with this population rewarding.

REFERENCES

Bradford, M. (2004). The bisexual experience: Living in a dichotomous culture. *Journal of Bisexuality*, *4*(1/2), 7-23.

RESOURCES

Bisexual Anthology Collective (Ed.). (1995). *Plural desires: Writing bisexual women's realities*. Toronto: Sister Vision Press.

Bradford, M. (2004). Bisexual issues in same-sex couples therapy. *Journal of Couple and Relationship Therapy*, *3*(3/4), 43-52.

Dworkin, S. H. (2001). Treating the bisexual client. *Journal of Clinical Psychology*, *57*(5), 671-680.

George, S. (1993). *Women and bisexuality*. London: Scarlet Press.

Gregory, D. (1983). From where I stand: A case for feminist bisexuality. In S. Cartlege & J. Ryan (Eds.), *Sex and love: New thoughts on old contradictions* (pp. 141-156). London: The Women's Press.

Hutchins, L., & Kaahumanu, L. (Eds.). (1991). *Bi any other name: Bisexual people speak out*. Boston: Alyson Publications.

Ochs, R. (Ed.). (2001). *Bisexual resource guide* (4th ed.). Cambridge, MA: Bisexual Resource Center.

Orndorff, K. (Ed.). (1999). *Bi lives: Bisexual women tell their stories*. Tucson, AZ: Sharp Press.

Rust, P. C. (1995). *Bisexuality and the challenge to lesbian politics: Sex, loyalty, and revolution*. New York: New York University Press.

Shuster, R. (1997). Sexuality as a continuum: The bisexual identity. In Boston Lesbian Psychologies Collective (Eds.), *Lesbian psychologies: Exploration and challenges* (pp. 56-71). Urbana, IL: University of Illinois Press.

Weasel, L. H. (1996). Seeing between the lines: Bisexual women & therapy. *Women & Therapy*, *19*(2), 5-16.

Weise, E. R. (Ed.). (1992). *Closer to home: Bisexuality and feminism*. Seattle, WA: Seal Press.

Whitman, J. S., & Boyd, C. J. (2003). *The therapist's notebook for lesbian, gay, and bisexual clients: Homework, handouts, and activities for use in psychotherapy*. New York: Haworth Press.

Affirmative
Psychotherapy
with Bisexual Men

Leo Goetstouwers

Available online at http://www.haworthpress.com/web/JB
© 2006 by The Haworth Press, Inc. All rights reserved.
doi:10.1300/J159v06n01_03

[Haworth co-indexing entry note]: "Affirmative Psychotherapy with Bisexual Men." Goetstouwers, Leo. Co-published simultaneously in *Journal of Bisexuality* (Harrington Park Press, an imprint of The Haworth Press, Inc.) Vol. 6, No. 1/2, 2006, pp. 27-49; and: *Affirmative Psychotherapy with Bisexual Women and Bisexual Men* (ed: Ronald C. Fox) Harrington Park Press, an imprint of The Haworth Press, Inc., 2006, pp. 27-49. Single or multiple copies of this article are available for a fee from The Haworth Document Delivery Service [1-800-HAWORTH, 9:00 a.m. - 5:00 p.m. (EST). E-mail address: docdelivery@haworthpress.com].

SUMMARY. This article describes the range of issues that are of concern to bisexual men seeking psychotherapy. In addressing these issues with bisexual clients, the therapist is well advised to recognize the diversity that exists within this population regarding the pathways that individuals take in the course of acknowledging and coming to terms with their sexual orientation. It is important for the therapist to recognize that for most bisexual clients, the presenting issues are those that are common to most psychotherapy clients, such as anxiety, depression, stress, and relationship issues. For others, however, there are questions about sexual identity, coming out bisexual, and the implications of their sexual attractions to both women and men. An individual may have concerns regarding whether or not to disclose his sexual orientation at the start of a new relationship, or regarding realizing for the first time that he has bisexual feelings within an already established same-sex or other-sex relationship or marriage. There may also be questions and concerns regarding HIV/AIDS. In these situations, the personal impact of living in a social context in which sexuality is thought of in dichotomous either/or terms will be a realistic concern. Current trends in the research and clinical literature regarding bisexual men will also be discussed. The variety of manifestations of bisexuality across racial, ethnic, and cultural groups will be examined, including the challenges that this may pose for clients and therapists who identify with dominant definitions of sexuality within their respective social communities. Finally, the practical value and shortcomings of the main therapeutic schools will be examined in terms of providing bisexual men with effective and affirmative psychotherapy. *[Article copies available for a fee from The Haworth Document Delivery Service: 1-800-HAWORTH. E-mail address: <docdelivery@haworthpress. com> Website: <http://www.HaworthPress.com> © 2006 by The Haworth Press, Inc. All rights reserved.]*

KEYWORDS. Bisexuality, bisexual men, bisexual identity, sexual identity, biphobia, psychotherapy, relationships, cultural diversity

Bisexuality has been viewed in many ways in psychological theory and by psychotherapists (Angelides, 2001; Dworkin, 2001; Firestein, 1996; Fox, 1996; Klein, 1993); Matteson, 1996; Paul, 1984, 1996; Wolff, 1992; Zinik, 1985). Empirical research has also found wide variation in how bisexuality is conceptualized and experienced (Fox, 1996; Klein, Sepekoff, & Wolf, 1985; MacDonald, 1982; Rust, 1996d, 2002a,

2002b; Weinberg, Williams, & Pryor, 1998). Similarly, bisexual individuals experience their own sexual orientation in a multitude of ways as well (Bradford, 2004b; Hansson, 1990; Hutchins & Kaahumanu, 1991; Ochs & Rowley, 2005; Off-Pink Collective, 1988; Rose, Stevens, & The Off-Pink Collective, 1996).

There are several typical issues that bisexual men may bring to therapy related to their sexual orientation, including: identity; coming out to self and others; relationships; sexuality; and issues of cultural diversity. In addition to client issues, there are also issues that may arise for therapists in working with bisexual clients, which often have their sources in stereotypes about bisexuality from psychological theory and from the individual experience of the therapist.

WHAT IS BISEXUALITY?

The question of how to define bisexuality is important not only in terms of theory and research, and in terms of the experiences of individual bisexual people, but also in terms of the way psychotherapists view and work with clients. Historically speaking, one of the difficulties in conceptualizing bisexuality has come from viewing sexual orientation in dichotomous terms (Angelides, 2001; Fox, 1996, Rust 2002a). While Kinsey and his associates (Kinsey, Pomeroy, & Martin, 1948; Kinsey, Pomeroy, Martin, & Gebhard, 1952). viewed sexuality non-dichotomously along a continuum, Klein, Sepekoff, and Wolf (1985) took this approach further, viewing sexual orientation as multidimensional, including not only sexual attraction and sexual behaviour, but sexual fantasies, emotional preference, social preference, lifestyle and self-identification as well. The Klein Sexual Orientation Grid (KSOG) also takes past, present and ideal aspects of these dimensions into consideration. This approach makes for a much more detailed and accurate picture of sexual orientation and sexual identity, which is very helpful for the therapist working with clients for whom sexual orientation and identity are potential issues in psychotherapy.

There is a wide range of how bisexual people experience the many aspects of sexuality that make up a multidimensional view of orientation. For some bisexual men, the presence of same- and other-sex feelings is experienced as conflictual, while for others it is not. This is important for both client and therapist, because if either or both are seeing sexual orientation from a dichotomous perspective, this will complicate the exploration of the client's sexuality in a neutral and affirmative way.

There is also the question of self-identification and sexual behaviour. One individual might experience both same- and other-sex attractions and behaviour, but may or may not self-identify as bisexual. Another individual might identify as bisexual, and yet only have sex with persons of the same sex or only with persons of the other sex. That is, bisexual men are not necessarily in relationships with both men and women concurrently. Furthermore, some bisexuals may see their sexual orientation in terms of their love for the person with whom they are involved, regardless of whether that person is a man or a woman. For these individuals, it is not that the biological sex is not important, but rather that the biological sex of their partners is only one of the factors involved in the choice of the particular person with whom they are in relationship (Coleman, 1987, 1998; Ross & Paul, 1992).

COMING-OUT BISEXUAL AND BISEXUAL IDENTITY

Several theories have been developed describing the coming out process for lesbians and gay men (Cass, 1979; Coleman, 1987). There are also theories describing the coming out process for bisexual women and bisexual men (Bradford, 2004b; Weinberg et al., 1998). Although stage theories describe typical experiences that most people have during the process of coming to terms with their sexual orientation, research has shown that coming out is not a linear process for most people, whether lesbian, gay, or bisexual (Cass, 1984; Fassinger & Miller, 1996; McCarn & Fassinger, 1996; Reynolds & Hanjorgiris, 2000; Rust, 1996a, 1996d, 2002a). Nevertheless, the stages described in these theories do point to the issues that people in the process of coming out have to face, and therefore being acquainted with the stages and issues particular to coming out bisexual is relevant for therapists working with bisexual clients.

The coming out model developed by Bradford (2004b) characterizes the coming out experiences of most bisexual people and includes four stages: *questioning reality; inventing identity; maintaining identity;* and *transforming adversity* (pp. 19-20). This model begins where most bisexual people begin when becoming aware of their same- and other sex attractions: *questioning reality.* The individual has the feeling that he doesn't seem to fit in the social environment in which he lives. This can lead to feelings of doubt about his own experience of attractions to both men and women. This, in turn, can lead to feelings of alienation and difficulty in experiencing himself as a whole person.

While some bisexual men are able to validate their bisexuality for themselves, many have considerable difficulty due to social norms against which there may seem no room for attractions to both women and men (Eliason, 2001; Herek, 2002; Israel & Mohr, 2004; Mohr & Rochlen, 1999; Mulick & Wright, 2002). Individuals who come into therapy at this point in the coming out process often feel isolated from friends, family, and their community (Bradford, 2004b). They may also have had the experience of not really feeling understood by a health care professional with whom they may have already consulted (Page, 2004). It is not unusual for individuals to present for therapy with of range of possible conditions that are either preexisting or a reaction to the experience of the coming out process, e.g., anxiety, depression, chronic stress, psychosomatic reactions, or substance abuse (Dworkin, 2000).

With support and validation, however, the experience of the coming out process can lead through an internal search for meaning and what Bradford (2004b) calls *inventing identity* (p. 19). The therapist needs to be aware that however positive the experience of support may be in the therapeutic relationship, there is often the parallel lack of everyday external acknowledgment and validation. For some bisexual men, this lack of external validation leads to the dilemma of whether or not to disclose their sexual orientation to others. For many men, their bisexuality may first become evident to others when they end an existing relationship and become involved with a person of another gender. This can be just as true for men who move from a same-sex relationship to a heterosexual relationship as for those who move from a relationship with a woman to a relationship with a man. For example, bisexual men who have been gay identified may first become aware of their bisexuality when they begin a relationship with a person of the other sex. They may also have mixed feelings about disclosing their bisexuality and may experience negative reactions or loss of gay friends and community when they reveal their attractions to women or begin a heterosexual relationship.

For the individual who has come to terms with his bisexuality, there is the additional task of what Bradford (2004b) calls *maintaining identity* (p. 19). The individual needs other accepting and validating individuals in his life to counter considering some of the non-validating and disempowering reactions that are common experiences for most bisexual people. For some bisexual men, this means primarily friends, partners, and family members, while for others, especially those in non-urban areas where bisexual community groups may not be available, this may be via the Internet. Websites with listings for bisexual resources, mailing lists, chatrooms, and conferences on bisexuality all offer the possibility for the individual bisexual man to participate in an affirmative community on a local, regional, national, and international scale. Those individuals who do become involved with other bisexual women and men can involve themselves in what Bradford (2004b) calls *transforming adversity* by creating community, taking social action, and becoming leaders and role models for others (p. 20).

BISEXUALITY AND RELATIONSHIPS

There are several issues that may arise in therapy for bisexual men who are in a relationship. An individual may have a conflict or mix of thoughts and feelings about his bisexuality, about disclosing his sexual orientation to his partner, about discussing his bisexuality with his partner, and about the potential consequences for the relationship. There may also be issues related to monogamy and non-monogamy, risk for HIV/AIDS and other STDs, or the experience of being both bisexual and a member of a racial, ethnic, or cultural minority.

Self-Disclosure of Sexual Orientation in Bisexual Men's Relationships

Some bisexual men are aware of their attractions to both women and men prior to the start of a particular relationship, while others only become aware of their bisexuality during the course of a relationship. Some individuals make their partners aware of their bisexuality at the start of the relationship, while others do not. For bisexual men in relationships where their partner is aware and supportive of their sexual orientation, bisexuality may not be an issue for which they have come to therapy. For those men who reveal their bisexuality to their partner during the course of a relationship, however, this disclosure may lead to a crisis in the relationship. This crisis may be about the bisexual individual's sexual orientation, but may well be focused on the shock experienced by a non-bisexual partner who realizes that he or she is in a relationship with someone who kept an important part of himself hidden. As Buxton (1994) points out, for example, a wife in a traditional heterosexual marriage, in reaction to the revelation of her husband's bisexuality, may feel betrayed, yet also feel a strong need to keep her family together, especially if children are involved. She may not, and therefore focus on her own feelings about what is ahead of her if she decides to stay with her husband.

Renegotiating of the Status of the Relationship

When partners decide to stay together, they have to discuss and renegotiate the terms of their relationship. As research on relationships in which one partner is bisexual confirms, there are several issues that are key to the success of the process that partners have to go through (Buxton, 1994, 2001, 2004; Coleman, 1985; Edser & Shea, 2002; McLean, 2004; Wolf, 1985). First, there needs to be a desire on the part of both partners to maintain the relationship. This presupposes an attitude towards the relationship in which there is a willingness to look beyond the borders of romanticism. Second, open communication is also important, so that there is a place in the relationship for whatever there is that has to be said by both partners in order for the relationship to work. Here, the therapist can help either or both of the partners to find a constructive and satisfying way to talk with each other, including about feelings of discomfort, insecurity, and pain that are involved in being open about all facets of the relationship.

Sexuality and the Structure of the Relationship

Individuals differ in terms of needs and desires, flexibility about sexual expression, and factors such as personality, cultural norms and values, religion, and age (Rust, 1996c, 2000b; Weinberg, Williams, & Pryor, 2001). The therapist can facilitate the partners finding a mutually agreed upon way to discuss and address this issue (Bradford, 2004a; Matteson, 1996). This may mean that the couple may decide to put having sex on hold for a period of time, or there may be an agreement to continue having a sexual relationship. Some couples may agree to having sex only if the bisexual partner commits to monogamy, while others may agree to having sex only if a third party is involved, or, if the couple is living together, only if the bisexual partner has sexual experiences outside the house, via the phone or the Internet, or on special occasions. Other couples may decide to open the relationship to other sexual experiences or relationships for both partners. In general, some form of physical intimacy is necessary for both individuals to remain in the relationship (Coleman, 1981/1982).

Mutual Support During the Coming Out Process

An additional issue is the willingness of both to support each other during the coming out process. That is, it is important to realize that both partners are undergoing a transformative process in different ways.

While the bisexual partner experiences the issues described in the coming out model articulated by Bradford (2004a, 2004b), the non-bisexual partner goes through a process described by Buxton (1994, 2001, 2004). The bisexual partner has to be able and willing to invest emotionally and in time in the process of his partner, realizing he or she has an arrear in development of thoughts, feelings and wishes to the subject of bisexuality. Both partners need to adapt to each other with mutual respect and flexibility. The same can be said about children and members of extended families. Questions about timing of disclosures of the bisexual partner's sexual orientation and potential reactions will need to be explored.

The experienced psychotherapist will recognize that the process of working through relationship issues and renegotiation of aspects of a relationship is not exclusively a bisexual issue. It is an essential part of being partners in a changing and growing relationship. The impact on a relationship is more complicated if issues such as non-monogamy enter in to a formerly monogamous relationship, since the typical structure of a relationship is defined in terms of a particular social and cultural environment in which there are strong conventions about matters such as sexual freedom (Queen, 1996). For couples who reconfigure their relationship, this can lead to an additional "coming out" process as individuals who are non-monogamous or polyamorous. There may well be feelings of isolation and estrangement that are familiar from the process of coming out bisexual regarding others who formerly were seen as friends or intimates, but who the couple no longer regards as appropriate or safe to talk with about matters of sexual behaviour and non-monogamy. In this regard, Rust (1996c) points out that people who enter an open relationship do not have a cultural model to fall back on. Therefore, they have to explicitly discuss and set with each other the rules for starting or having secondary relationships. Since in most cases, partners have to rely on each other in this, the outcome can feel very rewarding and can lead to the experience of a deeply felt positive interpersonal bond.

BISEXUAL MEN AND HIV/AIDS

Bisexual men have been regarded by many epidemiologists and HIV/AIDS researchers as a group that is at risk for HIV infection (Chu, Peterman, Doll, Buehler, & Curran, 1992; Doll, Myers, Kennedy, & Allman, 1997; Ekstrand et al., 1994; Leaver, Allman, Myers, &

Veugelers, 2004; Stokes, McKirnan, Doll, & Burzette, 1996). That is, bisexual men who have sex with men who are HIV positive may be involved in the transmission of HIV/AIDS to the heterosexual population through women with whom they may also be having sex. Ekstrand et al. (1994), for example, cite U.S. national surveillance data which indicated that among men in the United States who had been diagnosed with AIDS at that time, ". . . at least 14% were behaviorally bisexual." (p. 915) The data further indicated that " . . . nearly one quarter of bisexual men with AIDS who died were married at the time" (Ekstrand et al., 1994, p. 915). Doll et al. (1997) cite similar statistics: "Through December 1996, 76,075 men with a history of bisexual behavior since 1977 had been reported with AIDS to the Centers for Disease Control and Prevention (CDC). This figure represents 21% of the cumulative total of AIDS cases in men who have reported sex with men" (p. 120). Other research, however, indicates that there is no simple one to one relationship between the sexual behaviour of bisexual men and spreading of HIV/AIDS to other sexual orientation groups (Stokes, McKirnan, & Burzette, 1993). For example, Stokes et al. (1993) found that although most bisexually active men in their research did not disclose their same-sex behaviour to most people in their surroundings, including their female partners, the participants in their study reported being careful not to expose their female partners to unsafe sex.

Worth (2003) points out that it is overly simplistic to look only at the sexual behaviour of bisexual men when there appear to be other equally important factors that codetermine the spread of HIV/AIDS to women. She relies on social, epidemiological and virological evidence to make her argument by saying that. ". . . the rate of new HIV diagnoses amongst men who have sex with men is now in decline in some countries . . . worldwide, the numbers of women with HIV are rapidly increasing" (Worth, 2003, pp. 73-74). She further indicates that "Now the source of 40% of the new HIV diagnoses is sex between men and women. In the United States, HIV is now primarily transmitted through drug use and sex between men and women" (Worth, 2003, p. 83). She also argues against the assumption that "HIV is equally transmitted by vaginal or anal sex, and that different subtypes of the virus do not have different infectivity, means the explanation for infection is solely behavioral or environmental" (Worth, 2003, p. 83). Therapists should be careful about making any assumptions about bisexual men as a risk group just because of the sexual activity they may be having, since it is more a matter of whether it is safe or unsafe sex and what the motivations are for each.

Chu et al. (1992), McKirnan, Stokes, Doll, and Burzette (1995), and Matteson (1997) point to issues such as cultural differences, the role of religion, and the social stigma attached to bisexual behaviour as important factors to take into consideration while interpreting research findings on the relationship between bisexual behaviour and HIV/AIDS. Furthermore, the existence of contradictory research findings and the many possible factors involved in HIV transmission suggest how important it is for the psychotherapist working with bisexual men to take the initiative in being educated and aware about both HIV/AIDS and the diversity that exists within bisexual men as a group. This also points to the need for the therapist to be able to provide bisexual male clients with current and accurate information about HIV/AIDS. This is especially important since many bisexual men see themselves and their sexual behaviour and relationships in ways that are not addressed by HIV/AIDS researchers or by outreach and prevention workers who may be thinking either in terms of identity, i.e., gay men, or in terms of "men who have sex with men (MSM)." Many men do not regard themselves as either gay or bisexual, or do not use sexual identity as a way of thinking about their sexual behaviour. It becomes essential for the therapist to be able to think about and address his client using terms that fit the internal experience of the bisexual client.

McKirnan et al. (1995) and Israel and Mohr (2004) point to the importance of recognizing and lessening the stigma which is related to bisexuality. The therapist may be in the position of being a rational supportive person in a world where, in terms of general attitudes, many bisexual men have the feeling that everyone is against them, particularly in regard to general attitudes regarding HIV/AIDS and bisexuality. The therapist can also serve to support and promote the client's experience of self-respect and self-validation. This can help the individual bisexual male client to consider, where available, accessing a community of other bisexuals, where he may find a supportive source of information, education and prevention materials focused specifically on bisexuals and HIV/AIDS.

BISEXUALITY AND CULTURAL DIVERSITY

Within the population of individuals with same-sex attractions, behaviour, and relationships, there is significant diversity in terms of race, culture, and ethnicity (Bohan, 1996; Fukuyama & Ferguson, 2000; Manalansan, 1996; Stokes, Miller & Mundhenk, 1998). As Rust

(1996b) points out, Western bisexual, gay, and lesbian communities in the United States are predominantly European-American. This same phenomenon may well be true in other Western countries. This leads to the experience for many individuals of being a member of multiple minorities, i.e., being a racial, cultural, or ethnic minority and being a sexual minority. Even more complex is the experience of being bisexual, and therefore being a triple minority.

Working with bisexual men of colour can be a challenge to the therapist in terms of having an understanding of the mechanisms of prejudice and discrimination experienced by racial, cultural, and ethnic minority men in general, and the status of bisexuality and homosexuality in different cultures and sub-cultures as well. For example, there is a range of ways that individuals experience belonging to more than one group and therefore having multiple group identifications and allegiances (Collins, 2004; Dworkin, 2002; Fukuyama & Ferguson, 2000; Rust, 1996b). While some bisexual men may see their membership in multiple groups as a source of strength and pride, others may experience this as a source of conflict and pain. They may feel caught in another either/or situation and significant difficulty coming to terms with the demands that they may feel from either or both groups to make their primary allegiance to and identification with that group.

According to Bohan (1996), the core concept in the double discrimination experienced by individuals who are members of both sexual and racial, ethnic, and cultural minorities is the presence of *discredited* and *discreditable identities* (pp. 124-125). In particular, a discredited identity requires the development of a coping technique in order to handle the prejudice and discrimination with which a person is confronted primarily due to visibly being a member of a racial, ethnic, or cultural minority. This can vary from experiences of more blatant to more subtle prejudice and discrimination.

A bisexual identity, however, is an example of a discreditable identity in that disclosure is necessary for people to know that a person is bisexual. This requires the bisexual person to make decisions on an ongoing basis about whether or not and how to reveal this part of his or her identity. By not disclosing his bisexuality, an individual may be able to experience the support of the racial, ethnic, or cultural community in which he is a member within that context. At the same time he might also be seen as a gay or bisexual man who refuses to come out and so experience a sense of distance or rejection from the bisexual, lesbian, and gay communities. The stress involved in this kind of isolating experience can lead to a variety of symptoms, such as anxiety, depressed mood, and suicidal ideation (Diaz, Ayala, Bein, Henne, & Marin, 2001).

There is also the fact that although the concepts of sexual orientation and sexual identity that are routinely used in Western psychology are an attempt to represent sexual reality, these are in fact abstractions that are culturally based and biased (Collins, 2004; Fukuyama & Ferguson, 2000; Rust, 2000b; Smith, 1997). Muñoz-Laboy (2004) attempted to address this issue by using the term *configuration* instead of *identity* in describing the lives of the bisexually active Latino men in his research. A term like *MSM* (men who have sex with men) can also be seen as culturally biased as it does not accurately describe the perspective of the many racial, ethnic, and cultural minority individuals, for whom the culturally specific meanings that they have for their sexual experiences with women and men may be significantly at variance with those of the dominant culture (Carrier, 1985; Zamora-Hernandez & Patterson, 1996).

In most of the coming out models that have been developed to describe lesbian, gay, and bisexual identity development, there is an emphasis on the empowering effect of disclosing one's sexual orientation to others (Bradford, 2004b; Cass, 1979; Coleman, 1982; Weinberg et al., 1998). For bisexual and gay men who are not members of the dominant culture, however, non-disclosure may be a healthier option, given the possible negative personal consequences of disclosure in the racial, ethnic, or cultural community context in which they live (Dworkin, 2001).

Muñoz-Laboy (2004), Carrier (1985), and Zamora-Hernandez and Patterson (1996) have shown that bisexual men can be influenced by and adhere to strong male dominated norms and values in cultures in which there is little or no validation for other then heterosexual attractions, behaviour, and relationships. In the United States, this is evident in the lives of bisexual men regarding the experiences of men of colour in terms of the greater influence of more conservative political ideologies both in their communities and in the more general dominant culture. In Europe, a similar trend is visible in the impact of more conservative political and religious influences on being visible and to speak out as being gay, lesbian, bisexual, or transgender. The bisexual person of colour in any European country lives in both a more traditional cultural environment and in the dominant culture, and is affected both by established more conservative values regarding sexual expression and by the more liberal values of the dominant culture. For European bisexual people whose religious and cultural background is

Islamic, for example, there is a strong influence on patriarchal thinking on the one hand, and a parallel development of an Islamic based European feminist movement. The therapist needs to take into account the influence of these countervailing trends as they raise issues of multiple identity and loyalty issues for this diverse group of bisexual men.

SOME THERAPEUTIC IMPLICATIONS FOR WORKING WITH BISEXUAL MEN

The focus here will be on looking at the kinds of issues discussed above in terms of the theoretical and practical approach of the therapist working with bisexual men. In order to work in an affirmative way with bisexual clients, it is first of all most important to honor the experience of the client and to keep in mind the fact that power can hurt people, which makes it imperative as a psychotherapist never to impose your ideas and or values on the client. This means developing an awareness of personal, social, and cultural prejudices that might come into play in working with bisexual men (Lourea, 1985; Wolf, 1992). This is particularly true in metropolitan urban areas, where the therapist may not have knowledge in any detail about all the diverse racial, ethnic, and cultural groups in the general population. The therapist who is willing to learn about the client's culture and community, through reading the literature and by consulting with knowledgeable colleagues, will be in a better position to understand and empathize issues that are related to the interaction of culture and sexuality for that particular person.

As described above, bisexual men are a very diverse group of people socially, culturally, and in terms of their relationships. Therefore, it is not surprising that the issues with which bisexual men come into therapy are a reflection of this diversity. The research and current clinical literature indicates that issues, questions, and problems regarding their sexual orientation may be involved in why bisexual men seek out a therapist; however, other concerns, common to any psychotherapy, are most often of equal or greater importance in their decision to seek professional guidance (Lourea, 1985; Matteson, 1995; Page, 2004; Wolf, 1985, 1992).

Fassinger (2000) describes the advantages and disadvantages of several psychotherapeutic approaches in treating bisexual men and women, including psychodynamic, humanistic, cognitive-behavioural, and systems perspectives. For example, in comparison to other approaches, Fassinger (2000) thinks that psychodynamic approaches are more effective for those bisexual clients who are "at more advanced stages of identity formation; such individuals have successfully navigated much of the stress of coming out to self and others . . . or they may wish to develop deeper understandings of themselves" (p. 119). The concepts of psychodynamic theory, however, can be used throughout the therapy process, e.g., the ways in which transference can affect the interaction with a client, or the different forms in which resistance can show itself. All can be very useful to understand the feelings and behaviours of the bisexual client. This is in contrast to one of the classical concepts of psychoanalysis in which unresolved intrapsychic conflicts are seen as a primary source of psychopathology in general and bisexuality in particular. The challenge of the psychodynamic approach, however, is the tendency to disregard or diminish the importance of external influences in the culture, like dichotomous thinking about sexual orientation, which shape attitudes toward bisexuality and also play a role in the thoughts, feelings, and behaviour of bisexual men.

For those individuals who are suffering from symptoms of anxiety and depression, which the literature indicates are among the most commonly reported issues that bisexual clients bring to therapy (Diaz et al., 2001; Dworkin, 2000; Page, 2004), one may use a cognitive-behavioural approach. Here, the primary focus for the therapy is on unlearning negative cognitive thought patterns, relearning pleasurable activities, relaxation methods, and regular mood monitoring to promote insight in the relationship between thoughts and feelings. However, one has to be careful with applying these methods if depressive symptoms appear to be linked with a client's experience of his bisexuality. Since stress is known to be related to depression, there is a possibility that depressive symptoms are caused by the repression of a client's own bisexual feelings, isolation from the bisexual community, or a lack of information about bisexuality. In such cases, a humanistic psychotherapy approach would be more appropriate, with a primary focus on exploring feelings, needs, values, and wishes. This is not to say that cognitive-behavioural approaches do not have a potential role here. On the contrary, if a client needs support in terms of anxiety about exploration, e.g., visiting gay, lesbian, bisexual bars, seeing particular (bisexual) films, attending meetings of bisexual organisations, or receiving sex education or advice, then a cognitive-behavioural approach may be therapeutically more appropriate. This is also a very appropriate approach for men who may be caught in their own negative thought processes, offering practical ways to challenge and cope with these thoughts, and making it possible to shift their cognitive frame to more affirmative ways of thinking.

Systems therapy, along with feminist and multicultural based theory, is an effective approach when working with bisexual men on relationship issues or issues arising out of the experience of living as a racial, ethnic, or cultural minority person in a dominant Western cultural context (Collins, 2004; Fassinger, 2000; Israel & Selvidge, 2003). The helpfulness of a feminist theoretical framework is that it makes it possible for the therapist to understand and discuss the influence of power on the experience of belonging to a minority group. Power, in this regard, comes with imposed ideas and values regarding what is and is not normal sexual behaviour. As we have seen, this can take the form of dichotomous thinking in which there is no place for bisexuality, having the effect of making bisexual people invisible in cultural context. The need for a conceptual framework that helps in analyzing the mechanism of discrimination becomes clear in terms of understanding the experiences of bisexual and gay men who are not member of the dominant culture.

For all of these groups of bisexual men, it is important to understand how male domination works in the heterosexual world as well as in the gay community. Herek (2002), for example, describes the relationship between heterosexuality, negative attitudes towards bisexuals, and general belief systems in which a high level of religiosity is included. He found that in the social milieu of rural areas in the South of the United States, there was a relationship between age and negative attitudes toward bisexuality, which he explained by saying that these areas have been less influenced by feminism and gay and bisexual movements. The common theme in these different examples is that it is male domination in religion and the influence of patriarchal thinking during different timeframes of history that contributes to bisexuality being seen as a deviation from what is viewed as "normal." As one can imagine, a feminist theoretical and clinical approach has much to offer regarding issues like these that can be helpful to understand the underlying mechanisms at work in regard to bisexual men.

On the basis of his research findings, Herek (2002) reports that while gay men are seen by heterosexual men as a threat to their masculinity, bisexual men appear to be seen by gay men as a challenge to their sense of security about their own sexuality. As Ochs (1996) implies, for some gay-identified men, who in fact have sexual attractions to women as well as to men, bisexuality may be experienced as threatening because of a fear of having to go through the painful process of a second coming out. From this point of view, the dominant culture's hetero-normative ideal is stress producing for men, regardless of sexual orientation. For men whose sexual attractions and relationships deviate from that ideal, there is the potential that the resulting dissonant experience will result in distressing psychological symptoms such as anxiety and depression (Diplacido, 1998; Meyer, 2003). The research literature indicates these kinds of symptoms are also present among a certain proportion of bisexual male adolescents (Rotheram-Borus, Hunter & Rosario, 1994; Rosario, Schrimshaw, Hunter & Gwadz, 2002; Savin-Williams, 1994).

Therapists who are aware of the potential issues raised by the experience of multiple identities and community loyalties will be in a better position to support the bisexual client in assessing the potential psychological and emotional consequences for that particular person of disclosure or non-disclosure. In this, the chosen therapy method should be moulded to the issues a client comes with to practice, and therapists who have the knowledge, skills and flexibility to adjust themselves and their methods according to the needs and issues of their clients will notice a qualitative better rapport and therapy results.

CONCLUDING REMARKS

In this article, I have argued that a good working definition of bisexuality is necessary for the therapist in order to understand the issues that bisexual men bring with them when seeking out psychotherapy. These issues are not necessarily problems around bisexuality; however, the subject of bisexuality may arise in the course of therapy in many different ways. At the same time, some clients may show signs of depression or anxiety, or they may have problems in dealing with intimate relationships, that may or may not be related to their bisexuality. Furthermore, individual clients' experiences of their sexual orientation and their interpretations of these experiences can be negatively influenced by the dominant culture's dichotomous view of sexual orientation and sexual identity. This can create specific difficulties in the coming out process which require particular attention and support on the part of the therapist.

It is clear, on the basis of the current research and clinical literature, that the social and cultural context in which bisexual men and their partners live, along with personal factors, codetermine the possibilities that are open in terms of the structure and experience of the relationships in which they may be involved. In this respect, it is essential for therapists to keep in mind existing prejudices related to bisexuality in general, and also the impact of decades of romanticism and dichotomous thinking about sexual orientation and identity on socially accepted concepts of relationship norms and values. Psychotherapists must therefore keep themselves informed about the diversity of experiences in the relationships of bisexual men in order to be able to offer constructive interventions in any couple or family therapy offered to bisexual men and their partners.

A special issue for bisexual men is HIV/AIDS, as there is an ongoing discourse in which bisexual men are seen as a source of transmission of HIV/AIDS to the "general" population. There is also an argument to the contrary, based on a different interpretation of the epidemiological data available in the research literature. However, there is the risk of misinterpreting the epidemiological data when it comes to understanding the sexual behaviour of individual bisexual men in regards to HIV prevention. It is therefore important that the therapist stay informed about current literature to be able to give accurate and helpful information to the client about HIV/AIDS in relation to bisexuality.

The manifestations of bisexuality across racial, ethnic, and cultural groups are very diverse and show considerable differences. Special attention should be given to the potential prejudice and discrimination faced by bisexual men of colour confronted on the one hand by the cultural norms and values of the dominant culture and on the other hand by the definitions of sexuality within their respective cultural communities. The issues with which bisexual men come to the therapy should provide the main cue for the therapist in terms of the choice of psychotherapeutic method or approach. It is a principle of affirmative psychotherapy with bisexual men to make the client, his family, and their questions and concerns the primary focus of the therapy process, with the therapist's choice of interventions being those that respect and validate the desire and goals of the client and his loved ones.

REFERENCES

Angelides, S. (2001). *A History of Bisexuality*. Chicago: University of Chicago Press.
Bohan, J. S. (1996). *Psychology & sexual orientation: Coming to terms*. New York: Routledge.
Bradford, M. (2004a). Bisexual issues in same-sex couples therapy. *Journal of Couple and Relationship Therapy*, *3*(3/4), 43-52.
Bradford, M. (2004b). The bisexual experience: Living in a dichotomous culture. *Journal of Bisexuality*, *4*(1/2), 7-23.

Buxton, A. P. (1994). *The other side of the closet: The coming out crisis for straight spouses and families.* New York: John Wiley & Sons.

Buxton, A. P. (2001). Writing our own script: How bisexual men and their heterosexual wives maintain their marriages after disclosure. *Journal of Bisexuality, 1*(2/3), 155-189.

Buxton, A. P. (2004). Works in progress: How mixed-orientation couples maintain their marriages after the wives come out. *Journal of Bisexuality, 4*(1/2), 57-82.

Carrier, J. M. (1985). Mexican male bisexuality. *Journal of Homosexuality, 11*(1/2), 75-86.

Cass, V. C. (1979). Homosexual identity formation: A theoretical model. *Journal of Homosexuality, 4*(3), 219-35.

Cass, V. C. (1984). Homosexual identity formation: Testing a theoretical model. *Journal of Sex Research, 20*(2), 143-167.

Chu, S. Y., Peterman, T. A., Doll, L. S., Buehler, J. W., & Curran, J. W. (1992). AIDS in bisexual men in the United States: Epidemiology and transmission to women. *American Journal of Public Health, 82*(2), 220-224.

Coleman, E. (1981/1982). Bisexual and gay men in heterosexual marriage: Conflicts and resolutions in therapy. *Journal of Homosexuality, 7*(2/3), 93-103.

Coleman, E. (1982). Developmental stages of the coming out process. *Journal of Homosexuality, 7,* 31-43.

Coleman, E. (1985). Integration of male bisexuality and marriage. *Journal of Homosexuality, 11*(1/2), 189-208.

Coleman, E. (1987). Assessment of sexual orientation. *Journal of Homosexuality, 14*(1/2), 9-24.

Coleman, E. (1998). Paradigmatic changes in the understanding of bisexuality. In E. J. Haeberle & R. Gindorf (Eds.), *Bisexualities: The ideology and practice of sexual contact with both men and women* (pp. 107-112). New York: Continuum.

Collins, J. F. (2004). The intersection of race and bisexuality: A critical overview of the literature and past, present, and future directions of the 'Borderlands.' *Journal of Bisexuality, 4*(1/2), 99-116.

Diaz, R. M., Ayala, G., Bein, E., Henne, J. & Marin, B.V. (2001). The impact of homophobia, poverty and racism on the mental health of gay and bisexual Latino men: Findings from 3 U.S. cities. *American Journal of Public Health, 91*(6), 927-930.

Diplacido, J. (1998). Minority stress among lesbians, gay men, and bisexuals: A consequence of heterosexism, homophobia, and stigmatization. In G. M. Herek (Ed.), *Stigma and sexual orientation: Understanding prejudice against lesbians, gay men, and bisexuals* (pp. 138-159). Thousand Oaks, CA: Sage.

Doll, L. S., Myers, T., Kennedy, M., & Allman, D. (1997). Bisexuality & HIV risk: Experiences in Canada & the United States. *Annual Review of Sex Research, VIII,* 102-147.

Dworkin, S. H. (2000). Individual therapy with lesbian, gay, and bisexual clients. In R. M. Perez, K. A. DeBord, & K. J. Bieschke (Eds.), *Handbook of counseling and psychotherapy with lesbian, gay, and bisexual clients* (pp. 157-181). Washington, DC: American Psychological Association.

Dworkin, S. H. (2001). Treating the bisexual client. *Journal of Clinical Psychology, 57*(5), 671-680.

Dworkin, S. H. (2002). Biracial, bicultural, bisexual: Bisexuality and multiple identities. *Journal of Bisexuality, 2*(4), 93-107.

Edser, S. J., & Shea, J. D. (2002). An exploratory investigation of bisexual men in monogamous, heterosexual marriages. *Journal of Bisexuality, 2*(4), 5-43.

Ekstrand, M. L., Coates, T. J., Guydish, J. R., Hauck, W. W., Colette, L. & Hulley, S. B. (1994). Are bisexually identified men in San Francisco a common vector for spreading HIV infection to women? *American Journal of Public Health, 84,* 915-919.

Eliason, M. (2001). Bi negativity: The stigma facing bisexual men. *Journal of Bisexuality, 1*(2/3), 137-154.

Fassinger, R. E. (2000). Applying counseling theories to lesbian, gay, and bisexual clients: Pitfalls and possibilities. In R. M. Perez, K. A. DeBord, & K. J. Bieschke (Eds.), *Handbook of counseling and psychotherapy with lesbian, gay, and bisexual clients* (pp. 107-131). Washington, DC: American Psychological Association.

Fassinger, R. E., & Miller, B. A. (1996). Validation of an inclusive model of sexual minority identity formation on a sample of gay men. *Journal of Homosexuality, 32*(2), 53-78.

Firestein, B. A. (1996). Bisexuality as paradigm shift: Transforming our disciplines. In B. A. Firestein (Ed.), *Bisexuality: The psychology & politics of an invisible minority* (pp. 261-291). Thousand Oaks, CA: Sage.

Fox, R. C. (1996). Bisexuality in perspective: A review of theory & research. In B. A. Firestein (Ed.), *Bisexuality: The psychology & politics of an invisible minority* (pp. 3-50). Thousand Oaks, CA: Sage. Thousand Oaks, CA: Sage.

Fukuyama, M. A., & Ferguson, A. D. (2000). Lesbian, gay, and bisexual people of color: Understanding cultural complexity and managing multiple oppressions. In R. M. Perez, K. A. DeBord, & K. J. Bieschke (Eds.), *Handbook of counseling and psychotherapy with lesbian, gay, and bisexual clients* (pp. 81-105). Washington, DC: American Psychological Association.

Hansson, H. (Ed.). (1990). *Bisexuele levens in Nederland.* Amsterdam: Orlando.

Herek, G. M. (2002). Heterosexuals' attitudes toward bisexual men and women in the United States. *Journal of Sex Research, 39*(4), 264-274.

Hutchins, L., & Kaahumanu, L. (Eds.). (1991). *Bi any other name: Bisexual people speak out.* Boston: Alyson.

Israel, T., & Selvidge, M. M. D. (2003). Contributions of multicultural counseling to counselor competence with lesbian, gay and bisexual clients. *Journal of Multicultural Counseling & Development, 31*(2), 84-98.

Israel, T., & Mohr, J. J. (2004). Attitudes toward bisexual women and men: Current research, future directions. *Journal of Bisexuality, 4*(1/2), 117-134.

Kinsey, A. C., Pomeroy, W. B., & Martin, C. E. (1948). *Sexual behavior in the human male.* Philadelphia: W. B. Saunders.

Kinsey, A. C., Pomeroy, W. B., Martin, C. E., & Gebhard, P. H. (1952). *Sexual behavior in the human female.* Philadelphia: W. B. Saunders.

Klein, F. (1993). *The bisexual option* (2nd ed.). New York: Harrington Park Press.

Klein, F., Sepekoff, B., & Wolf, T. J. (1985). Sexual orientation: A multi-variable dynamic process. *Journal of Homosexuality, 11*(1/2), 35-50.

Leaver, C.A., & Allman, D., & Meyers, T., & Veugelers, P.J. (2004). Effectiveness of HIV prevention in Ontario, Canada: A multilevel comparison of bisexual men. *American Journal of Public Health, 94*(7), 1181-1185.

Lourea, D. N. (1985). Psycho-social issues related to counseling bisexuals. *Journal of Homosexuality, 11*(1/2), 51-62.

MacDonald, A. P. (1982). Bisexuality: Some comments on research and theory. *Journal of Homosexuality, 6*(3), 21-35

Manalansan, M. F. (1996). Double minorities: Latino, Black, & Asian men who have sex with men. In R. C. Savin-Williams & K. M. Cohen (Eds.), *The lives of lesbians, gays, & bisexuals: Children to adults* (pp. 393-415). Fort Worth, TX: Harcourt Brace.

Matteson, D. R. (1995). Counseling with bisexuals. *Individual Psychology, 51*(2), 144-159

Matteson, D. R. (1996). Counseling & psychotherapy with bisexual & exploring clients. In B. A. Firestein (Ed.), *Bisexuality: The psychology & politics of an invisible minority* (pp. 185-213). Thousand Oaks, CA: Sage.

Matteson, D. R. (1997). Bisexual and homosexual behavior and HIV Risk Among Chinese-, Filipino- and Korean-American Men. *Journal of Sex Research, 34*(1), 93-104.

McCarn, S. R., & Fassinger, R. E. (1996). Revisioning sexual minority identity formation: A new model of lesbian identity and its implications. *Counseling Psychologist, 24*(3), 508-534.

McKirnan, D. J., Stokes, J. P., Doll, L, & Burzette, R. G. (1995). Bisexually active men: Social characteristics & sexual behavior. *Journal of Sex Research, 32*(1), 65-76.

McLean, K. (2004). Negotiating (non)monogamy: Bisexuality in intimate relationships. *Journal of Bisexuality, 4*(1/2), 83-97.

Meyer, I. H. (2003). Prejudice, social stress, and mental health in lesbian, gay, and bisexual populations: Conceptual issues and research evidence. *Psychological Bulletin, 129*(5), 674-697.

Mohr, J. J., & Rochlen, A. B. (1999). Measuring attitudes regarding bisexuality in lesbian, gay male, and heterosexual populations. *Journal of Counseling Psychology, 46*(3).

Mulick, P. S., & Wright, L. W., Jr. (2002). Examining the existence of biphobia in the heterosexual and homosexual populations. *Journal of Bisexuality, 2*(4), 45-64.

Muñoz-Laboy, M. A. (2004). Beyond 'MSM': Sexual desire among bisexually-active Latino men in New York City. *Sexualities, 7*(1), 55-80.

Ochs, R. (1996). Biphobia: It goes more than two ways. In B. A. Firestein (Ed.), *Bisexuality: The psychology & politics of an invisible minority* (pp. 217-239). Thousand Oaks, CA: Sage.

Ochs, R., & Rowley, S. E. (Eds.). (2005). *Getting bi: Bi: Voices of bisexuals around the world*. Boston: Bisexual Resource Center.

Off Pink Collective. (1988). *Bisexual lives*. London: Off Pink Publishing.

Page, E. (2004). Mental health services for bisexual women and bisexual men: An empirical study. *Journal of Bisexuality, 4*(1/2), 137-160.

Paul, J. P. (1984). The bisexual identity: An idea without social recognition. *Journal of Homosexuality, 9*(2/3), 45-64.

Paul, J. P. (1996). Bisexuality: Exploring/exploding the boundaries. In R. C. Savin-Williams & K. M. Cohen (Eds.), *The lives of lesbians, gays, & bisexuals: Children to adults* (pp. 436-461). Ft. Worth, TX: Harcourt Brace.

Queen, C. (1996). Bisexuality, sexual diversity, & the sex-positive perspective. In B. A. Firestein (Ed.), *Bisexuality: The psychology & politics of an invisible minority* (pp. 103-124). Thousand Oaks, CA: Sage.

Reynolds, A. L., & Hanjorgiris, W. F. (2000). Coming out: Lesbian, gay, and bisexual identity development. In R. M. Perez, K. A. DeBord, & K. J. Bieschke (Eds.), *Handbook of counseling and psychotherapy with lesbian, gay, and bisexual clients* (pp. 35-55). Washington, DC: American Psychological Association.

Rosario, M., Schrimshaw, E. W., Hunter, J., & Gwadz, M. (2002). Gay-related stress and emotional distress among gay, lesbian, and bisexual youths: A longitudinal examination. *Journal of Consulting and Clinical Psychology, 70*(4), 967-975.

Rose, S., Stevens, C., & The Off-Pink Collective. (Eds.). (1996). *Bisexual horizons: Politics, histories, lives*. London: Lawrence & Wishart.

Ross, M. W., & Paul, J. P. (1992). Beyond gender: The basis of sexual attraction in bisexual men and women. *Psychological reports, 71*, 1283-1290.

Rotheram-Borus, M. J., Hunter, J., & Rosario, M. (1994). Suicidal behavior and gay-related stress among gay and bisexual male adolescents. *Journal of Adolescent Research, 9*(4), 498-508.

Rust, P. C. (1996a). Finding a sexual identity & community: Therapeutic implications & cultural assumptions in scientific models of coming out. In E. D. Rothblum, & L. A. Bond (Eds.), *Preventing heterosexism & homophobia* (pp. 87-123). Thousand Oaks, CA: Sage.

Rust, P. C. (1996b). Managing multiple identities: Diversity among bisexual women & men. In B. A. Firestein (Ed.), *Bisexuality: The psychology & politics of an invisible minority* (pp. 53-83). Thousand Oaks, CA: Sage.

Rust, P. C. (1996c). Monogamy & polyamory: Relationship issues for bisexuals. In B. A. Firestein (Ed.), *Bisexuality: The psychology & politics of an invisible minority* (pp. 127-148). Thousand Oaks, CA: Sage.

Rust, P. C. (1996d). Sexual identity and bisexual identities: The struggle for self-description in a changing sexual landscape. In B. Beemyn, & M. Eliason (Eds.), *Queer studies: A lesbian, gay, bisexual, & transgender anthology* (pp. 64-86). New York: New York University Press.

Rust, P. C. R. (2002a). Bisexuality: The state of the union. *Annual Review of Sex Research, 13*, 180-214.

Rust, P. C. R. (2000b). Review of statistical findings about bisexual behavior, feelings, and identities. In P. C. R. Rust (Ed.), *Bisexuality in the United States: A social science reader* (pp. 129-184). New York: Columbia University Press.

Savin-Williams, R. C. (1994). Verbal and physical abuse as stressors in the lives of lesbian, gay male, and bisexual youths: associations with school problems, running away, substance abuse, prostitution, and suicide. Special section: mental health of lesbians and gay men. *Journal of Consulting & Clinical Psychology, 62*(2), 261-269.

Smith, A. (1997). Cultural diversity and the coming-out process: Implications for clinical practice. In B. Greene (Ed.), *Ethnic and cultural diversity among lesbians and gay men* (pp. 279-300). Thousand Oaks, CA: Sage.

Stokes, J. P., McKirnan, D. J., & Burzette, R. G. (1993). Sexual behavior, Condom use, disclosure of sexuality, and stability of sexual orientation in bisexual men. *Journal of Sex Research, 30*(3), 203-213.

Stokes, J. P., McKirnan, D. J., Doll, L., & Burzette, R. G. (1996). Female partners of bisexual men: What they don't know might hurt them. *Psychology of Women Quarterly, 20*, 267-284.

Stokes, J. P., Miller, R. L., & Mundhenk, R. (1998). Toward an understanding of behaviourally bisexual men: The influence of context and culture. *Canadian Journal of Human Sexuality, 7*(2), 101-113.

Weinberg, M. S., Williams, C. J., & Pryor, D. W. (1998). Becoming and being "bisexual." In E. J. Haeberle & R. Gindorf Eds.), *Bisexualities: The ideology and practice of sexual contact with both men and women* (pp. 169-181). New York: Continuum.

Weinberg, M. S., Williams, C. J., & Pryor, D. W. (2001). Bisexuals at midlife: Commitment, salience, and identity. *Journal of Contemporary Ethnography, 30*(2), 180-208.

Wolf, T. J. (1985). Marriages of bisexual men. *Journal of Homosexuality, 11*(1/2), 135-148.

Wolf, T. J. (1992). Bisexuality: A counseling perspective. In S. H. Dworkin, & F. J. Gutierrez (Eds.), *Counseling gay men and lesbians: Journey to the end of the rainbow* (pp. 175-187). Alexandria, VA: American Association for Counseling and Development.

Worth, H. (2003). The myth of the bisexual infector? HIV risk and men who have sex with men. *Journal of Bisexuality, 3*(2), 69-88.

Zamora-Hernandez, C. E., & Patterson, D. G. (1996). Homosexually active Latino men: Issues for social work practice. In John F. Longres (Ed.), *Men of color: A context for service to homosexually active men* (pp. 69-91). New York: Harrington Park Press.

Zinik, G. (1985). Identity conflict or adaptive flexibility? Bisexuality reconsidered. *Journal of Homosexuality, 11*(1/2), 7-19.

Affirmative Psychotherapy with Bisexual Transgender People

Nick Embaye

Available online at http://www.haworthpress.com/web/JB
© 2006 by The Haworth Press, Inc. All rights reserved.
doi:10.1300/J159v06n01_04

[Haworth co-indexing entry note]: "Affirmative Psychotherapy with Bisexual Transgender People."
Embaye, Nick. Co-published simultaneously in *Journal of Bisexuality* (Harrington Park Press, an imprint of
The Haworth Press, Inc.) Vol. 6, No. 1/2, 2006, pp. 51-63; and: *Affirmative Psychotherapy with Bisexual
Women and Bisexual Men* (ed: Ronald C. Fox) Harrington Park Press, an imprint of The Haworth Press, Inc.,
2006, pp. 51-63. Single or multiple copies of this article are available for a fee from The Haworth Document
Delivery Service [1-800-HAWORTH, 9:00 a.m. - 5:00 p.m. (EST). E-mail address: docdelivery@
haworthpress.com].

SUMMARY. Affirmative psychotherapy positively affirms identity without promoting a particular perspective, making it a particularly effective technique for individuals exploring GLBT identities. This article explores the application of affirmative therapy with bisexual transgender individuals. Definitions of transgender and bisexual identities, as well as their intersections, are discussed to illustrate the particular relevance of affirmative psychotherapy. Case examples illustrate the benefits of affirmative psychotherapy with bisexual transgender individuals. *[Article copies available for a fee from The Haworth Document Delivery Service: 1-800-HAWORTH. E-mail address: <docdelivery@haworthpress.com> Website: <http://www.HaworthPress.com> © 2006 by The Haworth Press, Inc. All rights reserved.]*

KEYWORDS. Bisexuality, transgender, transsexual, gender, psychotherapy, counseling

INTRODUCTION

Bisexual and transgender issues share some interesting commonalities and intersections of history, visibility and emergence in the field of psychology. Very few theorists considered the possibility of both identities occurring in one individual (Denny & Green, 1996; Devor, 2000). Until recently, these issues have been the subject of limited attention, misunderstanding and pathologizing in both popular culture and as subjects of scientific study. Currently, the body of literature on bisexuality enjoys steady growth; the literature on transgender is in earlier stages of development but is growing as well. Current research and theory have revealed enough commonalities that therapists can consider the use of techniques effective in therapy with lesbians and gays with bisexual and transgender clients (Devor, 1997; Dworkin, 2000; Gainor, 2000).

Affirmative psychotherapy provides support for identity without promoting a particular perspective or imposing the therapist's value system on the client's identity construction process. Affirmative therapy is an effective technique for individuals exploring any aspect of identity, but it is particularly useful for individuals with GLBT identities.

Most sexual orientation theories utilize a rigidly categorized object vs. perceiver to describe orientation (Bohan, 1996; Klein et al., 1985; Rust, 2000). Thus, if a male is attracted to both males and females, he would be considered bisexual. If the same man is attracted to males only he would be characterized as homosexual. How does the characterization change if the individual declares himself "third gendered (neither man nor woman)"? The object of his attention remains male, but homosexual behavior is defined as male with male. Is the individual in question still homosexual? We could call him bisexual, but what would he call himself? In order to understand the application of affirmative therapy with bisexual transgender individuals it will be helpful to review some theory which describes transgender and bisexual behavior. This will help in understanding some of the intersections of these identities as well as highlight some unique applications of affirmative therapy.

To avoid the confusion which would arise by attempting to accommodate all labeling strategies or by attempting to use labels with uncertain definitions, I will use behavioral definitions of both bisexuality and transgender and will be working from within the binary gender system. There is a risk of compromising individual self determination if we include individuals in a population using a label which they would not endorse. As will be seen below, an individual who endorses one label at one point in their life may reject it and adopt another at a another time. However, terms such as bisexuality and transgender depend upon these dimorphic gender categorizations and labeling framework.

For the purpose of this discussion, *opposite gender* can be understood to mean the gender category to which the individual was not assigned at birth. *MtF* should be understood as female, *FtM* should be understood as male. The term transition refers to the changing of one's outward appearance (hormone surgery and/or sexual reassignment surgery) or legal status to reflect identification with the target or opposite gender.

Bisexuality and transgender discourse both challenge the sex/gender binary and move us closer to accurate descriptions of human behavior (Owen, 2003). Within psychiatry and psychology, there has been a recent trend toward non pathological views of both transgender and bisexual individuals (Alexander & Yescavage, 2003; Mathy, Lehmann, & Kerr, 2003). The literature on bisexuality has reflected this trend longer (Firestein, 1996; Fox, 1996; Klein, 1993; Rust, 2000).

Both transgender and bisexual people have history within the gay and lesbian community; both have been there from the beginning, and both share a history of lack of acceptance and validation within the gay and lesbian community (Alexander & Yescavage, 2003). Both groups share a history of pathologizing, sensational and misleading treatments by popular media.

For both bisexual and transgender people, there is a wide variety of sexual behavior, leading to some confusion about how to apply the terms. For example, some people identify as transgender until they transition, and afterwards use a sex-dichotomous label. Others identify as transgender whether or not they transition (Gagne & Tewkesbury, 1998). In the same way, some identify as bisexual and then later identify as hetero or homosexual, and later may return to identifying as bisexual (Klein, 1993). A more dynamic view of both would more closely reflect the reality of these identity development processes.

TRANSGENDER IDENTITY

Transgender is a term which refers to individuals who do not fit into the predominately dimorphic structure of gender in Western society. Transgender people report that their experience, internal sense or expression of gender does not correspond with what is required of them according to the gender assigned to them at birth (Pauling, 1999). Historically, literature in the medical community treated transgender issues as pathological, excluding from consideration individuals who never requested treatment. This view is reflected in popular culture's almost exclusive attention to individuals who transition (transsexual) or cross-dress. The growth in literature in psychology reveals a diversity of transgender identities and a concomitant need to understand all facets of transgender life.

Transgender identity has been discussed from both essentialist and social construction perspectives (Gagne & Tewkesbury, 1998; Hart 1984). The essentialist position supports the assignment of gender identity based on biological factors, as well as the maintenance of rigid gender boundaries through categorization, pathologizing and sex reassignment. The social construction perspective argues that gender is dynamic, and supports affirmative practices, which allow for individualized identitity development and expression.

Pauling (1999) proposed a five state model of transgender identity development, based on a social construction perspective. These are called states, rather than stages, to acknowledge the fact that identity development does not always proceed in a linear fashion and that an individual's commitment to an aspect of identity is not always permanent.

Nascience is a naïve state where identity is not salient or the individual is unaware of it. *Salience* is when transgender identity becomes critically salient and becomes the subject of problem solving. Another state is a process of *Exploration* of gender identity and alternate sexual identities. *Internalization/extermination* comprises an attempt to *internalize* the target identity, versus assigned gender, or an attempt to *exterminate* target gender characteristics and thereby reinforce or internalize assigned gender characteristics. *Commitment* involves an adherence to gender dichotomy and assigned or reassigned gender, or movement to gender diversity and identity as transgendered.

Klein (1993) posited four types of bisexuality. The *transitional* type is where bisexuality is considered a stage in the process of coming out gay or lesbian. *Historical* bisexuality is when there are both homosexual and heterosexual attractions, behaviors, or relationships in a person's life. *Sequential* bisexuality refers to monogamous relationships, and *concurrent* bisexuality is the maintenance of more than one relationship at the same time, at least one of which could be characterized as homosexual or bisexual.

Therapists need to be aware of personal and professionally based preconceptions (thoughts, feelings and perceptions based on outdated literature) about gender and sexual orientation in order to be able to provide effective therapy. The following issues may be of particular interest.

Assumptions Made on the Basis of Bisexual Identity

Historically, when considering sexual reassignment, individuals risked being considered not ready for transitioning because they were seen as not having made a choice regarding their sexuality (Bolin, 1988). Confusion about the object of sexual desire creates confusion about gender. Also, therapists' values may divert attention from issues the client considers more relevant; for example, a therapist may identify bisexuality as infidelity and address it as a contributing factor to a client's distress about sexual and/or gender identity.

Invisibility Is an Important Factor

When the perceiver and object fit the description of heterosexuality, their queerness becomes invisible and invalidated. For transgender people with same gender partners who, in effect, become opposite gender partners after transition, the connection with queer community disappears as the couple appears heterosexual in public. Bisexuality is invisible unless announced or otherwise known. Both cases create barriers to connection to and forming of community.

Fluidity of Identity Development

The fluidity of identity development is more visible for bisexual transgender individuals: they may identify as bisexual, then reject this label in favor of another, and later may return to acceptance of the label. As they transition (or not), the process of sexual and gender identification becomes apparent in their choice of partners. Thus, the dynamic process of identity development often is seen as pathological.

CLINICAL CASE EXAMPLES

The details of the cases described below (including names) have been altered to preserve the anonymity of the clients. Transition issues are not discussed in describing therapy with these individuals to avoid the controversial issues that arise when doing therapy with the goal of transition, and to emphasize the fact that transition is not the only reason transgender people request treatment. All of these clients identified as bisexual, either in the past or while in treatment. Two clients identified as transgender when they elected to have surgery since it was required to do so; they no longer identify as transgender.

The Case of Jenny

Jenny was a 28-year-old European American, a lifelong New England resident who said by way of self-identification, "I am a woman." At the time of treatment, she had been transitioning for four years. She had undergone electrolysis, was undergoing hormone therapy, and had received breast implants. The presenting issue was relationship issues, and the diagnosis was *Adjustment Disorder*. She was in therapy for six months, with treatment terminating when she moved to another community.

Jenny is MtF. She takes hormones, has had breast implants, but does not intend, at least right now, to have "bottom surgery." She lives as a woman. This is part of her relationship history. Until 10 years ago she exclusively dated women and had gone so far as to propose to one. Then for several years she explored relationships with men while continuing to date women. She then underwent a period of celibacy and decided to transition. For the past five years she has dated only biological males who, she says, are interested in dating transgender women.

Jenny's requested therapy to help her resolve issues which she says keep her from being able to find a long term partner. Her initial concern was that she was still in a period of bisexuality as transition and she wondered if she should try dating women.

Jenny's treatment lasted about 6 months before she moved out of the area. The move was part her strategy to establish herself in a new area where fewer people would know her history. Before she left her understanding of her attractions was more crystallized, and she described herself this way: "I thought I was interested in women, but I think what I'm looking for there is more like the intimate friendships I see them have. That's hard for me because before (she means before she transitioned), I turned all those relationships into sexual relationships." Jenny feels she's clearly interested in a male long term relationship partner, and has closed off other options. She also resolved to continue working on this in her new location.

For Jenny, it was important to have the label "transsexual" in order to obtain the medical treatment she needed. Otherwise she would not accept it. She was clearly uncomfortable with the label bisexual, but did feel that it described her behavior. She was willing to accept it as past behavior. Depending on the criteria used, we might be tempted to categorize Jenny's sexual behavior as male with male. If we used the criteria I used for this article, Jenny would be categorized as a bisexual transgender individual. I might attempt to help Jenny come to terms with her bisexual behavior and accept the label. An affirmative stance allowed room for her to come to the conclusion that she was no longer bisexual. Jenny's period of celibacy saved her from having to declare an attraction to men, a sometime criteria for sexual reassignment. She told me that when she got her letters she had every intention of remaining celibate, but was interested in men. She minimized her attraction to women because at the time she felt it was not relevant.

I included Jenny because her case raised for me an interesting question about transgender states: could the same criteria proposed by Klein (1993) be applied in the case of transgender individuals? Jenny would meet the criteria for a transitional transgender (as well as bisexual). Individuals who never transition, as well as most individuals who alternate (cross dressers, drag kings and queens, transvestites) would meet the criteria for sequential transgender. Historical transgender individuals would include those who tried forms of transgender expression and no longer engage in the behavior or in any transgender self-labeling. Finally, individuals who identify with both or neither gender would meet the criteria for concurrent transgender.

The Case of Bill

Bill is a 51-year-old African American who describes himself as possibly a gay male, but more likely bisexual. He identified as transsexual while transitioning but now feels this is less descriptive of him now. He is a New England resident who moved here from Philadelphia 10 years before starting current treatment. He underwent full transition, including surgery and hormones, between the ages of 48 and 49, and came in for counseling for depression related to relationship problems. He was seen for six sessions.

Bill is FtM and a person of color. These are, he says, his two most visible characteristics. No one questions his sexuality, though they did before his transition. His family was comfortable with his lesbian identity. They are less comfortable now that he has completed his transition and come out as bisexual. Bill requested therapy when his relationship with his long term female partner was failing, possibly due to his emergent bisexuality. Bill struggled with her characterization of his explorations as cheating on her. She was not convinced of his attraction or commitment to her and eventually left him. This was his last relationship with a biological woman, but he doesn't rule out the option.

Bill noted that as he began to explore relationships with men, he found himself drawn to group of gay men, and once socializing with them, became sexually attracted to them. It is interesting to note that similarly to Peter, Bill felt attracted to men before he transitioned. He often fantasized about sex with them, but never followed through because he feared being treated as a woman.

Bill was seen for a few sessions in which he addressed his attraction to men and resolved his grief about the loss of his long term partner. He terminated treatment as he felt he could continue to resolve his grief with the help of friends and his new cohort. He felt that the most valuable part of the treatment was the validation of his identity as bisexual. He did not feel any need to address transgender issues as he felt he had resolved those in earlier treatment.

The Case of Paul

Paul is a 42-year-old who has not undergone any hormonal or surgical transition, and prefers to be called a Black (vs. African American) man. He is a New England resident who moved from New York 7 years ago. His issues are depression, PTSD, transition questions. He is currently in therapy, ongoing since 18 months ago.

Paul reports that it never occurred to him to think of himself as particularly female, even after he was raped. He reports that he has worn men's clothing since high school, and was not challenged by his family or peers. People most often think he is a male, and he does not do anything to correct them. He has a deep voice, wears his hair short and shaves once a week. He uses the men's room in emergencies but otherwise does not use public restrooms.

Paul originally identified itself as a lesbian then as a bisexual and finally as a bisexual male. He says that he had dealt successfully with his PTSD symptoms and terminated from therapy when he discovered a biography of a female to male transsexual and witnessed the transition of a store owner in his neighborhood. He researched the issue and joined a support group. He started therapy again to deal with issues of identity, but has not decided whether he wants to undergo any medical process. He is afraid it is too expensive (he does not have health insurance) and risky. He is requesting therapy to address this feeling that he is a male but not wanting to lose his female history, to make a decision about transitioning, and to get support about coming out to family and friends. He also wants to get more information and support from transgender organizations. His main complaint is that he cannot find a therapist that is knowledgeable about transsexuality unless he travels a long distance from his rural town.

The Case of Peter

Peter is a 40-year-old European American FtM, a New England resident, who relocated from New York State. He has completed top surgery, and is currently on hormone therapy, with no further surgeries planned. He has been diagnosed with bipolar disorder and he has questions about his sexual behavior. He was in treatment one month, and transferred when his therapist left the agency where he was being seen. He describes himself as a bisexual man.

Peter says he's always been a man, so transgender terms have no meaning for and should not be applied to him. He has had hormonal treatment and some surgery to correct the most prominent of his birth defects, but some corrective surgery is inaccessible to him because of cost. He has always been bi, but says his appearance had made relationships with men impossible because they inevitably treated him like a woman and engaged in sexual behavior that left him cold. Since the surgery he has had moderate success attracting the kind of male he'd like to engage with, but his encounters with females have suffered. He questioned whether his medical treatment resulted in some changes that made him less attractive to women. He openly identifies as bi, and tells dates about his physical condition before engaging in sexual activity. This is a new strategy: before starting therapy, he would wait until someone questioned his condition; if there were no questions asked (he says often there weren't), he did not give any answers.

Peter has had a number of experiences with more than one partner; he was unsure how to identify his relation to his partners. In one case partners were a man and a woman, an ongoing relationship, in the other case there were several different encounters with two women. Peter was questioning his sexual activity when he started therapy as his psychiatrist questioned its relationship to his being bipolar; one of the possible symptoms of a manic episode is hypersexuality.

Peter was included because although he does not identify as transgender, most practitioners would assign this label to him. He identified as transsexual in order to facilitate his medical treatment. He did identify as bisexual. It was important for him to find a therapist who did not judge his lifestyle or automatically attribute it to his being bipolar.

A PERSONAL NOTE

How do I describe myself? I'm a black man. I've spent most of my life trying to be a woman, and gladly gave up when I realized I didn't have to do that. I came out to my family as bisexual years before I came out as transgender. I didn't use therapy to explore either of these identities. I identify as transgender and bisexual depending on the audience. At work, circumstances forced a change in pronouns, and the transgender aspect is highlighted because some days I look female. An interesting note is that my clients seem to have an easier time than some of my colleagues with adjusting to the information.

Even living in a community reputed as open and accepting, I have encountered a substantial amount of ignorance and prejudice. Sadly, incidents occur frequently. Recently two colleagues argued with me that an adult client's parent was seriously mentally ill; one because the parent was "having a sex change" and came to a family gathering cross-dressed; the other argued that the parent must be mentally ill because the parent was too old to be transitioning. The parent's transgender status was initially suggested to be the client's delusion, and later the source of the client's crisis. Another time, a colleague expressed disapproval of an eighteen-year-old who had completed sexual reassignment surgery, calling the process a double mastectomy, and opining that the client was too immature to make such a decision.

As I considered sexual reassignment surgery, I shopped for therapy and encountered resistance from therapists who, among other things, stated that they thought I was too pretty to be a man, that I should make a feminist statement by not changing my body, or that I should immediately make plans to have surgery. I found no one willing to consider both paths (transitioning or living as a man without transitioning) equally. Most questioned whether my bisexuality was an accommodation of my transgender status. Others felt it was an excuse for infidelity, since at the time I had two partners: one who acknowledged my masculinity and one who struggled with it. These experiences reinforced my philosophy of therapy: that I am here to help people make informed decisions, not to "help" them in any particular direction.

Many of the issues discussed here are issues I've dealt with, and as a therapist who is a person of color, transgender, and also bisexual, it is important for me to make the world a safe place for me and people like me. Affirmative therapy appears to hold promise for making that safety a reality, if not in the larger world, then at least in the therapy room.

REFERENCES

Alexander, J., & Yescavage, K. (2003). Bisexuality and transgenderism: InterSEXions of the others. *Journal of Bisexuality, 3*(3/4), 1-23.

Bohan, J. S. (1996). *Psychology & sexual orientation: Coming to terms.* New York: Routledge.

Bolin, A. (1988). *In search of Eve: Transsexual rites of passage.* South Hadley, MA: Bergin & Garvey Publishers.

Chase, T. (2003). The story so far. *Journal of Bisexuality, 3*(3/4), 111-116.

Denny, D., & Green, J. (1996). Gender identity and bisexuality. In B. A. Firestein (Ed.), *Bisexuality: The psychology and politics of an invisible minority* (pp. 84-102). Newbury Park, CA: Sage.

Devor, H. (1993). Sexual orientation identities, attractions, and practices of female-to-male transsexuals. *Journal of Sex Research, 30*(4), 303-315.

Devor, H. (1997). *FTM: Female-to-male transsexuals in society.* Bloomington: Indiana University Press.

Diamond, M. (2002). Sex and gender are different: Sexual identity and gender identity are different. *Clinical Child Psychology and Psychiatry, 7*(3), 320-334.

Drechsler, C. (2003). We are all others: An argument for queer. *Journal of Bisexuality, 3*(3/4) 265-275.

Dworkin, S. H. (2000). Individual therapy with lesbian, gay, and bisexual clients. In R. M. Perez, K. A. DeBord, & K. J. Bieschke (Eds.), *Handbook of counseling and psy-*

chotherapy with lesbian, gay, and bisexual clients (pp. 157-181). Washington, DC: American Psychological Association.

Fox, R. (1996). Bisexuality in perspective. In B. Firestein (Ed.), *Bisexuality: The psychology and politics of an invisible minority* (pp. 3-50). Thousand Oaks, CA: Sage.

Fukuyama, M. A., & Ferguson, A. D. (2000). Lesbian, gay, and bisexual people of color: Understanding cultural complexity and managing multiple oppressions. In R. M. Perez, K. A. DeBord, & K. J. Bieschke (Eds.), *Handbook of counseling and psychotherapy with lesbian, gay, and bisexual clients* (pp. 81-105). Washington, DC: American Psychological Association.

Gagne, P., & Tewksbury, R. (1998). Conformity pressures and gender resistance among transgendered individuals. *Social Problems, 45,* 81-101.

Gainor, K. A. (2000). Including transgender issues in lesbian, gay, and bisexual psychology: Implications for clinical practice and training. B. Greene, & G. L. Croom (Eds.), *Education, research, and practice in lesbian, gay, bisexual, and transgendered psychology: A resource manual* (pp. 131-160). Thousand Oaks, CA: Sage.

Green, J. (1998). FTM: An emerging dance. D. Denny (Ed.), *Current concepts in transgender identity* (pp. 145-162). New York: Garland.

Klein, F. (1993). *The bisexual option (2nd ed.).* New York: Harrington Park Press.

Klein, F., Sepekoff, B., & Wolf, T. J. (1985). Sexual orientation: A multi-variable dynamic process. *Journal of Homosexuality, 11*(1/2), 35-50.

Mathy, R. M., Lehmann, B. A., & Kerr, D. L. (2003). Bisexual and transgender identities in a nonclinical sample of north americans: Suicidal intent, behavioral difficulties, and mental health treatment. *Journal of Bisexuality, 3*(3/4), 93-109.

Meyer, M. D. E. (2003). Looking toward the InterSEXions: Examining bisexual and transgender identity formation from a dialectical theoretical perspective. *Journal of Bisexuality, 3*(3/4), 151-170.

Owen, M.K. (2003) Overstepping the bounds: Bisexuality, gender and sociology. *Journal of Bisexuality, 3*(2), 31-39.

Pauling, M. L. (1999). *A conceptualization of transgender issues: Research and treatment ideas.* Poster presented at the 107th Annual Convention of the American Psychological Association. Boston, MA.

Rosenberg, M. (2003). Trans/positioning the (drag?) king of comedy: Bisexuality and queer Jewish space in the works of Sandra Bernhard. *Journal of Bisexuality, 3*(3/4) 171-179.

Denny, D. (Ed.). (1998). *Current concepts in transgender identity.* New York: Garland.

Rust, P. C. R.. (2000). Alternatives to binary sexuality: Modeling sexuality. In P. C. R. Rust (Ed.), *Bisexuality in the United States: A Social Science Reader* (pp. 33-54). New York: Columbia University Press.

Promoting Well-Being: An Ecology of Intervening with African American Bisexual Clients

Raymond L. Scott

Available online at http://www.haworthpress.com/web/JB
doi:10.1300/J159v06n01_05

[Haworth co-indexing entry note]: "Promoting Well-Being: An Ecology of Intervening with African American Bisexual Clients." Scott, Raymond L. Co-published simultaneously in *Journal of Bisexuality* (Harrington Park Press, an imprint of The Haworth Press, Inc.) Vol. 6, No. 1/2, 2006, pp. 65-84; and: *Affirmative Psychotherapy with Bisexual Women and Bisexual Men* (ed: Ronald C. Fox) Harrington Park Press, an imprint of The Haworth Press, Inc., 2006, pp. 65-84. Single or multiple copies of this article are available for a fee from The Haworth Document Delivery Service [1-800-HAWORTH, 9:00 a.m. - 5:00 p.m. (EST). E-mail address: docdelivery@haworthpress.com].

SUMMARY. Many African American bisexuals must resolve a dilemma of how to form alliances with multiple social reference groups in the construction and maintenance of multiple identities. Often the ideologies espoused by these reference groups conflict in relation to their normative standards for gendered and sexual behavior. Until this dilemma is resolved, many bisexuals experience a fragmented sense of self. In the promotion of subjective well-being, therapists may assist African American bisexuals to deconstruct these hegemonic forms of femininity and masculinity, demoralized public media representations of their being, and the stigma and shame attached to homoerotic expressions of sexuality. Deconstructions of hegemonic femininities and masculinities are often accompanied by a need to resist the nature of a particular self, constructed by indigenous Africentric patriarchal psychologies. This construction of the self equates African American bisexual identities with a pathological personality disorder known as misorientation. The psychotherapist who is aware of these aspects of the experiences of African American bisexuals is in a better position to offer affirmative mental health services to this population. *[Article copies available for a fee from The Haworth Document Delivery Service: 1-800-HAWORTH. E-mail address: <docdelivery@haworthpress.com> Website: <http://www.HaworthPress.com> © 2006 by The Haworth Press, Inc. All rights reserved.]*

KEYWORDS. African American bisexuals, Africentricism, bisexuality, bisexual women, bisexual men, African American women, African American men, identity politics, gender, well-being, hegemony, cultural diversity, culturally competent psychotherapy

INTRODUCTION

There is a synergism between gender, identity formation, and the development of a coherent sense of self that affects the well-being of African American bisexuals (Volanen, Lahelma, Silventoinen, & Suominen, 2004). For clarity, the terms identity, self-concept, self-awareness, and self-consciousness are used interchangeably in this manuscript, as are black and African American. Bisexuality as a sexual identity among African Americans is simultaneously embodied in the femininities and masculinities performed under what may seem disparate labels including *bisexual, dykes, heterosexually-identified men who have sex with men* (MSM), and *heterosexually-identified women who have sex with women* (WSW) (Brandt, 2000; Emig, 2000; Gonzalez, 2000; Hunter & Alexander, 1996). Trends emerging in various communities indicate that additional labels such as *homo thugz* or *on the down low* (DL) are being adopted by some groups of African American MSM (King, 2003; Trebay, 2000; Wright, 2001). Labeling oneself as a homo thug or DL "has become a way for some black men to admit they like guys without resorting to words like gay, bisexual, or queer" (King, 2003, p. 38).

The use of disparate labels contributes to the fact that bisexuality has been and continues to be *invisible* in many African American communities. Visibility or *coming out* comes at the cost of caricature, stereotyping, fear, ostracism, and possible violence associated with *difference* in these communities (Carbado & Weise, 2004; Giroux, 1993). The cost is also experienced as injustice, racism, invalidation, and exploitation that is associated with the emergence of ill health, suffering, and oppression (Prilleltensky & Nelson, 2002). Some of these costs are offset through affirmative efforts by African American scholar-activists (Gates, 1997; Harris, 1994; Hemphill, 1991; hooks, 1989, 1994; Lubiano, 1998b; Reid-Pharr, 2001; West, 2001; Wyatt, 1997) that challenge such heteronormative-hegemonic practices. These efforts assist bisexuals to find supportive communities and develop their voices to advocate for social and political policy revisions locally and nationally (Conerly, 1996).

My exploration here draws from indigenous black psychologies (Parham & Brown, 2003; White & Cones, 1999), feminism (Butler, 1993; Garnets, 2002; Moraga & Anzaldua, 2002) and critical, ecological, and political theorists (Foucault, 1972, 1978; Gates, 1997). I move beyond situating bisexuality solely within love relationships. Rather I focus on the complexity of bisexuals' relationships to each other and to heteronormative-hegemonic structures that contribute to their sense of fragmentation and undermine their subjective well-being (Loiacano, 1989; Nero, 2004; Peplau & Spalding, 2003; Reid-Pharr, 2002; Weinberg, Williams, & Pryor, 2004). My goal is to assist therapists in providing culturally competent psychological services to African American bisexuals.

Toward this goal, I begin with a discussion of well-being and social capital. Three sections follow that address the hegemonic-heteronormative structures related to gender, identity, and sex systems; representations of bisexuals as *Other*; and the pathologization of bisexuality within the media, educational curriculum, and religion. I conclude with sections that address therapist variables and the use of integrative therapy in the promotion of well-being for these individuals.

WELL-BEING AND SOCIAL CAPITAL

Subjective well-being conveys how the clients evaluate their lives along various dimensions including life and relationship satisfaction; the absence of depression, anxiety, and other forms of psychological distress; and the maintenance of self-cohesion (Diener, Suh, & Oishi, 1997). It refers to the client's experience of life satisfaction, frequent joy, and their ability to cope with sexism, discrimination, and invalidation. An assessment of subjective well-being allows the clinician to determine what factors in the client's experiences contribute to the onset and maintenance of psychological distress, as well as what factors promote well-being (Volanen, Lahelma, Silventoinen, & Suominen, 2004).

Well-being and good mental health derive from participation and membership in family groups, social networks, or other social structures that enhance self-acceptance, personal growth, trust, safety, and reciprocity (Frumkin, 2003). Social capital is broadly defined here by these important predictors of mental health that arise directly and/or mediated through the role of informal networks, as well as formal associational ties (Henderson & Whiteford, 2003). The concept of social capital directs attention to the quantity and/or quality of resources that a client can access through her or his location in one or more social networks (Lin, 2000). Because social capital accounts for the role of social networks and social activities in preventing disease, facilitating recovery from illness, or adaptation to chronic illness (Pilkington, 2002); its absence may represent the foundation of African American bisexuals' sense of fragmentation.

HEGEMONIC IDENTITY SYSTEMS AND WELL-BEING

Therapeutically, identity negotiation may become highly salient given the risks associated with coming out and its impact on group membership and self-coherence as discussed above. Clients may find it beneficial to explore how hegemonic representational practices serve as manifestations of alterity through the defamation of non-heterosexual identities/subjectivities (Felski, 1997). In these instances, the exploration of the *Other* (Said, 1993) often involves assisting clients to understand how and why stereotypical, disparaging, and demoralized public media representations of bisexuals are created and circulated and how they maintain power imbalances and oppression. Significant challenges to these power imbalances and attendant oppression occur as clients recognize why the endorsement of a bisexual identity destabilizes the heterosexist identity politics inherent to the *jargon of authenticity* (Thomas, 1997).

Bisexuality may cut across multiple identities given that it involves an emotional bonding between individuals that may not rest on their perceived gender and, as such, this relational bonding may or may not include concomitant expressions of sexual behaviors (D'Augelli & Patterson, 1995; Esterberg, 1997; Firestein, 1996; Fox, 2003; Labriola, 2003). As such, bisexual identities represent subversive forms of self-organization and regulation that undermine two binaries common to the dominant U.S. culture and patriarchal Africentric worldviews. These dichotomous systems include the male-female gender/sex system and the homosexual-heterosexual binary (Butler, 1993; Gambs, 2003). African American bisexual identities also undermine the notion of authentic racial/ethnic identities promulgated through master narratives such as the jargon of authenticity that circulate within many African American communities. A subjective awareness of these subversive qualities on the client's part suggests a high degree of political sophistication. Thus, a clinician should not assume such awareness on the client's part; rather she or he must understand that this subversion destabilizes heteronormative standards sufficiently such that it decreases the likelihood of amassing social capital and developing a coherent sense of self.

Gender identity represents the transformation of one's anatomical sex through the performance of culturally defined social scripts that signal masculinity and/or femininity to one's audience (Felluga, 2003). Henson and Rogers (2004), for example, conceptualize gender as hierarchical relationships where heterosexual performances of gender are equivalent to "doing masculinity" and, by extrapolation, to doing femininity (p. 298). They use the term *doing* to connote performance and situate heterosexual performances of femininity and masculinity as hegemonic in relation to non-heterosexual performances of gender. Often linked to the writings of Antonio Gramsci (e.g., 1977; 1985), but by no means exclusive to him, *hegemony* means predominant influence, especially when it involves defining heterosexual performances of gender as desirable, natural, and normative (Mellstrom, 2002; Wood,

2000). This in turn makes the meanings chosen by the dominant heterosexual groups appear to be universal by conceptualizing *women* and
men as two distinct homogenous groups. This practice of elevating
group specific behavior to an universal etic serves to communicate to
American females and males expectancies for conformity to the
dichotomized construction of gender as female or male.

Contrary to indigenous black psychologies (Parham & Brown, 2003;
White & Cones, 1999; Wyatt, 1997), this practice of elevating group
specific behavior to a universal etic serves to communicate to African
American bisexuals expectancies for conformity to the dichotomized
construction of gender conceptualized such that *women* and *men* represent two distinct homogenous groups. That is, a fundamental premise
underpinning this type of indigenous psychologies is the understanding
that gender and sexual identities are social constructions (Abreu, Goodyear, Campos, & Newcomb, 2000)–structured by particular ideologies
and material environments and expressed through performativity
(Felluga, 2003).

Many of the attitudes, norms, mores, and symbols within many black
communities are informed by a specific variant of Africentric ideology
(Baldwin, 1989; Baldwin, Brown, & Rackley, 1990). This ideology as-
sumes an authentic *black* self and equates African American identity
with the concept of African self-consciousness (Atwell & Azibo, 1991;
Baldwin, Brown, & Rackley, 1990; Dennard, 1998). For Baldwin
(1989), an African self-consciousness describes:

> the 'conscious' expression of the social theory of African people
> (i.e., the practice by Black people of our Africentric social theory).
> Under normal and natural conditions, it reflects: (a) the recogni-
> tion of oneself as 'African' (biologically, psychologically, cultur-
> ally, etc.) and of what being African means as defined by African
> Worldview; (b) the recognition of African survival as one's first
> priority value; (c) respect for and active perpetuation of all things
> African, African life and institutions; (d) a standard of conduct to-
> ward all things and peoples non-African, and toward all things and
> peoples, etc., that are 'anti-African' (e.g., active opposition against
> all things that are anti-African). Collectively, these standards and
> activities represent the 'survival thrust' of African people as dic-
> tated by our Africentric social reality. (p. 74)

From an ecological perspective, this equation of an authentic *black*
self with the concept of African self-consciousness is embodied within

a macro-level narrative referred to as the *jargon of authenticity* (Bush, 1999; Thomas, 1997). At meso- and micro-levels, this narrative manifests in demoralized public media representations that attach shame and stigma to bisexual desires, identities, and behavior (Flannigan-Saint-Aubin, 1993; Hunter & Alexander, 1996; Lubiano, 1998a, 1998b; May & Strikwerda, 1992; Stokes & Peterson, 1998), and in the conflation of femininity, masculinity, and sexual behavior with compulsory heterosexuality (see Constantine-Simms, 2000; Hemphill, 1991; for excellent reviews of relevant literatures).

The jargon of authenticity marks boundaries that establish compulsory heterosexuality as the *norm* within many black subcultures and, thereby, polices emotional and sexual bonding between bisexuals (Carbado & Weise, 2004; Scott, 2004). Such policing has been effective through the languaging of all forms of homoeroticism as deviant or pathological (Atwell & Azibo, 1991; Azibo, 1989; Baldwin, 1989; Baldwin, Brown, & Rackley, 1990; Jackson, 1970, 1990; Nobles, 1985, 1986) and through forms of identity politics that marginalize sexual minorities (Eggerling-Boeck, 2002; Harrison & Harrison, 2002; Tate, 1988). These constructs continue to function as forms of oppression that effectively dislodge and excommunicate bisexuals from African American communities and ethnicities by framing them as inauthentic or not *truly black* (Adeleke, 1998). In consequence, the public disclosure of a bisexual identity, constructed by the Africentric scholars list above, may lead to the loss of a coherent self, a loss of place, as well as social inequity, and mental slavery.

HEGEMONIC REPRESENTATIONS OF THE BISEXUAL AS OTHER

To repeat, many African American bisexuals encounter demoralized and stereotypical social representations of themselves. I use the concept of positionality to denote the social position of the knower (here, it is the bisexual client) as shaped by variables such as class, race, gender, and sexual orientation. Questions of positionality are epistemological in nature in that they relate to how knowledge is produced and how the knower obtains knowledge of her- or himself. Given that many African American bisexuals are not members of the privileged classes, they may benefit from a therapeutic focus on how the limited perspective and ignorance of members of the privileged class shape their identities and their subjective appraisals of their well-being.

Epistemology involves theorizing about knowledge and the exploration of the nature, scope, and legitimacy of knowledge claims. As
Foucault (1972, 1978) points out throughout much of his work, that
which is determined to be true is largely the product of who has the
power to assert and insert a specific discourse into the public's or a specific sector's awareness. "Wherever truth is claimed, so is power; the
claim to truth is a claim to power" (Richardson, 1981, p. 173). Research
on homosexuality, for example, has been frequently framed within a social deviance paradigm that *produced knowledge* by situating lesbian,
gay, and bisexual people within certain theoretical assumptions that in
turn contributed to negative conceptions of their lives and their identities (Tierney, 1993). Clearly, the stance these theorists brought to their
studies shaped what were purported to be objective findings. Foucault's
work (1972, 1978) has consistently illustrated the role of power expressed through language and discourse in situating sexual identities. It
is difficult to refute Foucault's contention that a variety of social practices have served to situate heterosexuality in a hegemonic relationship
to homosexuality that marginalizes the latter. The power of the *norm* is
central to Foucault and his explanation of how homosexuality has come
to occupy the margins of social life. As Foucault argues, the emergence
of *homosexual* as a category of people has brought about the possibility
of large-scale oppression of these individuals.

Other critical postmodern and feminist theorists also call attention to
the idea that knowledge is relational (Agger, 1991; Benhabib, 1986; Fox,
2003; Hall, 1990; Kellner, 1988, 1990; Maroda, 2000; Munoz, 1999;
Somerville, 2000; Tolman & Diamond, 2001). Truth claims do not exist
on their own (Lyotard, 1984). Instead, they must be grounded in specific
assumptions (i.e., the jargon of authenticity) that first must be accepted
within a particular community of individuals. Like notions of truth, identities are also framed by discourses contingent to a large degree on power
relations. Power is evident through the ability to control the discourse or
language of identity. The notion that identities are essentially unstable because they are shaped within historical and cultural discourses elaborates
on this idea (Hall, 1990). The contentious nature of history and culture
situates identities within a contested field resulting in ongoing struggle,
which is often played out within identity politics.

PATHOLOGIZING BISEXUALITY

As discussed above, the failure of many black subcultures to affirm the
lived experiences of bisexuals is expressed through linguistic constructs

such as hegemony, positionality, and identity politics (Eggerling-Boeck, 2002; Harrison & Harrison, 2002). In consequence, therapists may assist African American bisexuals to continually deconstruct hegemonic forms of femininity and masculinity, demoralized public media representations of their being, and the stigma and shame attached to homoerotic expressions of sexuality (Greene & Croom, 2000; Norton, 2002; Williams, 1997). Deconstructions of hegemonic femininities and masculinities are often accompanied by a need to resist the nature of a particular self, constructed by indigenous Africentric patriarchal psychologies. Indigenous Africentric patriarchal psychologies, for the purposes of this manuscript, refer to a set of ideas put forth by theorists including Atwell and Azibo (1991), Baldwin (1989), Dixon and Azibo (1998), and Nobles (1985, 1986) that equate African American bisexual identities with a pathological personality disorder, misorientation, in which the consequence is a "loss of self." The main tenets of these theories hold that misorientation is disease-like; that it is constituted of particular behaviors; that it is a self-diagnosed but widespread condition; and that its cure hinges on a therapeutic recovery process (reparative therapy).

Through the propagation of concepts such as an *African self-consciousness*, *African's psychological blackness*, and *psychological misorientation* (Atwell & Azibo, 1991; Baldwin, Brown, & Rackley, 1990; Dennard, 1998), these ideologies perpetuate hegemonic discourses that link specific identities to psychopathology. For example, these theorists conceptualize African American bisexual identities within a disease model and posit that these identities have an onset, a definable course, and if left untreated, a predictable psychopathic outcome (see the diagnostic nosology of APA, 2000). Despite disagreement on its ontological basis–whether or not it is a disease, these theorists agree that it is a painful and ultimately self-destructive "physical, mental, emotional, and spiritual condition" (Atwell & Azibo, 1991).

THERAPIST VARIABLES

Providing affirmative therapy represents the adoption of particular stances that include a degree of advocacy in promoting an explicit agenda of raising experiences of oppression into consciousness, deprogramming, undoing negative conditioning associated with negative stereotypes of bisexuals, and minimizing the effects of direct violence and oppression (Milton & Coyle, 1999; Palma & Stanley, 2002).

Therapeutic work with this population requires an understanding of black indigenous psychologies and the social constructionist literature to highlight how identities, gender, and the expressions of sexuality are socially constructed (Butler, 1993; Felluga, 2003; Garnets, 2002; Norton, 2002; Schueller, 1999; Wyatt, 1997). Clinical work with this population also requires an understanding of how general psychological constructs within the rubrics of cognition, perception, and emotional bonds are often conflated with sexual behaviors. Clinicians must possess the ability to distinguish emotional and cognitive bonding from manifestations of behavioral bisexuality (McKirnan, Stokes, Doll, & Burzette, 1995; Peterson, 1991; Stokes, McKirnan, & Burzette, 1993; Stokes, McKirnan, Doll, & Burzette, 1996). Belief and praxis are not always consistent.

More specifically, providing affirmative psychotherapy to African American bisexual clients requires that the clinician has worked through her or his own sexual identity formation and has reached a point where he or she is comfortable with this identity (or identities) and have transcended the sex-role and gender binaries that constrain these behaviors in the United States. For gay, lesbian, and other bisexual therapists working with this sub-population requires comfort with their own homoerotic feelings and the ability to address and work with erotic transferences and counter-transferences when these arise (Book, 1995; Frost, 1998; Maroda, 2000; Rosiello, 2000).

As discussed above, an understanding of how social and political practices have and continue to police the sexuality of African Americans is essential to assisting bisexuals within these subcultures in finding meaning in and validating their experiences (Carbado, McBride, & Weise, 2002; Carby, 1992; Munoz, 1999; Somerville, 2000). This emphasis on the experiential in the production of meaning and knowledge requires a departure from positivist approaches and the etic formulations produced within these paradigms. By contrast, an ignorance of the diversity that exists among African American bisexuals leads to imposing particular stereotypical identities on these clients while simultaneously silencing other possible constructions and expressions of their identities. Similarly, overemphasizing the role of bisexual identities has been found to be harmful to the content and process of the therapeutic encounter. This phenomenon often manifests when clinicians situate *all or most* of the clients' concerns within or arising from their bisexual identities. Overemphasizing the role of bisexual identities represents an indirect form of pathologizing these identities (Milton & Coyle, 1999).

PROMOTING WELL-BEING
THROUGH INTEGRATIVE THERAPY

The recognition that bisexuality involves emotional and cognitive bonding with another regardless of his or her perceived gender is the antithesis of the doctrine that gendered behavior can only be interpreted within one of two categories, female or male, and that sexual and romantic bonds are only possible between rather than within these categories. Therapeutically, such recognition allows the clinician to move beyond situating bisexuality solely within love relationships. Rather, each case conceptualization addresses the complexity of African American bisexuals' identities and their relationship to each other and to heteronormative-hegemonic structures. Therapists working with this population are advised to be cognizant of how social and political forms of invalidation become languaged as psychopathology to silence the voices of these individuals. Thus, one aspect of promoting well-being for these clients may involve incorporating an overt acknowledgement of social and political issues into the therapeutic content and process, as appropriate (Carbado & Weise, 2004; Dennard, 1998).

From a narrative therapy perspective, African American bisexuals are cast as readers and writers, both read and written upon, who can only be understood within the ecology of U.S. culture. Here, African American bisexuals actively construct (and are actively constructed by) the moral, political, and ideological concerns of their families of origin and communities (Esterberg, 1997; Firestein, 1996; Harris, 2002; Nobles, 1985). Reading bisexuality in this manner redirects the therapeutic focus toward intersecting narratives of cultural histories, worldviews, and class dynamics that shape bisexuality and homoerotic desire. At times the story line reflects a critical reflexive movement away from the individual's psyche toward a socially and historically informed focus on the particulars in that client's experiences of oppression and/or liberation (Prilleltensky & Nelson, 2002). To address this complexity, it may prove efficacious for each case conceptualization to address the following broad themes for problem identification and resolution:

1. The sociocultural and political dimensions that shape identity development for African American bisexuals;
2. The client's experience of invalidation, marginality and oppression as related to heterosexist and patriarchal gender and sexual ideologies that are often prevalent in African American communities; and

3. An exploration of the benefits accrued through amassing sufficient social capital toward the promotion of mental health and well-being in their lives.

Theoretically, it is recommended that clinicians ground each case conceptualization in an integrative therapy model, where narrative therapy serves as a meta-theory that emphasizes the important role of language, context, and a collaborative approach to working with clients. This collaboration allows each client to construct her or his problems as stories that have been reinforced by dominant narratives circulating within his or her cultural histories and which are often internalized as a habitual pattern for construing reality. Here African American bisexuals actively construct (and are actively constructed by) the moral, political, and ideological concerns of their families of origin and communities.

Clinicians can use theories and techniques from a variety of models in a compatible way to facilitate the change processes of narrative therapy. Such change typically involves assisting the client in achieving desired outcomes through creating more preferred stories about problems and their lives. Developing alternate narratives becomes liberating because they enable these clients to re-author their lives and resist impoverishing, subjugating and disenfranchising dominant narratives such as the jargon of authenticity. In particular, it is crucial for therapists to assist clients in understanding how ostracism and social invalidation signify an absence of social capital that may contribute to their psychological distress. That is, garnering access to valued resources improve the likelihood that physical, psychological, and political well-being will ensue as well as social capital for problem identification and resolution.

A dual emphasis on the resources embedded in social relations and network or network characteristics has been empirically demonstrated to bolster well-being (Volanen, Lahelma, Silventoinen, & Suominen, 2004). That is, social capital has been demonstrated to enhance the likelihood of instrumental returns, such as better jobs, earlier promotions, higher earnings or bonuses, and expressive returns, such as better mental health. The presence of such health-promoting factors at all ecological levels can have positive and synergistic effect on well-being. Because good mental health derives from participation and membership in family groups, social networks, or other social structures that enhance self-acceptance, personal growth, trust, safety, and reciprocity, assisting the client in achieving social capital may be one goal of the therapy. As such, the accrual of social capital represents a desired outcome toward preventing disease and facilitating recovery from illness or adaptation to chronic acculturative stress.

Therapists may also assist African American bisexuals to deconstruct hegemonic narratives of femininity and masculinity, demoralized public media representations of their being, and the stigma and shame attached to homoerotic expressions of sexuality. Deconstruction is another strategy used to assist clients to create alternate stories that contest hegemonic narratives. To repeat, hegemony means predominant influence, especially when it involves defining heterosexual performances of gender as desirable and natural. In accord with African American traditions of subversion and identity politics (Conerly, 1996; Firestein, 1996; Icard, 1985; Munoz, 1999; Ongiri, 1997; Reid-Pharr, 2002; Somerville, 2000), African American bisexual identities represent subversive discourses that undermine two binaries common to the dominant U.S. culture and patriarchal Africentric worldviews. These dichotomous systems include the male-female gender/sex system and the homosexual-heterosexual binary (Butler, 1993; Gambs, 2003).

An understanding of these subversive features of gender and sexual identities will permit clinicians to reconceptualize identities, desire, and the expression of sexual behavior as located along intra-cultural and intra-ethnic continuums. Conceptualized in these ways, bisexuality emerges as a more inclusive category than sexual activity alone. Depending on the client's goals, a therapeutic focus on the subversive qualities of the client's identities may assist the client to achieve psychic and social liberation. For some clients, this therapeutic focus may germinate the seeds for emancipatory cultural politics. It becomes emancipatory through advocacy and activism that deconstructs the oppressive, homosexual-heterosexual binary and the male-female gender/sex system in contemporary U.S. society as well as the jargon of authenticity.

Therapists may assist these clients to understand that this narrative is predicated on the notion that homoerotic desire (Tolman & Diamond, 2001) or homosexuality did not exist in pre-colonial Africa (Black, 1997; Jackson, 1970, 1990). Patton (1992) and more recent scholar-activists (Epprecht, 2002; Eskridge, 1993; Forché, 1993; Mkhize, 2001; Murray & Roscoe, 1998; Summers, 2002) refute this heteronormative-hegemonic revisioning of collective memory by proponents of Africentricism. In rebuttal, they demonstrate that homoerotism and homosexual emotional bonding and cohabitation were not unusual in pre-colonial African cultures. While increasing a client's understanding of this hegemonic myth may foster their development of a more coherent sense of themselves, it may also be necessary to assist the client to find heterosexual and homosexual allies, and alternate spaces and communities for support, validation, emotional bonding, and liberation.

REFERENCES

Abreu, J. M., Goodyear, R. K., Campos, A., & Newcomb, M. D. (2000). Ethnic Belonging and Traditional Masculinity Ideology among African Americans, European Americans, and Latinos. *Psychology of Men & Masculinity, 1*, 75-86.

Adeleke, T. (1998). *Unafrican Americans: Nineteenth-century black nationalists and the civilizing mission.* Lexington: University Kentucky Press.

Agger, B. (1991). Critical theory, poststructuralism, postmodernism: Their sociological relevance. *Annual Review of Sociology, 17*, 105-131.

American Psychiatric Association. (2000). *Diagnostic and statistical manual of mental disorders* (4th ed.; Text revision: DSM-IV-TR). Washington, DC: Author.

Atwell, I., & Azibo, D. A. (1991). Diagnosing personality disorders in Africans (blacks) using the Azibo Nosology: Two case studies. *The Journal of Black Psychology, 17*, 1-22.

Azibo, D. A. (1989). African-centered theses on mental health and a nosology of Black/African personality disorder. *The Journal of Black Psychology, 15*, 173-214.

Baldwin, J. A. (1989). The role of black psychologists in black liberation. *The Journal of Black Psychology, 16*, 67-76.

Baldwin, J. A., Brown, R., & Rackley, R. (1990). Some socio-behavioral correlates of African self-consciousness in African-American college students. *The Journal of Black Psychology, 17*, 1-17.

Benhabib, S. (1986). *Critique, norm, and utopia.* New York: Columbia University.

Black, D. P. (1997). *Dismantling black manhood: An historical and literary analysis of the legacy of slavery.* New York: Garland Publishing.

Book, H. E. (1995). The "erotic transference:" Some technical and countertechnical difficulties. *American Journal of Psychotherapy, 49*, 504.

Brandt, S. (2000). American Culture X: Identity, homosexuality and the search for a new American hero. In R. West & F. Lay (Eds.), *Subverting masculinity: Hegemonic and alternative versions of masculinity in contemporary culture* (pp. 67-93). Atlanta, GA: Rodopi.

Bush, L. (1999). Am I a man?: A literature review engaging the sociohistorical dynamics of black manhood in the United States. *Western Journal of Black Studies, 23*, 49-58.

Butler, J. (1993). *Bodies that matter: On the discursive limits of "sex."* New York: Routledge.

Carbado, D. W., McBride, D. A., & Weise, D. (2002). *Black like us: A century of lesbian, gay, and bisexual African American fiction.* San Francisco: Cleis Press.

Carbado, D. W., & Weise, D. (2004). The Civil Rights Identity of Bayard Rustin. *Texas Law Review, 82*, 1133-1196.

Carby, H. V. (1992). Policing the black woman's body in an urban context. *Critical Inquiry, 18*, 738-755.

Conerly, G. (1996). The politics of black lesbian, gay, and bisexual identity. In B. Bleemyn & M. Eliason (Eds.), *Queer studies: A lesbian, gay, bisexual & transgendered anthology* (pp. 133-145). New York: New York University Press.

Constantine-Simms, D. (2000). *The greatest taboo: Homosexuality in black communities.* Los Angeles: Alyson Books.

D'Augelli, A. R., & Patterson, C. J. (Eds.). (1995). *Lesbian, gay, and bisexual identities over the lifespan: Psychological approaches.* New York: Oxford University Press.

Dennard, D. (1998). Application of the Azibo Nosology in clinical practice with black clients: A case study. *The Journal of Black Psychology, 24,* 182-195.

Diener, E., Suh, E., & Oishi, S. (1997). Recent findings on subjective well-being. Retrieved May 7, 2005 from: *http://www.psych.uiuc.edu/~ediener/hottopic/paper1.html*

Eggerling-Boeck, J. (2002). Issues of Black identity: A review of the literature. *African American Research Perspectives, 8,* 17-26.

Emig, R. (2000). Queering the straights: Straightening queers: Commodified sexualities and hegemonic masculinity. In R. West & F. Lay (Eds.), *Subverting masculinity: Hegemonic and alternative versions of masculinity in contemporary culture* (pp. 207-226). Atlanta, GA: Rodopi.

Epprecht, M. (2002). Male-male sexuality in Lesotho: Two conversations. *Journal of Men's Studies, 10,* 373-384.

Eskridge, W. N., Jr. (1993). A history of same-sex marriages. *Virginia Law Review, 79,* 1419-1513.

Esterberg, K. G. (1997). *Lesbian & bisexual identities: Constructing communities, constructing selves.* Philadelphia: Temple University Press.

Felluga, D. (June 25, 2003). Modules on Butler: On performativity: Introductory guide to critical theory. Retrieved October 11, 2003 from: *http://www.purdue.edu/guidetotheory/genderandsex/modules/butlerperformativity.html.*

Felski, R. (1997). The doxa of difference. *Signs, 23,* 1-22.

Firestein, B. A. (Ed.). (1996). *Bisexuality: The psychology and politics of an invisible minority.* Thousand Oaks, CA: Sage.

Flannigan-Saint-Aubin, A. (1993). Black Gay Male discourse: Reading race and sexuality between the lines. In C. Fout & M. S. Tantillo (Eds.), *American sexual politics: Sex, gender, and race since the Civil War* (pp. 381-403). Chicago: The University of Chicago Press.

Forché, C. (Ed.). (1993). *Against forgetting: Twentieth-century poetry of witness.* New York: W. W. Norton & Company.

Foucault, M. (1972). *The archaeology of knowledge and the discourse on language* (A. M. S. Smith, Trans.). New York: Pantheon Books.

Foucault, M. (1978). *The history of sexuality, Volume I: An introduction* (R. Hurley, Trans). New York: Vintage.

Fox, R. C. (2003). Bisexual identities. In L. D. Garnets & D. C. Kimmel (Eds.), *Psychological perspectives on lesbian, gay, and bisexual experiences* (pp. 86-129). New York: Columbia University Press.

Frost, J. C. (1998). Countertransference considerations for the gay male when leading psychotherapy groups for gay men. *International Journal of Group Psychotherapy, 48,* 3-24.

Frumkin, H. Healthy places: Exploring the evidence. *American Journal of Public Health, 93,* 1451-1459.

Gambs, D. (2003). Bisexuality: Beyond the binary? *The Journal of Sex Research, 40,* 317-320.

Garnets, L. (2002). Sexual orientations in perspective. *Cultural Diversity and Ethnic Minority Psychology, 8,* 115-129.

Gates, H. L. (1997). *Thirteen ways of looking at a black man.* New York: Random House.

Giroux, H. A. (1993). *Living dangerously: Multiculturalism and the politics of difference.* New York: Peter Lang.

Gonzalez, M. (2000). The Moor's Last Sigh (Salman Rushdie): Marginal alternatives, the reconstruction of identity through the Carnival of Indetermination. In R. West & F. Lay (Eds.), *Subverting masculinity: Hegemonic and alternative versions of masculinity in contemporary culture* (pp. 128-143). Atlanta, GA: Rodopi.

Gramsci, A. (1977). *Selections from political writings (1910 1920)* (J. Mathews, Trans.). London: Lawrence & Wishart; International Publishers.

Gramsci, A., Forgacs, D., & Nowell-Smith, G. (1985). *Selection from cultural writing.* (W. Boelhower, Trans.). London: Harvard University Press.

Greene, B., & Croom, G. L. (Eds.). (2000). *Education, research, and practice in lesbian, gay, bisexual, and transgendered psychology: A resource manual* (pp. 1 45). Thousand Oaks, CA: Sage.

Hall, S. (1990). Cultural identity and diaspora. In J. Rutherford (Ed.), *Identity: Community, culture, difference* (pp. 222-237). London: Lawrence & Wishart.

Harris, E. L. (1994). *Invisible life: A novel.* New York: Anchor Books.

Harris, L. A. (2002). Black feminism and queer families: A conversation with Thomas Allen Harris. *African American Review; 36,* 273-282.

Harrison, L., & Harrison, C. K. (2002). African American racial identity: Theory and application to education, race, and sport in America. *African American Research Perspectives, 8,* 35-46.

Hemphill, E. (Ed.). (1991). *Brother to brother: New writings by black gay men.* Boston: Alyson.

Henderson, S., & Whiteford, H. (2003). Social capital and mental health. *The Lancet, 362,* 505-508.

Henson, K. D., & Rogers, J. K. (2004). "Why Marcia You've Changed!" Male clerical temporary workers doing masculinity in a feminized occupation. In M. S. Kimmel & M. A. Messner (Eds.), *Men's lives* (6th ed.). Boston: Pearson.

hooks, b. (1989). *Talking back: Thinking feminist, thinking black.* Boston: South End Press.

hooks, b. (1994). *Outlaw culture: Resisting representations.* New York: Routledge.

Hunter, J., & Alexander, P. (1996). Women who sleep with women. In L. D. Long and E. M. Ankrah (Eds.), *Women's experiences with HIV/AIDS: An international perspective* (pp. 42-55). New York: Columbia University Press.

Icard, L. (1985). Black gay men and conflicting social identities: Sexual orientation versus racial identity. *Journal of Social Work and Human Sexuality, 4,* 83-93.

Jackson, G. (1970). *Soledad brother: The prison letters of George Jackson.* New York: Bantam Books.

Jackson, G. (1990). *Blood in my eye.* Baltimore: Black Classic Press.

Kellner, D. (1988). Postmodernism as social theory: Some challenges and problems. *Theory, Culture & Society, 5,* 239-269.

King, J. (2003). Remixing the closet. *Village Voice, 48,* 38-46.

Labriola, K. (2003) What is bisexuality? Who is bisexual? Retrieved October 13, 2003 from: *http://www.bayarea.net/~stef/Poly/Labriola/bisexual.html*

Lin, N. (2000). Inequality in social capital. *Contemporary Sociology, 29,* 785-795.

Loiacano, D. K. (1989). Gay identity issues among black Americans: Racism, homophobia, and the need for validation. *Journal of Counseling and Development, 68,* 21-25.

Lubiano, W. (1998a). Black nationalism and black common sense: Policing ourselves and others. In W. Lubiano (Ed.), *The house that race built: Black Americans, U.S. terrain* (pp.232-252). New York: Pantheon Books.

Lubiano, W. (Ed.). (1998b). *The house that race built.* New York: Pantheon Books.

Lyotard, J. F. (1984). *The postmodern condition.* Minneapolis: University of Minnesota Press.

Maroda, K. J. (2000). On homoeroticism, erotic countertransference, and the postmodern view of life: A commentary on papers by Rosiello, Tholfsen, and Meyers. *Journal of Gay & Lesbian Psychotherapy, 4,* 61-70.

May, L. & Strikwerda, R. (Eds.). (1992). *Rethinking masculinity: Philosophical explorations in light of feminism.* Lanham, MD: Rowman & Littlefield Publishers.

McKirnan, D. J., Stokes, J. P., Doll, L., & Burzette, R. G. (1995). Bisexually active men: Social characteristics and sexual behavior. *The Journal of Sex Research, 32,* 65-76.

Mellstrom, U. (2002). Patriarchal machines and masculine embodiment. *Science, Technology & Human Values, 27,* 460-479.

Milton, M., & Coyle, A. (1999). Lesbian and gay affirmative psychotherapy: Issues in theory and practice. *Sexual and Marital Therapy, 14,* 43-60.

Mkhize, V. (2001). A gay Zulu language: Behind the mask. Retrieved October 24, 2003 from: *www.mask.org.*

Moraga, C. L., & Anzaldua, G. E. (Eds.). (2002). *This bridge called my back: Writings by radical women of color.* Berkeley: Third Women Press.

Munoz, J. E. (1999). *Disidentifications: Queers of color and the performance of politics.* Minneapolis: University of Minnesota Press.

Murray, S. O., & Roscoe, W. (Eds.). (1998). *Boy-wives and female husbands: Studies of African homosexualities.* New York: St. Martin's Press.

Nero, C. I. (2004). Black queer identity, imaginative rationality, and the language of home. In A. Gonzalez, M. Houston, & V. Chen (Eds.), *Our voices: Essays in culture, ethnicity, and communication* (pp. 74-79). Los Angeles: Roxbury Publishing Company.

Nobles, W. W. (1985). *Africanity and the Black family: The development of a theoretical model* (2nd ed.). Oakland, CA: Institute of the Advanced Study of Black Family Life and Culture.

Nobles, W. W. (1986). *African psychology: Toward its reclamation, reascension, and revitalization.* Oakland, CA: Institute of the Advanced Study of Black Family Life and Culture.

Norton, R. (June 2002). A critique of social constructionism and postmodern queer theory: Essentialism. Retrieved October 11, 2003 from: *http://www.infopt.demon.co.uk/social03.htm.*

Ongiri, A. A. (1997). We are family: Black nationalism, Black masculinity, and the Black gay cultural imagination. *College Literature, 24,* 280-294.

Palma, T. V., & Stanley, J. L. (2002). Effective counseling with lesbian, gay, and bisexual clients. *Journal of College Counseling, 5,* 76-90.

Parham, T. A., & Brown, S. (2003). Therapeutic approaches with African American populations. In F. D. Harper & J. McFadden (Eds.), *Culture and counseling: New approaches* (pp. 81-98). Boston: Allyn and Bacon.

Patton, C. (1992). From nation to family: Containing "African AIDS." In A. Parker, M. Russo, D. Sommer, & P. Yaeger (Eds.), *Nationalisms & Sexualities* (pp. 218-234). New York: Routledge.

Peplau, L. A., & Spalding, L. R. (2003). The close relationships of lesbians, gay men, and bisexuals. In L. D. Garnets & D. C. Kimmel (Eds.), *Psychological perspectives on lesbian, gay, and bisexual experiences* (pp. 449-475). New York: Columbia University Press.

Peterson, J. L. (1991). Black men and their same sex desires and behaviors. In G. Herdt (Ed.), *Gay culture in America: Essays from the field* (pp. 147-164). Boston: Beacon Press.

Pilkington, P. (2002). Social capital and health: Measuring and understanding social capital at a local level could help to tackle health inequalities more effectively. *Journal of Public Health Medicine, 24,* 156-159.

Prilleltensky, I., & Nelson, G. (2002). *Doing psychology critically: Making a difference in diverse settings.* New York: Palgrave Macmillan.

Reid-Pharr, R. F. (2001). *Black gay man: Essays.* New York: New York University Press.

Reid-Pharr, R. F. (2002). Extending queer theory to race and ethnicity. *The Chronicle of Higher Education; 48,* B7-B9.

Richardson, B. B. (1981). Racism and child-rearing: A study of Black mothers. (Doctoral dissertation, The Claremont Graduate University). *Dissertation Abstracts International, 42,* 125A.

Rosiello, F. (2000). On lust and loathing: Erotic transference/countertransference between a female analyst and female patients. *Journal of Gay & Lesbian Psychotherapy, 4,* 5-26.

Said, E. W. (1993). *Culture and imperialism.* New York: Knopf.

Schueller, M. J. (1999). Performing whiteness, performing blackness: Dorr's cultural capital and the critique of slavery. *Criticism, 41,* 233-256.

Scott, D. M., III. (2004). Harlem shadows: Re-evaluating Wallace Thurman's The Blacker the Berry. *MELUS, 29,* 323-340.

Somerville, S. B. (2000). *Queering the color line: Race and the invention of homosexuality in American culture.* London: Duke University Press.

Stokes, J. P., McKirnan, D. J., & Burzette, R. G. (1993). Sexual behavior, condom use, disclosure of sexuality, and stability of sexual orientation in bisexual men. *The Journal of Sex Research, 30,* 203-213.

Stokes, J. P., McKirnan, D. J., Doll, L., & Burzette, R. G. (1996). Female partners of bisexual men: What they don't know might hurt them. *Psychology of Women Quarterly, 20*, 267-284.

Stokes, J. P., & Peterson, J. L. (1998). Homophobia, self-esteem, and risk for HIV among African American men who have sex with men. *AIDS Education and Prevention, 10*, 278-292.

Summers, M. (2002). "This immoral practice:" The prehistory of homophobia in black nationalist thought. In T. Lester (Ed.), *Gender nonconformity, race, and sexuality* (pp. 21-43). Madison, Wisconsin: The University of Wisconsin Press.

Tate, G. T. (1988). Black nationalism: An angle of vision. *Western Journal of Black Studies, 12*, 41-47.

Thomas, K. (1997). "Ain't nothing like the real thing:" Black masculinity, gay sexuality, and the jargon of authenticity. In W. Lubiano (Ed.), *The house that race built* (pp.116-135). New York: Pantheon Books.

Tierney, W. G. (1993). *Building communities of difference: Higher education in the 21st century*. Westport, CT: Bergin & Garvey.

Tolman, D. L., & Diamond, L. M. (2001). Desegregating sexuality research: Cultural and biological perspectives on gender and desire. *Annual Review of Sex Research, 12*, 33-74.

Trebay, G. (2000). Homo thugz blow up the spot. *The Village Voice, 45*, 44-48.

Volanen, S-M., Lahelma, E., Silventoinen, K., & Suominen, S. (2004). Factors contributing to sense of coherence among men and women. *European Journal of Public Health, 14*, 322-331.

Weinberg, M. S., Williams, C. J., & Pryor, D. W. (2004). Becoming bisexual. In M. Stombler, D. M. Baunach, E. O. Burgess, D. Donnelly, & W. Simonds (Eds.), *Sex matters: The sexuality and society reader* (pp. 23-30). Boston: Pearson.

West, C. (2001). *Race matters*. Boston: Beacon Press.

White, J. L., & Cones, J. H. (1999). *Black man emerging: Facing the past and seizing a future in America*. New York: W. H. Freeman and Company.

Williams, R. M. (1997). Living at the crossroads: Explorations in race, nationality, sexuality, and gender. In W. Lubiano (Ed.), *The house that race built: Black Americans, U.S.* terrain (pp.136-156). New York: Pantheon Books.

Wood, S. W. (2000). Prison masculinities. *Library Journal, 125*, 167.

Wright, K. (2001). The great down-low debate. *The Village Voice, 46*, 23-25.

Wyatt, G. E. (1997). *Stolen women: Reclaiming our sexuality, taking back our lives*. New York: John Wiley & Sons, Inc.

Affirmative Psychotherapy with Older Bisexual Women and Men

Bobbi Keppel

Available online at http://www.haworthpress.com/web/JB
© 2006 by The Haworth Press, Inc. All rights reserved.
doi:10.1300/J159v06n01_06

[Haworth co-indexing entry note]: "Affirmative Psychotherapy with Older Bisexual Women and Men."
Keppel, Bobbi. Co-published simultaneously in *Journal of Bisexuality* (Harrington Park Press, an imprint of
The Haworth Press, Inc.) Vol. 6, No. 1/2, 2006, pp. 85-104; and: *Affirmative Psychotherapy with Bisexual
Women and Bisexual Men* (ed: Ronald C. Fox) Harrington Park Press, an imprint of The Haworth Press, Inc.,
2006, pp. 85-104. Single or multiple copies of this article are available for a fee from The Haworth Document
Delivery Service [1-800-HAWORTH, 9:00 a.m. - 5:00 p.m. (EST). E-mail address: docdelivery@
haworthpress.com].

SUMMARY. When bisexual clients come to therapy, they are likely to bring specific bisexual aging issues, including coming out, isolation, lack of supportive social networks, and the impact of agism, homophobia, bi-negativity and biphobia in their personal and professional lives. Many have been ignored, patronized, and/or discounted because of their bisexual orientation and will not reveal their identity until the therapist demonstrates an understanding, accepting, and supportive attitude toward bisexuality. This article discusses ways in which therapists can be most helpful. They can increase their knowledge and comfort levels with bisexuality and with polyamory so they can fully support bisexual identity and behaviors. They can use language which is comfortable for the client since language choice varies within the age range referred to as the "aging" population. Some clients may not self-identify as bisexual, particularly those who reached adulthood before *bisexual* and *bisexuality* appeared in the media. Therapists can develop expertise and guide clients in finding and using community and online bisexuality-related resources. They can look for resources to support bisexual end of life and other spiritual needs. They can find resources for safer sex education and develop some ability to provide that education when resources cannot be found. They can refuse to assume that everyone is either *straight* or lesbian/gay male whether or not she or he is coupled, married, divorced, and/or a parent. They can make themselves allies for bisexuals by speaking supportively and accurately about bisexuality with their own and other professional colleagues, and by supporting bisexual visibility in their communities and their professional organizations. *[Article copies available for a fee from The Haworth Document Delivery Service: 1-800-HAWORTH. E-mail address: <docdelivery@haworthpress.com> Website: <http://www.HaworthPress.com> © 2006 by The Haworth Press, Inc. All rights reserved.]*

KEYWORDS. Bisexuality, bisexual, psychotherapy, counseling, bisexual women, bisexual men, aging, elders, older bisexual women, older bisexual men

INTRODUCTION

The issues that older bisexual women and men bring to therapy are similar in many ways to more general therapeutic issues for seniors and for bisexuals. There are also differences for this group that are specific to being older and bisexual. What is different about therapy with older bisexuals from therapy with non-bisexual elders and with younger bisexuals? What will be helpful to you and your clients in working together?

As therapists, you know how to look through several lenses at once. Think of looking through one of those teleidoscope toys which show many views of the same object at the same time. While you can't focus on all of the images at once, all are important in understanding the whole. Each image shows a different aspect of the same person; in this case, for example, bisexual, senior, or gender. If you integrate all of the images, you may see one bisexual elder. Looking at me in that way, some of the images you will see are bisexual, clinical social worker, senior (72), bisexual activist, safer sex educator, and female. I came out as bisexual 30 years ago in a midwestern city. I was married, and we had two young children at home.

My therapy practices have all been in small cities. I have never practiced in the few large metro areas which have big bisexual populations, although I have been part of the Boston area bisexual movement for 18 years, and I have been working with the Bisexual Health Project's safer sex outreach program in Boston for 5 years. I have now lived in urban southern Maine for almost 20 years. Most of the population is European American. The state is as rural as Nebraska, where I lived before. For 15 years, I have been teaching mental health and health professionals, teachers, counselors, parents, religious educators, and others about bisexuality and how it fits into the larger picture of sexuality and sexual orientation. Here, I will focus on some of the most salient characteristics of older bisexuals, the kinds of issues that they are likely to bring to therapy, and ways for therapists and counselors to provide affirmative and appropriate mental health services to this population.

One way to get a sense of the issues on which you will be working with older bisexual clients is to put together a set of images that illustrate these issues. Start with images of the place where the oppression of older members of our society meets the oppression of bisexuals. Stripes might work, or you can make each image a different color. Now, try adding images for heterosexism and homosexism. Often you will also be working with additional oppressions such as ableism, racism, and ethnic differences. If each of these oppressions has a different color, the area could look like one of those fancy marbles where colors swirl around, sometimes blending, sometimes not; but it's all in one marble.

TERMINOLOGY

When I use the terms *bisexual women, bisexual men,* or *bisexuals,* I may be writing both about people who identify with the label and those whose attractions are to persons of more than one sex and gender, whether or not they choose the bisexual label, or any label at all. I use the term *queer* as a non-pejorative collective noun for non-heterosexuals, and *gay* for gay men. I use acronyms like *BGLT* (bisexual, gay, lesbian, transgender), and not always in the same order, and *G/L* or *L/G* (gay and lesbian). I use *GLH* for gay, lesbian, and heterosexual, the identities which are the "other" for bisexuals. Sometimes, I string a bunch together like *BGLTQI* for bisexual, gay, lesbian, transgender, questioning, and intersex.

Although bisexual women and men are often described as attracted to the same and opposite sexes, the attraction is more likely to be to gender than to sex, i.e., to the gender presentation of the person, rather than the biological markers of genes and chromosomes. Furthermore, since there are biologically more than two sexes, there is no "opposite" sex. "Other" or "another" are more appropriate words. Extensive explanations and examples are found in Natalie Angier's *Woman: An Intimate Geography* (1999) and Joan Roughgarden's *Evolution's Rainbow* (2004).

PRESENTING ISSUES

The chances are that your average older bisexual will not come in talking about bisexuality even if that is her or his major issue. Instead, older bisexual women and men are likely to come into therapy and counseling with the more usual therapeutic issues of older people, such as depression, loss, separation, relationships, and isolation. These are more likely starting points, in part because they are more acceptable topics for most therapists. By the time they come to you, most of these individuals will have had experiences of being discounted, patronized, and ignored because of age. They will compensate by looking for the most acceptable ways to be seen and heard. Similarly, if they have been ignored, patronized and discounted on account of their sexual orientation, they will start with another topic–one that they believe will be more acceptable to you.

IDENTITY AND LABELING

Even more so than with gay men and lesbians, bisexual men and bisexual women may choose not to reveal their sexual identity to the therapist. In many cases, clients may not use the labels *bisexual* or *bi* for themselves, although they may be attracted to, and sexually and/or emotionally involved with, persons of more than one sex and gender, concurrently or over time. Some sexuality educators have coined two very descriptive terms: *heteroflexible* for those who self-identify as heterosexual but have same-sex attractions and/or behaviors; and *homoflexible* for those who self-identify as lesbians or gay men and have other-sex attractions and/or behaviors. The *Sexual and Affectional Orientation and Identity Scales* (SAOIS) were developed to show how attractions, behaviors, labels, and other aspects of orientation and identity may differ for an individual and may change over time. The Scales are a very useful tool for both therapists and clients in understanding many sexual orientations and identities (Keppel & Hamilton, 1988, 2000).

If you, as a therapist, are open to many possibilities and establish your acceptance of bisexuality as normal and valid, you may be trusted. Even if you elicit information about same-sex and other-sex attractions and behaviors, you will need to be cautious about labeling to get the trust of bisexuals. References to "*homosexual . . .*" and "*heterosexual . . .*" are likely to be received by bisexual women and men as signals that you are engaged in binary thinking: either "straight" or gay/lesbian, and we will need to be wary of your assumptions about us. *Same-sex* and *same-gender* or *other-sex* and *other-gender* are friendlier and more accurate, and they are more likely to provide the client with the impression that your views of sexual orientation and sexuality extend beyond labels and either/or thinking. Cohorts within the *older than 50* population vary widely. The bisexual baby boomers, have seen *BGLT* words in print for most of their lives even if most of what they have seen has been negative. They probably have the vocabulary, although they may, or may not, apply it to themselves.

Many older people with same-sex and other-sex attractions, fantasies, and/or behaviors won't have the terms *bisexual* or *bi* in their vocabularies, because those in their 60s and beyond usually grew up without ever even hearing about gays and lesbians. When we did hear or see lesbians and gay men, the news and images we heard and saw were negative. Bisexuals, if reported about at all in the media, appeared much later and were often portrayed even more negatively than lesbians and gay men. In their contributions to the book *Bisexual Politics*, Tucker,

Highleyman, and Kaplan (1995), Amanda Udis-Kessler (1995) and Stephen Donaldson (1995) describe the emergence in the 1970s of the first bisexual movements in the United States.

Until 1973, gay men, lesbians, bisexuals, transgender people, and queer folks were considered mentally ill, as *homosexuality* was an official psychiatric diagnosis (Bayer, 1981). According to Donaldson (1995), even after the declassification of homosexuality as a mental illness, media articles reported psychiatrists as maintaining that bisexuality was still an indication of psychopathology. The effects have lingered on in all mental health professions with training and supervision conveying a "mental illness" slant when describing working with BGLT issues. Until recently, training programs and clinical supervision commonly avoided LGBTQ issues altogether, and some programs still have little or no training in working with LGBTQ clients (Phillips, 2000). In 2000, the American Psychological Association adopted official guidelines for working with lesbian, gay and bisexual clients, in which, for the first time, a major psychological professional organization made an official statement that neither homosexuality nor bisexuality are indicative of mental illness. In contrast, in 2004, the board of directors of the major accrediting body for marriage and family therapists and their supervisors, the American Association of Marriage and Family Therapists (AAMFT), while prepared to declare homosexuality is not, in and of itself, a diagnosable mental illness, were not yet ready to say the same about bisexuality.

INVISIBILITY

Wherever you start, the thread of invisibility will wind through your work with bisexual men and women and will need to be addressed repeatedly (Ochs, 1996). Because so few older bisexual women and men are willing to disclose their sexual orientation to others, they rarely find an accepting social networks or groups where they can feel completely comfortable with their identity. As the partner pool shrinks with age, finding long term partners can become more difficult. As friends die or become incapacitated, and as travel becomes more challenging, chances for expanding social networks tend to decrease. Coaching can be very helpful in terms of how much and which history to share for those individuals who move to a new community.

As an older bisexual, I remind myself:

- All seniors are invisible some of the time in an ageist society
- All queers are invisible some of the time in a heterosexist society
- All women are invisible some of the time in a sexist society
- All bisexuals are invisible some of the time in a gay male/lesbian society
- All bisexuals are invisible some of the time in a heterosexual society
- All bisexuals are invisible some of the time in dualistic and simplistic theories of sexual orientation and sexual identity

You can assume that those issues affecting older gay men and lesbians also affect bisexual men and women who affiliate and identify with gay and lesbian communities (Baron & Cramer, 2000). There is ample literature about older lesbians and gay men and the issues of separation, loss, family issues, health rights for partner care, and survival benefits. While these issues also affect older bisexuals, there are additional issues specific to the older bisexual population. For example, bisexuals can be unwelcome in lesbian and gay communities. Gay men and lesbians may ignore or oppress bisexuals. Being accepted as bisexual may be contingent on appearing to be lesbian or gay. Bisexuals who affiliate with lesbian and gay communities may feel they are in a special closet. They may feel that they cannot talk about their experience as bisexuals, including talking in a positive way about their other-gendered former or current spouses and partners. This silence may extend to talking about their children. Using language which includes bisexual and transgender people may be regarded suspiciously.

The isolation of living as an out bisexual may be worse for many individuals than the closet of homosexual disguise. Many gay men and lesbians experience a separation from their families of origin at some time in their coming out process, and the lesbian and gay community becomes their new family. Many community members who have other-sex attractions tend to keep these attractions to themselves, expressing their other-sex attractions and relationships secretly to avoid community disapproval or ostracism.

EXAMPLES FROM THE FIELD

One common sequence involves the question of support for a bisexual woman showing interest in same-sex relationships. When the woman continues to self-identify as bisexual rather than dismiss her other-sex relationships as "just going through a phase," she may lose the support of a lesbian partner and/or lesbian friends and may also feel excluded from her established social circle.

Quite a few older women currently self-identifying as lesbian have told me stories that illustrate another common experience. They married as young adults, lived in loving partnerships, had children, and then were divorced, widowed, or separated when their children were adolescent or had left home. At that time, each of these women was attracted to other women, started a relationship with a woman, and entered the lesbian community. Often, a price of joining the lesbian community was to deny the loving element of the previous partnership and that part of her history. After a few years of self-identifying as lesbian, each of these women had realized she was still or again attracted to men and that she no longer wanted to deny the loving family she had earlier in life.

In addressing the dilemma raised as a result of this experience, some of the women continue in relationships with other women but also have secret male partners, live in a different closet, are denied access to appropriate safer sex information when using lesbian health centers, and are very hesitant to mention or celebrate their earlier loving relationships with men when in the company of members of their lesbian community. Some leave the lesbian community for the bisexual community and are cut off by many of their lesbian friends. Some leave the lesbian community for a male partner and live their lives as heterosexuals although they have not lost their attractions to women. All of these are painful solutions which deny some parts of this person. If she is one of your clients, you will have much healing work to do starting with letting her tell her full story with all of its losses.

The issues affecting older heterosexual women and men also affect bisexual women and men who are living in the context of and identify with the dominant heterosexual/straight culture, such as separation, loss, family issues, health rights for partner care, and survivor benefits. There are issues particular to older bisexuals living in the heterosexual community: bisexuals, like gay men and lesbians, are often unwelcome in heterosexual communities. Women and men who have been part of straight communities may oppress or ignore bisexual men and bisexual women and, in most places, still have legal and social support for doing so. Acceptance from the heterosexual community may be contingent on staying in the closet, as there is the risk of social isolation as a consequence of coming out bisexual. There is also the risk of losing social networks, friends, and status, and loss of heterosexual privilege. It is not unusual for bisexual men and women to move to a different community after they come out and separate from a life partner.

As with bisexual women and men who have lived in the context of the lesbian and gay communities, the restrictions of living in the hetero-sexual community may indicate what may be most helpful from the therapist for elder bisexual clients: Use inclusive language. Talk about relationships including all partners and kids. Expose the stresses of liv-ing in a closet, any closet. Validate bisexuality and bisexual identity as normal. Discuss the risks of coming out and living as bisexual. Accept that the isolation of living as an out bisexual may be worse than the closet of heterosexual disguise. Expose the realities of heterosexual privilege and what its loss may include. Help your clients identify the trade offs. Confront fantasies that this client will be completely accepted into a gay male or lesbian community as a bisexual person.

Fortunately, there are some exceptions to these either/or models. As a bisexual social worker in a mostly rural state, I've been interested in how queer folks, especially women, fill their needs for communities. Based on my discussions with other social workers in this and adjoining states and with rural queer New England women, older bisexuals may participate in gay male or lesbian groups, and are accepted and cele-brated as lesbian or gay; however, they are usually careful not reveal their bisexuality. Sometimes, in rural Maine, bisexuals who are out, but not in-your-face out, are accepted as they are. For example, in mostly rural Maine, bisexuals participate in several senior older lesbian groups, Gay Men Together (a statewide, twice yearly gathering), GAYLA (a Unitarian Universalist based gay, bisexual and trans men's summer conference), Mainely Men (a mixed orientation quarterly retreat), In The Company of Women (a Unitarian Universalist based mostly older lesbian, bisexual and trans women's summer conference), Am Chofshi (a chapter of an international Jewish queer organization), other groups around the state with gay and/or lesbian names, and other informal re-gional social groups. Bisexuals from rural areas in other states report some similar semi-acceptances.

What can we learn from research in Australia? Taking their samples from the Canberra area voter registration rolls (registration is manda-tory in AU where failure to vote incurs a fine), Professor Anthony Jorm and his Canberra colleagues have interviewed large samples of persons ages 20-24, 40-44, 60-64 about their mental health (Jorm, Dear, Rodgers, & Christensen, 2002). These cohorts will be re-interviews ev-ery 5 years for 20 years to assess changes as they age.

Professor Jorm presented findings from their research at the 7th International Bisexual Conference in Sydney, Australia, in 2002. They found that a significantly greater proportion of lesbians, gay men, and bisexuals in their sample reported what they considered risk factors for mental health issues, compared to the heterosexuals in their sample. Furthermore, bisexual women and men reported a higher incidence of these same risk factors than the lesbians and gay men in their sample. These risk factors include adverse childhood experiences, current adverse life events, poor social support, and financial problems.

After his presentation, Professor Jorm asked his audience to give him their ideas and explanations for the differences this study showed between the mental health of bisexual men and women and that of gay men, lesbians, and heterosexuals. Regardless of the age and nationality of respondents in that audience, the stories and comments he received were of invisibility and oppression in the wider queer communities and of pervasive inadequacy and abuse in the mental and physical health care delivery for many bisexual women and bisexual men.

TRAINING ISSUES

At the 5th International Bisexual Conference held in Cambridge, Massachusetts, in 1998, Ron Fox, Ph.D., convened a panel to discuss bisexuality and mental health. In a large room, jammed with mental health professionals from all over the world, not one person reported even one graduate program providing adequate training for medical or mental health professionals working with bisexual clients. That is right: not psychologists, psychiatrists, social workers, marriage and family counselors, licensed professional counselors, physicians, or nurses. This was true even in professional training programs which do a competent job of training around gay male and lesbian issues.

When medical and mental health professionals are not informed about bisexuals and bisexuality, they are not likely to accept us or understand what kinds of help we need (Dworkin, 2000). Out and assertive bisexual women and men who go for help often spend their own time and, therefore, their own money, training their health care professionals about bisexuality and bisexual issues so they can work more productively regarding their health issues. This may be the case with bisexual clients seeing gay, lesbian, or heterosexual therapists.

To counter the general lack of acceptance of bisexuality experienced by bisexual women and bisexual men, assume that bisexual identity, attractions, and behaviors are normal and valid. Develop a resource list including those in your community, online, in films and in books. Stock some of the most helpful books and pamphlets and/or have information on how to obtain them.

MENTAL HEALTH PROFESSIONALS AS ALLIES FOR OLDER BISEXUALS

All bisexuals need advocates and allies. One way you can be helpful to your older bisexual clients is as an ally and advocate outside of therapy. You may scramble the BGLT letters so "gay and lesbian" don't always come first. You may ask questions and use inclusive language wherever bisexual elders being left out, reflecting the assumption that wherever there are elders, some of them are bisexual. You may invoke your profession's code of ethics, if it includes a "do no harm" phrase, and point out that failing to use inclusive language when talking about queer issues and BGLTQI people harms those who are left out, especially elders. If your code of ethics addresses support and advocacy for minorities, you may press for bisexual and elder inclusive policies and language in your professional association(s). Thank you, in advance, for every time and place you take these steps.

BISEXUAL ELDERS AND SEXUAL EXPRESSION

One of the most dangerous ways in which oppression of bisexual elders plays out is in the area of safer sex education. Americans over 50 have high rates of sexually transmitted infections/diseases (STIs/STDs), including HIV/AIDS (Ginty, 2004). The Centers for Disease Control (CDC) report rising rates of infection in this age group. At this time, there are no national programs for STI/HIV prevention among people over 50, so most of the state and local HIV prevention programs for them are in those states where HIV is already epidemic in some of their retirement facilities. The stereotype of older people is that they have given up sex and are not interested in sexuality or sexual activity. Most medical professionals have not been trained either to talk about sex or about aging. As a result, they are not likely to initiate conversations about sex or sexuality, especially when patients are a generation (or two) older. It is like talking to the parent whose sexuality most adult children, including doctors, have denied. It is easier to duck the issues

(Ginty, 2004). When health practitioners are uncomfortable talking about sexuality and about sexual orientation, especially about bisexuality, their patients cannot be properly assessed for STIs/STDs, may not have opportunities to discuss their sexual behavior, and may lose opportunities to prevent serious and sometimes life threatening infections.

As a therapist, you may find yourself a senior safer sex educator by default. There is a lot your clients need to know, and you may be the only available teacher. Quite literally, their lives may depend on your willingness to educate them. Get the facts. Your local Planned Parenthood program may either give a safer sex workshop or be able to direct you to one. Your city and/or state public health departments can probably do the same. Many shops that carry condoms, latex dams, lubricant, sex toys, and/or erotica have knowledgeable staff and a good selection of literature including "how to" instructions. Some give classes, and some have Websites that include safer-sex information.

Some Websites are set up to meet the assumed needs of bisexuals and others who have sexual relationships with persons of more than one sex/gender. One of the best and most explicit and current online sites is sponsored by the San Francisco Department of Public Health. You will find information about all STDs/STIs including prevention, transmission, symptoms, even a section on how to talk with partners, which you can use in working with your clients. Fenway Community Health in Boston, home of the BiHealth project, and San Francisco Sex Information also carry up to date information. As you use the one of these Websites and/or take a safer sex workshop, you can expect to become more knowledgeable and more comfortable with the information and its use. Then, you can get the equipment and be ready to do show and tell. "Here's how to put on a male condom, a female condom, use a latex dam, how to put on and take off gloves, and here's why you need to use them."

Remember that most of the current STIs were unknown when folks my age were growing up and partnering, e.g., chlamydia, genital warts, cervical cancer, herpes, hepatitis A and hepatitis C. Even syphilis and gonorrhea, the two STIs/STDs that we heard of in our youth, are now epidemic in antibiotic resistant strains. Let your clients know that having any STI increases the risk of contracting others because they use the same routes of transmission.

Your skills in teaching clients about other kinds of negotiation can be expanded to teach them how to talk about and negotiate about sex. If you make it fun, they can probably be relaxed enough to learn what they need to do. If they are connecting with new sexual partners, their health and survival may depend on their learning these skills now. Folks who are seniors now were not supposed to talk about sex. Most did not learn to negotiate as equals. They usually learned only a tiny sexual vocabulary. Remind them that many partners will not share their sexual histories, especially if they know they have one or more STIs. Many seniors will not even know they are carrying STIs.

Bisexuals attending gay or lesbian health and mental health centers, or getting individual care, may get some safer sex information but providers may assume that they only need same-sex safety education. This is inadequate not only for bisexuals, but also for many gay and lesbian and heterosexually identified people who are sexually active with persons of more than one sex and gender. Similarly, providers in mainstream medical and mental health centers may incorrectly assume that bisexuals only need other-sex safer-sex education, or they may not provide any safety safer-sex education at all.

When a therapist works with the assumption that elder clients have sexual feelings and activities, the knowledge to educate clients about the basics of sexuality and safer sex, and an indication that she/he knows about these matters, older bisexual clients are more likely to be open to talking about sexually related issues, such as loss of partners, sexual dysfunctions, and needs for safer sex education. Likewise, the therapist who is aware of and understands the phenomenon of multiple partners, and same-sex and other-sex partners and attractions, will be in a better position to provide opportunities for older bisexual clients to discuss these issues. You can learn a lot by looking up resources on responsible non-monogamy and/or polyamory where issues and solutions are discussed. All resources are not created equal. For example, the *Journal of Bisexuality* devotes most of its 2004 (Vol. 4, No. 3/4) issue to articles about polyamory and bisexuality and has one or more articles on the topic in nearly every past issue. The Website of the Bisexual Resource Center has a "Responsible Non-monogamy" pamphlet that can be downloaded and printed out. The Unitarian Universalists for Polyamory Awareness Website has links to other polyamory resources as well as a chat area for ongoing discussions of the issues.

SPIRITUALITY

Inevitably, nearly every older person addresses some end-of-life spiritual issues. You may be thinking, perhaps hoping, there will be religious professionals and/or spiritual leaders available to help clients. Unfortunately, most of those responsible for spiritual care have not had any training regarding the spiritual issues which are typically experienced by bisexual people. You can be helpful by screening spiritual care givers in the community to find those who are willing to support the spiritual work of bisexual women and men. Stay aware that although many faith traditions are at least somewhat accepting of gay and lesbian members, they may not be inclusive of bisexuals. Even where the faith group has signed on as "accepting" or "affirming," support your older bisexual client in being wary. Each specific congregation and its leaders will need to be checked out for the degree to which they are in fact accepting of bisexual people.

Out of the closet bisexual religious professionals and other spiritual leaders are rare. Even if lesbian and gay clergy and spiritual leaders are allowed and accepted within a denomination, those who are bisexual usually are not. Brainstorm with your client for ways of approaching a faith group's local leader(s) for spiritual care to maximize the possibilities for successful integration into a congregation. Resources for you may include directors of religious education and chaplains because they often have a broader view of acceptance and know the internal politics of particular congregations and groups. You can also help to increase the number of resources available by raising the issue of support for older bisexuals' spiritual needs when you attend meetings or gatherings that include religious professionals and spiritual leaders.

Many older queer people left their faith tradition, or were forced out of it, when they came out. To support bisexual clients as they seek to reconcile and/or clarify how their bisexuality has affected their spiritual journey, you might steer them to the anthology *Blessed Bi Spirit: Bisexual People of Faith* for explorations of bisexual spirituality in many different faith traditions (Kolodny, 2000). For those who have given up on a faith tradition and now seek some reconnection or new connection with a spiritual leader and/or congregation, the opportunity to compare opportunities and experiences of various faiths may lead them to the resources appropriate to their needs.

Mending relationships by forgiving others and/or reestablishing connections are end-of-life tasks that may be very painful and frustrating for people who were cut off from families and friends when they came out. As mentioned earlier, some bisexual men and women will have come out as gay men or lesbians and developed their bisexual identities later. They may have had two series of cut offs, one as they went from straight to lesbian or gay communities, and another as they went from gay or lesbian to bisexual communities. In some cases, your clients' families and friends may have accepted them as lesbian or gay, but cut off from them later because bisexuality was less understood and less accepted, especially if your clients were involved with multiple partners of different sexes and genders. Sometimes, the therapist needs to coach the bisexual woman or man in negotiating the reconnection process. Other times, the therapist helps hold the client's pain when reconnection is refused, supporting the client's bisexual identity as valid and healthy even though others are not accepting it.

HOUSING

For a variety of reasons, older bisexual women and men may need to change their living arrangements. These changes may raise a whole new set of concerns. Aging bisexuals may wonder whether or not to be out in the new location or facility and whether or not caregivers will give needed care to someone identified as different. New queer and queer-friendly retirement facilities are going up around the United States, but they are not necessarily bi-friendly. If you are helping your bisexual client through a housing choice process, urge careful investigation around acceptance and inclusion. The client may be best served by a two-pronged approach. Home health services may be increased to allow her or him to remain longer in the current independent living situation while, at the same time, efforts are made to increase acceptance of bisexuals in an otherwise suitable retirement facility.

RESOURCES FOR AND ABOUT BISEXUAL ELDERS

You have probably noticed that I urge you and your clients to look for some possible supportive resources, maybe online, or in films and books. If you think gay and lesbian aging is hard, bisexual is much harder because the usual resources do not yet exist. We do not yet have the body of valid research about older bisexuals that we have about older gay men, lesbians, and heterosexuals. To date, professionals in the field of aging, like those in the American Society on Aging (ASA), the National Council on the Aging (NCOA), and SAGE (Services and Advocacy for GLBT Elders) conferences have only given minimal attention and space to bisexuals and bisexual issues.

Conferences on aging often look better on paper or on an Internet Website than they are live. Sessions and groups may be listed as "GLBT"; however, this does not mean that data or experiences directly relevant to older bisexual women or men are covered or discussed in the session. While "GLBT" looks politically correct, in terms of actual conference programming, this does not necessarily reflect actual intent, information, or inclusivity.

Within ASA, you will find the LGAIN (Lesbian and Gay Aging Information Network), which publishes a newsletter online and in print. Their spring 2002 issue is all about bisexual aging. Therapists can also use the general aging literature and the aging literature on gay men and lesbians as places to start, since there will be many overlapping issues. You can also extrapolate some of the issues relevant to bisexual elders from the literature about younger bisexual men and women.

THE BISEXUAL RESOURCE CENTER (BOSTON)

The Website of the Bisexual Resource Center does not yet have specific resources for elders; however, it is a gold mine for all kinds of other information and for networking. The Website includes links to the bisexual bookstore, bisexual video store, bisexual music store, bisexual products, and gives information about films with bisexual characters. The site lists conferences, events, and news. Pamphlets covering many topics related to bisexuality can be read online and downloaded. You could have all of them available in your office. The *Bisexual Resource Guide*, formerly available in paper, is an international directory of bisexual and bisexual-friendly groups around the world now available online. You and your older clients can use it to seek out social support groups and connections around the world.

There are two anthologies that will give you and your clients glimpses into the experiences of a whole range of bisexual women. The first is *Bi Any Other Name*, which includes essays by three bisexual elders (Hutchins & Kaahumanu, 1991). The second is *Getting Bi*, a collection of 187 essays by bisexual women and men from 32 countries around the world, including several by bi elders (Ochs & Rowley, 2005). Both are available through the Bisexual Resource Center bookstore and elsewhere. Sadly, there are no books on bisexual parenting or grandparenting and no children's books for a bisexual parent or grandparent to read aloud. "Am I Blue" is a wonderful story for middle school and up (Coville, 1994). I have adapted it and told it aloud to groups of various ages.

CONCLUDING REMARKS

Never underestimate the power of an epiphany, otherwise known as an "aha" experience. In 1996, I prevailed upon a middle aged, bisexually-behaving friend in rural northern Maine to join nearly 1,000 other bisexual and bi-friendly folks at the *5th International Bisexual Conference* in Cambridge, Massachusetts. When I caught up with him after the first day, he said, "This is the first place I have ever been as an adult where I could just open my mouth and say what I think!" He also looked at the range of personal presentation styles and opined, "No matter how I dress, I will still be middle of the road in this crowd." He still lives in a rural part of Maine, but that is about all that has not changed.

On the first day of that same conference, a new bisexual acquaintance and I went up to every gray haired person whom we saw and asked them to join us for lunch. About a dozen of us seniors spent hours swapping stories, giving and receiving support for being and living as older bisexuals. Keep these stories in mind for your clients.

REFERENCES

American Psychological Association. (2000). Guidelines for psychotherapy with lesbian, gay, and bisexual clients. *American Psychologist, 55*(12), 1440-1451.

Andrew, E. J. (2000). *Swinging on the garden gate: A spiritual memoir.* Boston: Skinner House.

Angier, N. (1999). *Woman: An intimate geography.* New York: Anchor Books.

Baron, A., & Cramer. D. (2000). Potential counseling concerns of aging lesbian, gay, and bisexual clients, In R. M. Perez, K. A. DeBord, & K. J. Bieschke (Eds.), *Handbook of counseling and psychotherapy with lesbian, gay, and bisexual clients* (pp. 207-224). Washington, DC: American Psychological Association.

Bayer, R. (1981). *Homosexuality and American psychiatry: The politics of diagnosis.* New York: Basic Books.

Coville, B. (1994). Am I Blue? In M. D. Bauer (Ed.), *Am I Blue? Coming out from the silence.* (pp. 1-26). New York. Harper-Trophy.

Donaldson, S. (1995). The bisexual movement's beginnings in the 70s: A personal retrospective. In N. Tucker, L. Highleyman, & R. Kaplan (Eds.), *Bisexual Politics: Theories, queeries, & visions* (pp. 31-45). New York: Harrington Park Press.

Dworkin, S (2000) Individual therapy with lesbian, gay, and bisexual clients. In R. M. Perez, K. A. DeBord, & K. J. Bieschke (Eds.), *Handbook of counseling and psycho-*

therapy with lesbian, gay, and bisexual clients (pp. 157-181). Washington, DC: American Psychological Association.

Ginty, M. M. (2004). HIV/AIDS cases still rising among older women. Retrieved from *http://www.kccall.com/News/2004/0326/Community/082.html.*

Hutchins, L., & Kaahumanu, L. (Eds.) (1991) *Bi any other name: Bisexual people speak out.* Boston: Alyson.

Jorm, A. F., Korten, A. E.,Rodgers, B., Jacomb, P.A., & Christensen, H. (2002). Sexual orientation and mental health: Results from a community survey of young and middle-aged adults. *British Journal of Psychiatry, 180,* 423-427.

Keppel, B. (1991). Gray-haired and above suspicion. In L. Hutchins & L. Kaahumanu, (Eds.), *Bi any other name: Bisexual people speak out* (pp. 154-158). Boston: Alyson.

Keppel, B. (1999, Summer). Swimming upstream: Queer families and change. *Anything That Moves, 20,* 12-14.

Keppel, B. (2002). The challenges and rewards of life as an outspoken bisexual elder. *Outword: Newsletter of the Lesbian and Gay Aging Issues Network (LGAIN), 8*(4), 1, 6.

Keppel, B., & Firestein, B. (in press). Bisexual inclusion in addressing issues of GLBT aging: Therapy with older bisexuals. In B. A. Firestein, (Ed.), *Becoming visible: Counseling bisexuals across the lifespan.* New York: Columbia University Press.

Keppel, B., & Hamilton, A. (1998). *Using the Klein Scale to teach about sexual orientation.* Boston: Bisexual Resource Center. Retrieved January 10, 2005 from: http://www.biresource.org/pamphlets/klein_graph.html.

Keppel, B., & Hamilton, A. (2000). Your sexual orientation: Using the *Sexual and Affectional Orientation and Identity Scale* to teach about sexual orientation. In R. S. Kimball (Ed.), *Our whole lives: Sexuality education for adults* (pp. 157-161). Boston: Unitarian Universalist Association and United Church Board of Homeland Ministries.

Kolodny, D. R. (Ed.). (2000). *Blessed bi spirit: Bisexual people of faith.* New York: Continuum.

Ochs, R., & Rowley, S. (Eds.). (2005) *Getting Bi: Voices of bisexuals around the world.* Boston: Bisexual Resource Center.

Ochs, R., Biphobia: It goes more than two ways. In B. Firestein (Ed.), *Bisexuality: The Psychology and Politics of an Invisible Minority* (pp. 317-239). Thousand Oaks, CA: Sage.

Phillips, J. C. (2000). Training issues and considerations. In R. M. Perez, K. A. DeBord, & K. J. Bieschke (Eds.), *Handbook of counseling and psychotherapy with lesbian, gay, and bisexual clients* (pp. 337-358). Washington, DC: American Psychological Association.

Roughgarden, J. (2004). *Evolution's rainbow: Diversity, gender, and sexuality in nature and people.* Berkeley, CA: University of California Press.

Tucker, N., Highleyman, L., & Kaplan, R. (Eds.). (1995). *Bisexual politics: Theories, queeries, & visions.* New York: Harrington Park Press.

Udis-Kessler, A. (1995). Identity/politics: A history of the bisexual movement. In N. Tucker, L. Highleyman, & R. Kaplan (Eds.), *Bisexual Politics: Theories, queeries, & visions* (pp.17-30). New York: Harrington Park Press.

ONLINE RESOURCES

Bisexual Resource Center Website.The Bi Bookstore, Bi Video Store, Bi Music Store, Bi Products, bi news, downloadable pamphlets, health information, and links to just about everything you might want to know about bisexuals and bisexuality around the world including online chat groups and an index of bi-inclusive groups in every country. *http://www.biresource.org*

Fenway Community Health Center, Boston, home of the BiHealth project and its Safer Sex Educator team. *http://www.fenwayhealth.org/services/wellness/bihealth.htm*

Good Vibrations. Store plus online information about sex, sexuality, sex toys, resources. *http://www.goodvibes.com*

Grand Opening. Store plus online information about sex, sexuality, sex toys, resources. *http://grandopening.com*

Outword: Newsletter of the Lesbian and Gay Aging Issues Network (LGAIN). American Society on Aging, Spring, 2002 (Vol. 8, No. 4) issue, with the theme of bisexuals ages 50-plus. *http://wwwasaging.org*

San Francisco Department of Public Health website. Frequently updated information about sexually transmitted infections (STIs): prevention, incidence, transmission, treatment, education strategies, and just about anything else you and/or your clients might want to know. Good section on talking with partners about STIs. *http://www.sfdph.org*

San Francisco Sex Information. A bi-affirmative and bi-aware Website and hotline that has been providing sexuality information to diverse communities since the 70s. *http://www.sfsi.org/*

Unitarian Universalists for Polyamory Awareness. Thoughtful education and discussion about having more than one committed relationship at a time. Links to other resources. *http://www.uupa.org*

Counseling Heterosexual Spouses of Bisexual Men and Women and Bisexual-Heterosexual Couples: Affirmative Approaches

Amity P. Buxton

Available online at http://www.haworthpress.com/web/JB
© 2006 by The Haworth Press, Inc. All rights reserved.
doi:10.1300/J159v06n01_07

[Haworth co-indexing entry note]: "Counseling Heterosexual Spouses of Bisexual Men and Women and Bisexual-Heterosexual Couples: Affirmative Approaches." Buxton. Amity P. Co-published simultaneously in *Journal of Bisexuality* (Harrington Park Press, an imprint of The Haworth Press, Inc.) Vol. 6, No. 1/2, 2006, pp. 105-135; and: *Affirmative Psychotherapy with Bisexual Women and Bisexual Men* (ed: Ronald C. Fox) Harrington Park Press, an imprint of The Haworth Press, Inc., 2006, pp. 105-135. Single or multiple copies of this article are available for a fee from The Haworth Document Delivery Service [1-800-HAWORTH, 9:00 a.m. - 5:00 p.m. (EST). E-mail address: docdelivery@haworthpress.com].

SUMMARY. In approximately two million current or former marriages in the United States, one of the spouses is bisexual, gay, or lesbian. When lesbian, gay, or bisexual spouses disclose their sexual orientation, their heterosexual spouses face unique issues. Their coping proceeds through common stages from initial trauma to eventual transformation. Mixed-orientation couples, too, progress through typical stages as they deal with complex relationship challenges. Heterosexual spouses of bisexual partners and bisexual-heterosexual couples face the additional challenge of understanding bisexuality. Resolving the issues and coming to terms with the disclosure for spouses and couples may take more than three years. Peer support and counseling help spouses clarify their needs, goals, and values during this period. For therapists working with such clients, scant literature about heterosexual spouses in these marriages and bisexual-heterosexual couples and the general lack of knowledge about bisexuality and mixed-orientation relationships make it difficult to know how best to counsel spouses. Counseling is most effective when therapists know the core issues of heterosexual spouses, typical stages of their resolving them, and the common path through which bisexual-heterosexual couples progress. With effective counseling, heterosexual spouses and bisexual-heterosexual couples are more likely to resolve issues constructively and to grow in individual strength and mutual understanding. *[Article copies available for a fee from The Haworth Document Delivery Service: 1-800-HAWORTH. E-mail address: <docdelivery@haworthpress.com> Website: <http://www.HaworthPress.com> © 2006 by The Haworth Press, Inc. All rights reserved.]*

KEYWORDS. Bisexuality, bisexual wives, lesbian wives, bisexual husbands, gay husbands, heterosexual husbands of bisexual wives, heterosexual husbands of lesbian wives, heterosexual wives of bisexual husbands, heterosexual wives of gay husbands, mixed-orientation marriages, counseling, psychotherapy

INTRODUCTION

I want a therapist who can help me build up my self esteem, give me some direction (recommending reading or suggesting I join a support group), and challenge me and not necessarily make this process easy for me. (Heterosexual wife of bisexual man)

> *When a mixed-orientation couple comes for help and one spouse says, "I have same-sex attractions," and the other says, "I'm straight," the therapist needs to say, "I hear you both," and acknowledge the major ramifications for the spouse coming out AND the straight spouse coping with shattered illusions and self-esteem issues. (Heterosexual husband of bisexual woman)*

These two comments represent concerns common to many spouses whose husbands and wives are coming out as gay, lesbian, or bisexual in increasing numbers across the United States. This phenomenon presents three challenges for therapists: how to help the individuals who are coming out; how to work with their heterosexual husbands and wives, current or former, and how to provide support and guidance to these mixed-orientation couples. Traditional therapy for spouses is grounded in a body of knowledge based almost exclusively on relationships between presumably heterosexual persons. The relationship dynamics and factors involved in mixed-orientation marriages are much the same. However, working with spouses and couples in such marriages requires additional knowledge and additional sets of questions to get to and resolve core problems.

BACKGROUND

There are approximately two million couples who are or were in mixed-orientation marriages in the United States, a figure based on recent estimates of the percentage of the population that is gay, lesbian, or bisexual, the average proportion of those who marry, as documented in empirical research, and the latest census figures on the adult population (Buxton, 2001). While the breakdown of marriages in which one of the partners is bisexual is unknown, the proportion of those in bisexual-heterosexual marriages is sizable among the over 10,000 spouses with whom I have had contact in nineteen years of study and fourteen years of observation as Executive Director of the Straight Spouse Network. Anecdotal reports suggest that many of the heterosexual spouses in these marriages remain closeted to protect their bisexual, gay, or lesbian partners, are unaware of resources to help them, feel sufficiently satisfied by their marriage not to seek help, find alternative resources, or resolve their issues themselves, without therapy or the use of self-help resources.

Despite these numbers, there is scant literature about heterosexual spouses in mixed-orientation marriages to help therapists counsel them as effectively as they might (Buxton, 2001). The first studies of gay married men or their wives were clinical in nature, appearing in 1969 at about the same time as the Stonewall uprising launched Gay Liberation (Imielinsky, 1969). The studies that focused on closeted or troubled gay husbands or their wives (H. L. Hatterer, 1970; M. Hatterer, 1974). After the American Psychiatric Association removed homosexuality from the *Diagnostic and Statistical Manual of Mental Disorders* in 1973, several non-clinical studies appeared. This research examined gay husbands' struggles with their own negative views of homosexuality, acceptance of being gay, and integration of their homosexual orientation with their roles as spouses in heterosexual marriages and as fathers and divorced lesbian mothers' coping with child custody and parenting (Buxton, 1999, 2001). In one study only, openly gay/straight couples were described as enjoying satisfying relationships and were termed "the new couple" (Nahas & Turley, 1979).

In the 1980s, a multidimensional perspective on sexual orientation emerged with the development of the *Klein Sexual Orientation Grid* (Klein, Sepekoff, & Wolf, 1985). Several researchers examined the experiences of married bisexual spouses, mostly husbands, and bisexual/gay-heterosexual couples (Deabill, 1987; Kohn & Matusow, 1980; Wolf, 1985). The mid- to late eighties saw the first studies of heterosexual wives in mixed-orientation marriages (Hays & Samuels, 1985; Gochros, 1989) followed by a handful of books in the nineties, including two on lesbian wives (Abbott & Farmer, 1995; Strock, 1998), two on gay-straight relationships (Whitney, 1990; Whitehead, 1997) and one on heterosexual wives and husbands of gay, lesbian or bisexual spouses (Buxton, 1994). More recently, one report has appeared on wives of gay husbands (Grever, 2001) and two on marriages that continued after disclosure (Buxton, 2001, 2004).

All told, literature about heterosexual spouses and mixed-orientation married couples is minimal, especially empirical data about heterosexual husbands and bisexual-heterosexual couples. Moreover, in most research on gay, lesbian, and bisexual spouses, data gathered from bisexual participants are included in those from gay men and lesbians, thereby hiding singular characteristics of each orientation. Two additional issues present challenges for therapists working with spouses in bisexual-heterosexual marriages. One is the practice in our society of defining sexual orientation by the gender of a person's sexual partner without reference to his or her erotic, emotional or social attractions, sexual fantasies, or self-identification (Klein et al., 1985). The other challenging practice is the tendency to infer a person's sexual orientation based on the gender of his or her sexual partner, an assumption that can lead to mislabeling all spouses in opposite-gender relationships as heterosexual. In fact, some of these spouses may be bisexual, lesbian, or gay, each with her/his distinctive experience and expression of sexual orientation and sexual identity.

Compounding erroneous assumptions is a common "either gay or straight" view of sexual orientation. From this dichotomous perspective, the same-gender sexual behavior of bisexual persons renders them automatically gay. As a heterosexual wife told me, "If they have gay sex, they are not straight." This either/or perceptual frame negates the "both/and" actuality that bisexual persons embody, and to which, if married, their heterosexual partners need to relate in order for their relationship to be mutually satisfying. For therapists, holding an either/or view of sexual orientation, a one-dimensional concept of sexual orientation solely as sexual behavior, or the assumption that sexual orientation is defined by the gender of one's sexual partner keeps them from understanding bisexual-heterosexual relationships and offering effective counseling to either or both spouses in mixed-orientation relationships.

Acknowledging and understanding bisexuality as distinct from homosexuality and heterosexuality and knowing the many dimensions of sexual orientation provides therapists an essential knowledge base for working effectively with spouses in bisexual-heterosexual marriages. My years of study and experience with spouses in mixed-orientation marriages have convinced me of the reality of bisexuality. My working definition is that bisexual persons are sexually, emotionally, and erotically attracted to both men and women, usually in varying degrees that may fluctuate over time; and may or may not have sex with partners of both genders, in the same time period or over time; and self-identify as bisexual. Like homosexuality and heterosexuality, bisexuality is multidimensional, involving sexual fantasies, emotional and social attractions, sexual desires, and pleasurable lovemaking. The key difference is that the combination of factors operating for bisexual persons orients them toward attractions toward both genders.

Bisexual-heterosexual couples form a singular and complex dynamic in which the bisexual partners are sexually attracted to their spouses and experience pleasure from making love with them, while also being attracted to other persons of the same gender. They can form monogamous relationships with opposite- or same-gender partners and procreate with heterosexual partners. Those who are monogamous in a bisexual-heterosexual marriage forsake all others of both genders, in contrast to heterosexual spouses who are attracted to and forsake others only of the opposite gender. Some self-identified gay and lesbian persons, too, have sex with, marry, and form monogamous relationships with opposite-gender partners and produce children with them; yet they are not physically or sexually turned on by or tuned into the sexuality of their heterosexual spouses and remain attracted sexually exclusively to others of the same gender. Love, respect, a deep bond, and commitment motivate them to stay married, but they lack the sexual passion of bisexual spouses.

My aim here is to fill gaps in the literature about heterosexual spouses in bisexual-heterosexual marriages and about bisexual-heterosexual couples. With this broader knowledge base, therapists can more quickly identify core issues of heterosexual spouses whose partners come out as bisexual, typical stages through which they cope with those issues, and stages through which bisexual-heterosexual couples work through their issues, as well as a sounder sense of what heterosexual spouse and bisexual-heterosexual couples seek in therapy. Therapists will then be better able to help individual spouses and couples resolve their concerns constructively. While heterosexual spouses in bisexual-heterosexual marriages and bisexual-heterosexual couples are the focus here, they share with spouses of gay or lesbian partners and gay/lesbian-heterosexual couples many of the issues and progress through the same stages of coping that are described below.

COMMON ISSUES OF HETEROSEXUAL SPOUSES IN BISEXUAL-HETEROSEXUAL RELATIONSHIPS

When mixed-orientation couples marry, most heterosexual spouses are unaware of their partners' same-gender attraction. In some instances, their partners become aware of their same-gender attractions for the first time during the marriage. It is often the case that partners who are bisexual, lesbian, or gay minimize, deny, bury, or conceal that part of themselves or hope that marriage will weaken or end those feelings that many do not want. When they eventually become aware, can no longer deny their same-gender attractions, or begin to explore or act on them, many tell their spouses. Some make a commitment not to act on their same-gender attractions. In other cases, their spouses discover evidence of same-gender attractions or behavior, e.g., gay-related Websites, including those with pornography, love notes on greeting cards from a lover, e-mail replies to gay dating services or personal ads, telephone numbers on matchbooks from gay bars, or semen stains on underwear in the laundry basket. Disclosure or discovery may occur at any point in a marriage, early on when the couple has a newborn or toddlers, during a midlife crisis or after a parent's death, or much later, when the couple faces an "empty nest." Some partners remain closeted. Others deny their same-gender attractions despite evidence that their wives or husbands may have found out or their heterosexual spouses' "sixth sense" that their partners have inclinations toward homosexual or bisexual orientation or behavior.

Once a spouse discloses or acts on his or her same-sex attractions, the couple relationship typically follows one of three trajectories. About a third of the couples break up quickly, because the gay, lesbian, or bisexual partner has a lover or wants to live as "a gay person" in the gay community or the heterosexual partner cannot tolerate deception, an affair, non-monogamy, or homosexual behavior (Buxton, 1994, 2001, 2004). Another third stay together for two or three years to sort out alternatives, deciding finally to separate. The other third commit themselves to redefine the marriage so that they can stay together. Of these, about half determine after about three years that separation is best for their relationship, and the remaining half stay married for three or more years. In both cases, the couples form strong bonds that last even if marriage does not. Regardless of when husbands or wives come out or their spouses discover clues, the information revealed by the disclosure—same-gender attraction, experimentation, or a lover—raises common issues for heterosexual spouses: a challenge to the marriage, a sense of sexual rejection, parent-spouse conflict, and fragmentation of their own identity, integrity, and belief system.

The analysis below describes these concerns briefly in the order in which spouses most often become aware of them (Buxton, 1994, 2005). Although these issues are discussed separately, spouses' concerns intertwine and interact, making each problem more powerful and confusing. Isolating them, however, may make it easier for therapists to identify the heart of the matter that lies below the presenting concerns that spouses bring to counseling. The first three areas of concern, sexuality, the marriage, and children, arise immediately and stay in spouses' minds, whether at home, at work, or at night, when they should be sleeping.

Sexuality issues are one of the three unique concerns of heterosexual spouses. Once a spouse finds out that a husband or wife is gay, lesbian, or bisexual, sexual adequacy becomes an issue. Many feel rejected sexually as a man or a woman, and may wonder if they were not enough of a woman or man to maintain their partner's sexual attraction to them. Feeling short-changed or inadequate sexually leads some spouses to believe that they may be irrevocably dysfunctional as sexual beings. Most spouses, particularly wives, also fear exposure to sexually transmitted diseases, including HIV, and may get tested. A number question their own orientation.

Sexual rejection appears to be a more salient concern for spouses of gay or lesbian partners than for those whose husbands or wives are bisexual. The most challenging sexual issue for spouses of bisexual partners is to understand the nature of bisexuality: that their partners may be attracted to someone else as well as them or may or may not want to act on it. Some bisexual spouses simply want their bisexuality acknowledged and accepted, without a desire for a different partner. Once heterosexual spouses understand bisexuality, they do not feel quite as sexually rejected. Instead, they believe that their partners still desire them sexually and have the potential of being fully pleasured by them when making love, even if their partners may not demonstrate any sexual interest initially after coming out. Some partners are so immersed in their struggle to come to terms with their bisexuality that they put sex in their marriages on hold. While spouses of gay and lesbian partners question if they can satisfy them in all other ways but sex, those with bisexual partners include lovemaking among factors on which to work so that they can keep satisfying or once again satisfy their partners. Many wonder if they can continue keep their partner's desire alive alongside competing attractions toward persons of the same gender. Others feel they must prove that they are better sexual partners to their bisexual spouses than any potential or actual outside lover. This concern is heightened when their partners cease lovemaking for a period of time in order to come to terms with their bisexuality.

Marriage issues emerge at once. Disclosure or discovery that a partner is gay, lesbian, or bisexual and possibly having casual or intimate sex with someone of the same gender puts into question the continuation of marriage, traditional concepts of marriage, and the meaning of fidelity. Heterosexual spouses sense that the strength of the relationship is being tested and wonder what changes they might have to make to stay married. They wonder how to factor in their partners' same-gender desires if they continue the marriage. Like their partners, they struggle with how to integrate the heterosexual image the marriage projects with their partners' revealed orientation and suffer cognitive dissonance about that apparent contradiction. Many fear their partners will fall in love with someone of the same gender and leave. Spouses also struggle with concerns about monogamy and fidelity alongside negative opinions that may be expressed by members of both families of origin about non-monogamy or same-gender relationships. Spouses in bisexual-heterosexual marriages often receive more outside support from family and friends than do those in gay- or lesbian-heterosexual marriages, although they may experience just as much negativity about staying married or saying they are bisexual from members of the gay and lesbian communities (Buxton, 2001, 2004).

For spouses with children, the impact of the partner's disclosed orientation on their children is of major concern, as it is for their partners. As parents, heterosexual spouses want to support their children as they cope with the revealed orientation of their gay, lesbian, or bisexual parent and want to keep them from getting hurt from teasing or stigmatization by children, neighbors, or, in some cases, their faith community. As spouses, many also feel conflict between their own hurt from disclosure and their desire as a co-parent to preserve the children's bond with their parent who has come out.

Along with their partners, spouses wonder if, when, and how to tell their children that their parent is bisexual, gay, or lesbian. Most parents usually tell the children when they feel comfortable enough with the information and before the children hear the news from outsiders who may not be accepting or have appropriate knowledge. Some parents do not tell. Some children find out themselves. In cases in which the bisexual, gay, or lesbian parent does not have an outside partner or engage in gay-related social or other activities, parents choose not to tell, believing that it is a private matter and will not impact the children. If their children find/figure it out themselves, however, many feel that their parents did not trust them with the truth.

Once the children are told or find out and encounter negative attitudes outside the family about gay or lesbian persons or relationships, parents try to help them understand sexual orientation, bisexuality, and antigay attitudes in society. The heterosexual parents become models of how the children process the disclosure and relate to the disclosing parent. Most try to model acceptance, despite their own turmoil. Children aged from about 11 to 14 have the roughest time, while teenagers may act out, often against the straight parent, the safe one, adding to his or her stress from the disclosure. Most children, after initial shock, anger, or silence, become accepting over time (Buxton, 1999). As young adults, a number express pride in their gay, lesbian, or bisexual parent. In some cases, the disclosing parent may neglect the children for a period of time or engage in ineffective parenting behaviors that upset the children (without diminishing their love) and trouble the heterosexual parent. Divorce, which occurs in the majority of cases, exacerbates the children's issues related to the parents being bisexual, gay, or lesbian, especially separation anxiety, fear of abandonment, and division of loyalties (Buxton, 1994, 1999).

Problems related to sexuality, marriage and children concern heterosexual spouses for months, as they try to survive the devastation of the disclosure. As they cope, most slowly become aware of more complex issues that affect their inner being. Toward the end of the first year, questions arise about their own identify, integrity, and belief system.

Gradually, many spouses realize that their self-esteem has disappeared, their self-concept has become blurred, and their sense of self worth has plummeted. For many, pre-disclosure interaction with their partners fed into or created feelings of personal inadequacy. Lack of success in pleasing their partners as their partners struggled with their closeted issues chipped away some if not all their confidence in being worthwhile, strong, or competent. After the coming out, a number sympathize with their partners' pain, help them cope, or accommodate to their needs to keep the marriage going. In so doing, many lose track of who they are, what they need, and what their interests were. Simultaneously, their partners, being released from their self imposed "prisons" to some degree and absorbed with their struggle to understand and accept their true identities, often do not notice their spouses' discomfort. Some partners do not accept accountability for any negative consequences of the disclosure and blame their spouses for expressing hurt or anger. Experiencing inattention, blame or criticism, worries about the marriage and children, and effects on their partners' changes on them and the family, many spouses begin to feel worthless and to lose confidence in their ability to do anything about their concerns or discern what they want. Many ask, "What about me?," triggering a quest to find out who they are, what some call a "self search."

Perceived or actual deception of the partners' sexual orientation in the pre-disclosure period is the second issue unique to straight spouses and usually more troublesome than the fact the partner is bisexual, lesbian or gay. Regardless of how short or long a time partners hid their orientation or same-gender activities or to what degree that hiding was conscious or deliberate, most straight spouses feel they were deceived, duped, or living someone else's lie. They feel betrayed by the very persons with whom they thought they had most intimate of relationships and who should have trusted them with this core information about themselves. Not only was couple trust broken, but for spouses whose partners acted on their same-gender feelings, the marital vows were broken as well. For many, the disclosure opens a Pandora's box of previous secrets, lies, half-truths, or omissions. Some spouses wonder what role they may have played unconsciously in the deception and/or denial. Feeling led on and, for some, "used," most lose confidence in their own judgment of whom to trust, including themselves. They find it hard to trust their partner's word. Some become paranoid about what else might be hidden.

Some bisexual, gay, and lesbian partners continue to lie about their activities, and many criticize their spouses for disclosure-related behaviors, like not keeping the house clean because of exhaustion from the crisis, weeping about the disclosure, or becoming angry if the partners' lover comes to the house. Losing a sense of what's normal, some spouses accept the blame and wonder how much of the turmoil is their fault. Spouses whose partners stay in denial, despite evidence, sometimes search for more clues, for example, snooping on the Internet, even though they feel guilty doing so. Many spouses keep the disclosure and their partners' gay-related activities secret from friends and families of origin because their partners ask them not to tell or they fear that their partners may lose position or status in their jobs, faith community, or family of origin. Dissembling makes most of them feel uncomfortable. Acting as accomplices to the very deceptive behavior that hurt them causes moral confusion. Many begin to feel governed by the secret, rather than their conscience. They sense that their moral compass is shattered, feeling bereft of a lodestar to judge what is true or false, right or wrong.

Spouses with long-held views, based on societal, familial, or faith-based assumptions or doctrines that homosexual behavior is evil, immoral, or damnable feel the biggest moral challenge. Finding themselves married to a member of a group they previously condemned, someone who is also a parent to their children, prompts many to question their moral assumptions. Sometimes, liberal minded spouses are surprised to feel antigay sentiments and thoughts early on because of their devastation from the disclosure. As spouses ponder questions about what is right, keep the disclosure, dissemble, and feel impacted daily by their partners' new ideas, feelings, and behaviors that challenge their moral values, many feel powerless as moral agents in their lives.

Finally, the disclosure invalidates the spouses' belief system, the perceptual framework with which one makes sense of life and the world. The disclosure shatters their concepts of gender, marriage, family, sexual orientation, the meaning of life, and their future. This is the third unique issue that heterosexual spouses face. How to reconcile their previous conceptions of the way life is supposed to be with the reality of changes in their partners, marriage, and family presents a major challenge. Bisexuality itself challenges the either/or view of sexuality prevalent in our society. Losing their worldview that provides meaning in their lives is especially hard for spouses in conservative families, communities, or religious denominations, such as Mormon, Roman Catholic, Orthodox Judaism, or some evangelical churches. Lacking a blueprint for their lives, most spouses begin to feel hopeless. They cannot imagine what goals to set in order to become purposeful human beings. Without purpose, a number despair or become suicidal.

These issues alongside those with which their bisexual partners struggle can create a tragic situation for both spouses. Unlike gay and lesbian spouses who can find many supportive resources nationally, locally, and online, bisexual and heterosexual spouses have few outside support resources. At the same time, more support resources are available to validate the bisexual partners' struggle than exist for their heterosexual spouses. Feeling stigmatized by antigay social attitudes and not understood by most family members, friends, and often therapists, many heterosexual spouses cope alone. This self-imposed isolation aggravates feelings of inadequacy, hopelessness, and sometimes shame. Isolation and embarrassment, in turn, prevent their seeking help from the only support organization available for them, the Straight Spouse Network. Those who find this peer support system say that it provides the most effective help for coping constructively, in some cases, in conjunction with effective therapy.

STAGES OF COPING AMONG HETEROSEXUAL SPOUSES IN BISEXUAL-HETEROSEXUAL MARRIAGES

Stages through which spouses typically move as they cope with their issues provide a framework by which therapists can ascertain where a spouse is in the process of resolving them (Buxton, 2005). Presenting their coping in stages is misleading, since spouses do not proceed in lockstep fashion. Rather, they deal with one or more issues simultaneously and those concerns change in intensity or arise in diverse forms. At the same time, coping proceeds in a generally forward movement in the sequence described below, from shock through acceptance and healing to final transformation.

Initial Shock, Denial, and Relief

Once partners come out or their orientation is discovered, heterosexual spouses experience a mix of shock, denial, idealistic hope, or sense of relief. They do not deal directly with the disclosed information, hoping that it is a nightmare from which they will awaken, believing that love can resolve all problems or their partners will realize it is a mistake, or feeling relieved to know a reason for what was previously askew in the relationship, something that perhaps they can remediate.

Facing, Acknowledging, and Accepting Reality

Gradually, as consequences of the relationship impact their daily lives, spouses begin to face the reality of their partners' revealed sexual orientation, their own pain, and consequences of the disclosure on their marriage and family. Slowly they note and acknowledge changes in their partners' behavior, wardrobes, activities, and appearance; their own physical, mental, emotional, and spiritual health; their daily schedule and workplace performance; their attitudes toward life; the relationship and lovemaking; parenting behaviors; the partners' schedule at home and away; and family activities. Ever so slowly, spouses accept the fact that their partners' revealed orientation, their own devastation, and changes in their relationship, family, and daily life cannot become what they were before the disclosure.

Letting Go of the Past and Focusing on the Present

Accepting what is unchangeable leads to spouses' letting go of the past experiences as they thought them to be, while preserving memories of what was real in their marriage and family life. At this stage, spouses begin to look at themselves and their present lives, evaluating who and where they are and mapping steps toward controlling their own healing and growth.

Healing

Focusing on the present, spouses begin a many-pronged process of healing physical, sexual, emotional, cognitive, moral and spiritual wounds. Spouses generally seek help from varied sources, including: books and articles; Web sites; friends and family; professionals; education; and support or interest groups. As they begin to heal, they discover their core needs, wants, goals, and values.

Reconfiguring and Transforming

After many months, most reconfigure their self-image, moral compass, and belief system. This reconfigured blueprint provides an internal source of meaning and purpose. With this newly formulated outlook, spouses begin to transform their lives, whether within or outside of the marriage.

Key turning points in spouses' coping are signaled when they cease to ask "Why?" and instead ask, "What about me?" "Whom can I trust?" and "Where can I find meaning?" These three questions address their key issues of identity, integrity, and belief system, and propel them forward in coping constructively. As one spouse indicated, "The minute I stopped asking why questions and realized that didn't matter, it just is, I started to heal."

Four emotions are attached to one or more of the common issues, complicating the spouses' progress. Intense pain arises from finding out that their partners are gay, lesbian, or bisexual; feeling rejected sexually; or being left out of the partners' outside activities. Hurt feelings come up whenever they wonder, "How could he/she do this to me? I was the one who loved him/her the most?" Others sense that it is unfair that their partners seem to receive more outside attention and support than they do. As their self-concept crumbles, spouses often take every negative experience with their partners personally, exacerbating hurt feelings. Fear arises in spouses' initial stages of denial, apprehension when they face reality, and anxiety as they contemplate letting go of what they used to have and hoped to restore. Many feel frightened when imagining what might happen if their partners should leave or contemplate taking their own steps toward an unknown future. Many dread rejection of themselves, partners, or children because of their partners' orientation. Anger erupts with most issues, most often as they think about sexual rejection, deception, threats to their marriage, effects of the disclosure on their children, self-concept, values, and belief system, and changes they feel forced to make, such as divorce. Angry feelings often reemerge long after spouses accept and let go, when something reminds them of post-disclosure days as a happy couple and family. Grief, too, runs through most stages, from weeping as shock wears off, to crying as they acknowledge and accept reality, to sobbing when they finally let go of the past.

The power of these feelings helps most spouses move forward. A number, however, become stuck in one place because of the overwhelming force of one or more of these emotions. Hurt feelings, unresolved, lead to spouses' seeing themselves as victims and therefore powerless. Spouses overcome by fear and anxiety become unable to cope, succumbing to hopelessness. Those who cannot work through their anger become vindictive and vengeful, using the energy of anger to strike back at their partners or the gay community rather than to help themselves move forward. In some cases, unexpressed rage permeates all actions, causing illness and making spouses feel more worthless. Grief, unresolved, often turns into depression and suicidal thoughts or actions.

In many cases, spouses work through these feelings and issues alone. They are more likely to resolve them constructively if they have a support system of peers (face-to-face and online support groups, gatherings, and, one-on-one sharing), some family members, and a few friends who validate their feelings, provide reality checks for their situation, suggest ways to manage their emotions, and nurture their self concept and confidence. Some spouses, especially those who become stuck or overwhelmed by the confusion or challenges, seek therapists to help them untangle the issues and manage their feelings before they explode or implode. Few find therapists who also have knowledge about or experience with sexual orientation issues, bisexuality, or mixed-orientation couples. Without peer or therapeutic support, the process is slower, more erratic, and sometimes never completed.

Given the complex issues and emotional undercurrent, most spouses take from three to six years to work through their concerns The length of time to reach the transformation stage is often prolonged by various factors, including: the way in which the partners come out and what they do afterwards; the degree of devastation to the spouses' self concept and confidence; their emotional distress and shattering of belief system; the couples' financial situation; the presence of children at home; unexpected events such as family illness or accidents; divorce/custody issues if the couple divorces; and underlying psychological problems.

STAGES THROUGH WHICH BISEXUAL-HETEROSEXUAL COUPLES PROGRESS

The process by which heterosexual spouses resolve their issues proceeds side by side with their partners' processing their disclosure (or denial), and those two processes proceed alongside the couple's coping with relationship issues. Below are brief descriptions of stages through which mixed-orientation couples typically progress as they try to resolve post-disclosure challenges to the marriage. While a third of known couples separate right away without much coping, the remaining two-thirds stay together through two or more stages (Buxton, 1994, 2004, 2005).

Honeymoon Period

Once the partner's sexual orientation is shared or acknowledged after discovery, many (but not all) couples feel closer and more intimate, often increasing marital sex.

Awareness of Differences and Conflicts

Gradually, both spouses become aware of post-disclosure differences. As bisexual spouses struggle with or express their need or wish to interact with other bisexual men or women online and/or in the local community, their heterosexual spouses feel and express concerns about the impact of such activities on them and the children, often feeling left out and minimized in importance. Conflicts become apparent as bisexual partners explore their same-gender attractions (online or face to face), away from the family circle and often as their primary focus, while their heterosexual spouses express pain, fear, anger, or grief about these pursuits. These reactions in turn become potential or real obstacles to the bisexual spouses' explorations and outside same-gender activities, be they social or sexual. Simultaneously, these conflicts often bring to light underlying differences in the two spouses' communication styles, problem-solving habits, and/or personality traits. These differences hinder conflict resolution

Increase (or Decrease) of Couple Communication, and Mutual Adjustments

Some couples learn how to express or explain and understand each other's needs, wants, feelings, values, or priorities. Others do not and decide to separate. Spouses deciding to stay together at this point and understanding these differences between them try to respect and adjust to each other's needs, wants, feelings, values, and priorities, while negotiating boundaries and accepting non-negotiable items. Couples who cannot accomplish this next step separate.

Reinstatement (or Not) of Trust

Because of the breakdown of trust caused by the disclosure of closeted identity of behavior, heterosexual spouses work to restore belief in the partner's word. Together, they also look at the relationship itself to ascertain the quality of the relationship and whether or not they believe it is worth preserving. Some, while believing in its quality, fear that differences might eventually destroy their friendship and decide to separate to preserve their bond.

Increase (or Decrease) of Tolerance

Couples make mutually agreed upon changes so that each feels satisfied in the relationship. They adjust and adapt, as more changes become needed. Those who cannot tolerate them head toward divorce.

Integration of the Changes

Couples still together in his stage of adaptation learn to live with the changes as ongoing givens in their relationship. Both spouses accept them as integral parts of their relationship. Those who do not, separate.

Commitment to Work Jointly to Continue the Marriage

Having accepted and integrated the changes, couples who are still together commit to work jointly to develop a healthy interdependence that includes mutual support, nurturing, and respect for each spouse's autonomy and worth and a shared goal of a fulfilling, pleasureful relationship affirmed by demonstrated love and marital lovemaking that has continued throughout the process. As differences, changes, and challenges occur over time, these couples continually redefine and renegotiate the terms of their relationship.

Among couples who do not separate immediately after disclosure to sort out issues, the possibility of separating arises first at the tolerance and adaptation stage, as they try to mesh their two sets of needs. Additional numbers of couples decide to separate in each successive stage through reinstatement of trust and belief in the quality of the relationship. For couples who work through all stages to create an enduring marriage, the tolerance stage is the pivotal point at which they begin the renegotiating that enables them to do so.

Among couples who separate, early or late, some maintain an amicable relationship based on friendship and co-parenting responsibilities. Others separate with hostility because of intolerance or distrust, core differences, financial or custody battles, or intensifying reactions to post disclosure changes, such as the partner's finding a lover. These conflictual behaviors make it difficult for either spouse to resolve his or her individual issues.

In marriages in which the partners deny their same-gender attractions, spouses decide what to do based on their individual needs, wants, values, and priorities; the impact on the children; and increased negative behavior of their partners as they struggle with their coming out. Some couples accept the unspoken truth and do their best to maintain a functioning marriage and family out of love. In other cases, some heterosexual spouses stay married for a period of time, unsure and fearful; while some bisexual spouses remain, often guilt-ridden, afraid, depressed or resentful. Still other couples separate because of the toll wrought on them and the family by the denial or closeted behavior.

Compared to spouses in gay/lesbian-heterosexual marriages, more spouses in bisexual-heterosexual marriages report resilience and compromise and more feel supported by the couple's love and validation from their families of origin (Buxton, 2001, 2004).

COUNSELING HETEROSEXUAL SPOUSES
OF BISEXUAL PARTNERS

Given the triple challenge of the intertwined issues and unsynchronized stages of the heterosexual spouse, the bisexual spouse, and the bisexual-heterosexual couple, what counseling is most helpful? The following descriptions indicate the kind of counseling that heterosexual spouses of bisexual partners and couples have found or think would be most helpful, based on comments about therapy that I have gathered over the years and conversations with knowledgeable therapists.

Several premises are helpful to frame counseling of heterosexual spouses in this situation, so that the therapist can focus on discerning which issues underlie the presenting concerns of each spouse and guide them as they work out the best steps to take toward the future for them. A major point to keep in mind is that the areas of concern that trouble heterosexual spouses of bisexual partners (sexuality, marriage, children, identity, integrity, and belief system) mirror those with which their partners struggle. However, heterosexual spouses are way behind their disclosing partners in dealing with these concerns and need time to catch up. The two spouses are also dealing with bisexuality and their mixed-orientation relationship at different stages, levels of understanding, and personal experiences. That lack of synchronicity affects the spouses' ability to understand one another, especially during the first year or so after disclosure.

Another difference between the spouses is that issues that challenge heterosexual spouses are not initiated by them, but arise largely in response to their partners' disclosure and post-disclosure changes. This difference explains why many heterosexual spouses see themselves as casualties, albeit unintended, of someone else's actions and decisions.

Third, the two spouses bring two distinct sexual orientations to the relationship: bisexuality and its dual attraction as contrasted to the single vector attraction of heterosexual spouses. Also, each spouse's sexual orientation is separate from his or her personality traits, behavior, and individual psychological problems. Sexual orientation does not determine how either spouse reacts and copes or how the couple relates and communicates.

A fourth premise to keep in mind is that each spouse's experience is embedded in a family, societal, and cultural context that affects how he or she perceives and handles issues. Their family heritage and particular community in which the spouses grew up and live influenced the partners' deciding to marry, stay closeted, and come out and the way that the heterosexual spouse works through disclosure concerns. Both spouses are impacted by reactions of their families of origin, colleagues, friends, and fellow congregants to the partner's same-gender attraction or behavior or having outside lovers. Cultural factors play a strong role, too. Hispanic spouses, for example, keep close ties with their families of origin who are often hold cultural negativity toward homosexual behavior. African American spouses are affected by the denial of many persons in their communities and churches who deny the existence of gay or bisexual African American men; the number who have AIDS; and the number of married men who engage in same-gender sex on the "down low" (King, 2004). Some Asian-American heterosexual spouses do not seek therapy because that is a sign of shameful weakness in their cultures (Buxton, 1994).

Other factors that affect how spouses cope include their ages, length of the couple's relationship, and presence or absence of children in their homes. Age provides clues to dating practices, socializing patterns, and preferred sexual practices of and preferred social attitudes toward gay, lesbian, or bisexual persons at the time of the wedding and the post-disclosure period. The length of the relationship influences the relative strength of a couple's habits of relating and communicating. The longer they have been together, the more their history and connectedness are impacted by the disclosure and become more difficult to unravel if they divorce.

A sixth set of circumstances are personal crises that can sidetrack spouses' coping, such as job loss, a child's or family member's illness or death, a family move, financial troubles, or disclosure-related events like neighbors' gossip, a public outing, ostracism by their faith community, or their children's being teased or discriminated against by school mates.

A seventh point to remember is that a number of mixed-orientation couples have formed positive relationships even though they divorce and a number have created enduring marriages in various forms: monogamy, celibacy, open, triad, closed loop, or polyamory.

Finally, it takes time, usually three or so years for spouses and couples to develop a post-disclosure relationship that works for them. Resolving their issues cannot be rushed. Rushing to "move on" or make decisions often leads to a painful backlash for one or both spouses or a delayed upheaval in the family.

Heterosexual spouses seek therapy for an array of expressed concerns. They crave acknowledgement of the uniqueness and difficulty of their situation. Each presenting problem is the tip of a complex composite of the issues, coping behaviors, and emotions described above. Therapists, knowing this underlying and unspoken chaos, can help spouses trace their presenting issues to the heart of the matter that needs healing. The following are the most common concerns that heterosexual spouses present.

Health problems that some spouses bring to counseling include precipitous loss of weight from not eating or weight gain from gorging on comfort food or inactivity. Some spouses resume smoking or increase drinking to numb the pain, deny reality, and avoid action. Others cannot sleep, work, or take care of the house or children. Many bring sexuality concerns, such as alleged frigidity, loss of sexual desire, feelings that they are sexually starved or inadequate, or desire to enhance marital sex. Wives worry about sexually transmitted diseases, especially AIDS, and where to find confidential testing. Other problems range from hypertension and skin rashes to depression, suicidal thoughts, or self-cutting.

Some spouses arrive at the therapist's office after a heart attack, breakdown, or drug overdose.

Many spouses come with questions about how to keep the marriage alive, provide sexual satisfaction to their partners, or become more attractive to them. Some want to know ways to entice their partners back to an exclusive relationship, improve communication with them, get them to tell the truth, to avoid outbursts of anger or to resolve arguments. Still others want to know how to set boundaries on their partners' outside activities or how to distance themselves on the path to divorce. Some seek options other than monogamy or an open marriage. Many wonder if they can accept non-monogamy, and if not, how to tell their partners. Those in an open relationship want to manage their jealousy or fear that their partners might leave. Those whose partners are in denial would like reassurance that they are correct in believing their partners have same-gender attractions.

Psychological issues include the heterosexual spouses' denial or disbelief that their partners are bisexual, gay or lesbian. Others come with self-blame for their partners' turning to persons of the same gender, asking what they did wrong. Some express shame or embarrassment, suspecting that everyone probably knows is and wondering what is wrong with their own sexuality. Many seek help for low self-esteem, lack of confidence, and/or feelings of worthlessness, a self-perception often heightened by their partners' blaming. Feeling that they lost themselves through accommodation in the marriage, a number ask, "What about me? I have no idea who am I anymore?"

Many spouses present cognitive conflicts, feeling unable to comprehend their partner's attraction to both men and women or the partner's deception. Most are confounded as to how their partners could be straight one day and bisexual the next, asking, "If I am sexually satisfying, why did he/she turn to someone else?" Another quandary is how their partners could have known and not told them or are still in denial.

Most spouses present morality concerns, most often about the deception by the one person to whom they felt closest. They want to rebuild trust in their own judgment of truth, "right" and "wrong," and their partners' word. Some question if their marriage was only a sham or express embarrassment that they had no idea their partners were attracted to the same gender. Some show shame about their partners' current behavior. Still others are troubled by the conflict between their love of their partner and their religious beliefs that condemn homosexuality and condone only heterosexual marriage. Others fear being stigmatized or hurt from rejection or non-understanding from friends and ask, "How can I accept him/her when what they're doing is wrong?" or say, " I feel guilty going to church (or temple)." Others wonder, "Is non-monogamy infidelity if we both agree it's okay to have an outside lover?" Still others ask if it is wrong to be selfish to seek what they need, even a divorce.

Spiritual concerns are often a presenting issue. Feeling hopeless, many spouses feel bereft of anything they ever loved and complain they have nothing to live for. Despairing complaints include the sense of being alone or "empty" because life no longer has meaning. Many wonder in what they can believe. Others distrust their instinct to love people and do not dare enjoy what they have. Some call this state a spiritual death or dark night of the soul.

No matter what the presenting issue, at least one of the pervasive emotions discussed earlier, hurt, fear, anger and grief, colors how spouses state their concerns. Many do not specify a particular emotion but manifest it in their voices, on their faces, or through behaviors such as clenched fists or agitated movements. Other spouses specifically ask for help to manage feelings so overwhelming that they block any progress in coping. A number inquire, for example, "How can I get rid of this pain" or "stop feeling hurt?" Fearful clients murmur, "I'm anxious all the time," of "I'm having panic attacks." Angry spouses ask, "How can I handle my anger so our discussions don't turn into battles?" or "I'm so afraid I'll blow up at her in front of the children." Finally, grief and despair are shown or described in comments like, "I can't stop crying," or "I want to end it all."

Given these feelings that become overwhelming, heterosexual spouses want validation that their feelings are normal for anyone facing a husband's or wife's disclosure and help in handling them appropriately. They crave acknowledgement of the uniqueness and difficultly of their situation. At the same time, they usually arrive with action goals of which they are often unaware or unable to articulate. They want help to clarify their concerns, guidance for handling their emotions and suggestions of strategies to regain their self-esteem and confidence. They desire ways to change their ineffective behaviors, perceptions, and feelings so that they can progress more steadily in ways that fit their particular needs, wants, and values. Once therapists discern the underlying issues and current coping stage of spouse clients, they can help spouses achieve the desired action that will move them through the current stage onto the next. Therapists have a wide repertoire of tools to help clients meet these goals, especially strategies to manage pain, fear, anger and grief; to restore self esteem, self worth, and confidence; to communicate effectively; and to resolve couple conflicts. Spouses' action goals follow the typical order of their coping.

Face and Acknowledge

Spouses want to grasp the reality of their hurt and pain, and their partners' bisexual orientation and changes in their lives resulting from the disclosure of their partners' bisexuality.

Learn and Understand

They want to break through dualistic thinking to understand bisexuality and recognize needs of their partners that they cannot fill. Spouses also want know and understand the implications the range of possibilities for mixed-orientation marriages.

Accept and Let Go

Spouses want to be able to accept what has happened and to be able to let go of hopes that they can recreate their past situation. They want to release hopes and misassumptions and to stop asking "why" questions that can never be answered.

Take Care of Themselves

Spouses want to refocus on taking care of their own needs and restoring their own physical, sexual, emotional, mental, and moral spiritual health. They want to deal realistically with problems and needs related to their own growth and their relationship. This means working through hurt, anger, fear, and grief so that they do not see themselves as victims, feel paralyzed or vindictive, or become despairing or suicidal.

Reconfigure Identity, Integrity, Belief System

A major action goal is developing a clear self-concept of self worth, authenticity, and confidence in their ability to cope. They would like to cultivate flexibility, resilience, empathy, as well as self-esteem in order to live with more satisfaction whether or not they stay married. They aim to clarify their own wants, needs, and values to form a solid base of integrity by which to evaluate what future steps are "right" for them. They yearn to sort through their values to construct a reality-based moral compass with which to discern truth and falsehood and to learn how to trust their own judgment and the word of others, and particularly their partners. Finally, they want to recreate a belief system that gives them a wider perspective to view their suffering and the post-disclosure situation in such a way that is provides meaning and purpose in their lives.

Incorporate Reconfigured Perspective into Daily Life

Spouses want to incorporate their reformulated identify, integrity, and belief system into daily actions. They want to examine and evaluate alternative options in their lives as individuals and spouses. For those who decide to stay married, they wish to nurture and strengthen themselves and the relationship. Those who decide to separate want to distance themselves from the partners.

COUNSELING BISEXUAL-HETEROSEXUAL COUPLES

When heterosexual spouses come with their bisexual spouses for counseling, the couples bring two sets of issues in the same areas of sexuality, marriage, children, identity, integrity, and belief system in addition to relationship concerns. A couple's presenting issues reflect the stages through which couples redefine their relationship after the disclosure.

Communication problems are common. While most presenting concerns mirror communication difficulties that ordinary couples report, those of bisexual-heterosexual couples involve the complexity of bisexuality; a mixed-orientation relationship; and each spouse's sexual, emotional, cognitive, moral, and social issues that they need to express and explain to each other in order to reach a common ground of understanding.

Difficulties of adjusting to post-disclosure changes are often presented. Heterosexual spouses are angry that their partners go out frequently or spend long periods of time on the computer e-mailing other bisexual men. Bisexual partners who stay home or cut back computer time for their spouses' sake resent their "controlling" wives or husbands. Other concerns include bisexual spouses' disliking their spouses' constant questions about bisexuality or what they do when they go out; outbursts if the partners do not do their share of family affairs; or hostility after separation.

Both spouses frequently present concerns about negotiating and setting boundaries. They frequently seek ways to avoid conflicts so they can work out how to meet each other's needs, wants, and values with understanding. They voice concerns such as, "How can I keep her from worrying when I'm out late?" or "I don't want her bringing the girl friend to my house when the kids are here."

Deception and denial issues are common and sometimes not voiced, but apparent. If a partner still denies his or her same-gender attraction or behavior, the denial is a major and difficult concern to work through, if ever. For other couples, developing trust again is a major issue, especially if bisexual partners hid their sexual orientation for a long time or acted on it secretly. Post disclosure concerns include discomfort from keeping the secret from friends, family or colleagues.

Many couples want help evaluating the relationship to see if it is worth preserving. Comments may range from, "I'm not sure we have anything to save enough to work through the bi thing," to "How can we throw this all away?"

Distinctive of bisexual partners, contrasted with heterosexual spouses (and gay or lesbian spouses), is the need to develop strategies to withstand negativity against bisexuality expressed by some members of the gay and lesbian communities as well as negative feelings of either spouse. Negative feelings include fear, feeling isolated, resentment, jealousy, the bisexual wives' guilt, or the husbands' religious judgments (Buxton 2001, 2004).

With these presenting concerns as entry points, couples, too, come to therapy with action goals, not always articulated, to help them work through the relationship stages constructively and maintain a positive relationship, whether or not they stay married. Goals include those for each spouse within the relationship, interaction between the spouses, and actions for couples to take jointly.

Individual Actions

Spouses want to educate themselves about bisexuality and mixed-orientation marriages and to develop a personal support system of peers and at least one friend and family member. They each wish also to develop open-mindedness to alternatives and options, flexibility to try new behaviors, and understanding that failed trials are learning opportunities

Couple Interaction

Couples would like to engage honest communication so that each spouse can express his or her feelings, needs, hopes, values, and priorities candidly and the other spouse listens without interruption or defensiveness. Bisexual spouses, especially husbands, want to demonstrate their love of heterosexual spouses to them; while heterosexual spouses want reassurances that they are loved no less when their partners go out or have a lover. Both spouses want to respect each other's needs and wishes and support one another as each copes with his or her own problems. Another goal is practicing empathy, concerned about each other's struggle but not taking on the responsibility of solving the other's problem.

Couple Actions

Couples want to identify their reasons for marrying and positive elements of their marriage, love, and friendship, as a foundation from which to build a new relationship, whether or not they stay married. If the relationship problems threaten the couple's bond, they want to accept that reality and end the marriage before the friendship is harmed. If they are committed to staying together, they want to negotiate mutually satisfying compromises for the sake of the relationship, agreeing on boundaries and limitations and accepting non-negotiables. They want to schedule time to get away from disclosure issues for couple or family activities solely to enjoy each other's company and nurture the relationship. Finally, they realize they have to want to create their own context to support their decision, especially if family, friends, community, and/or faith community are against non-monogamy or same gender attractions or activities.

As therapists apply their counseling skills to help couples achieve these goals, they will want to focus on helping the spouses develop coping strategies cited most often as effective, despite internal or external obstacles, by the largest number of spouses studied from all mixes of mixed-orientation couples: honest communication, finding peer support, demonstrating love, the heterosexual spouse's acceptance, compromise, resilience, and empathy (Buxton, 2001, 2004). Empathy, an important strategy for navigating conflicts, is often achieved by a spouse's remembering the couple's core love and bond, rather than reacting to expressed emotions, behavior shown in many personal stories of bisexual and gay husbands (Klein & Schwartz, 2001) as well as of bisexual wives and heterosexual spouses of bisexual and gay partners (Buxton, 1994, 2004).

In view of the double agenda that couples bring to counseling and the complexity of the issues and of bisexuality, couples require time to work through their concerns. The most realistic and promising counseling objective is not to save or to end the marriage but rather to help the spouses work out as candidly and lovingly as they can ways to redefine their relationship so that it is meets both sets of needs, wants, and values regardless of the outcome of the marriage itself. The more help that couples receive to get through the tolerance stage, the more likely that more of them can create a marriage in which both spouses are satisfied and strong and more of them who decide to divorce will do so amicably and maintain a lasting bond.

Therapists need to help both spouses decide which actions would be best for them to take in the least stressful and most empowering ways as possible. Spouses who responded report they want counselors who, as one heterosexual wife told me, "See the issue they are dealing with from both gay/bi and straight perspectives, and help them sort out what they need to do about it, the options they have, and what they need to think about in considering the options to that end."

DISCUSSION

Therapy for heterosexual spouses in bisexual heterosexual marriages and bisexual-heterosexual couples is most effective when therapists understand bisexuality and mixed-orientation relationships, as well as acknowledge the unique issues of both the bisexual and heterosexual spouses. Understanding of the issues with which heterosexual spouses grapple is critical. As one of the spouses who shared with me concerns about therapy stated, "I wish the hopelessness, the intense sense of betrayal, the depth and complicated multitude of complex feigns and fears with which straight spouses are left after years of marriage were better understood." Therapists need to recognize these kinds of singular issues, discern the stage in which spouses are coping, validate their feelings and help them manage them, provide them with options, and help them take actions demonstrated to resolve spouse and couple issues constructively.

Heterosexual spouses want therapists who encourage them to face reality, help them restore self worth and confidence, reconfigure their moral compass and belief system; help them develop communication skills to share feelings and needs honestly with their partners and suggest effective relational strategies in general and those specific to bisexual-heterosexual couples. Therapists whom spouses find most helpful pay attention to the particulars of the heterosexual spouse's family and social context.

In couples therapy, addressing the heterosexual spouse's concerns as well as those of the bisexual spouse is essential. Couples also want therapists to isolate sexual orientation factors from relational and individual issues and to keep sessions from becoming discussions of personal irritations. They want therapists to listen to both sides of issues raised, acknowledge the individual idiosyncrasies of each spouse, follow up "obvious" clues to same-gender attractions of bisexual partners in denial, hold no preconceived idea about how the marriage "should" work out, and refrain from pushing spouses toward a particular outcome. As one heterosexual wife commented to me, "So much of marriage counseling is about compromise and meeting in the middle. The assumption is that there is actually a middle. With a mixed orientation marriage, there has to be an acknowledgement that the situation may be unworkable. Otherwise the straight spouse will continue to be beaten down by the whole thing."

In the end, both spouses are responsible to resolve their individual issues based on their wants, needs, values, and priorities, while the couple is responsible to evaluate jointly their post-disclosure relationship to decide what to do about the marriage. Key to their progress is finding peer support, individual and/or group, and taking time rather than rushing the process. Clinging to the marriage blinds them to options and prohibits them from developing flexibility to withstand natural mistakes that come with forging a relationship in new territory. The desired outcome is to develop constructive ways to create a positive relationship. Focusing on the present dynamics between the spouses rather than on the past or future holds greater promise for couples to develop a positive relationship. When the two spouses focus on themselves, what they value in the relationship, what they can create together, and what significant factors in their relationship need to be preserved, then they are better able to resolve their own issues and strengthen the best in each other as well as their bond, regardless of what happens to the marriage. Through this process, both the heterosexual and bisexual spouses typically become stronger, wiser, and more fulfilled in all dimensions.

REFERENCES

Auerback, S., & Moser, C. (1989). Groups for the wives of gays and bisexual men. *Social Work, 32*(4), 321-25.

Buxton, A. P. (1994). *The other side of the closet: The coming-out crisis for straight spouses and families.* New York: John Wiley & Sons.

Buxton, A. P. (2000). The best interest of children of lesbian and gay parents. In R. Galatzer-Levy & L. Kraus, (Eds.), *The scientific basis for custody decisions* (pp. 319-346). New York: John Wiley & Sons.

Buxton, A. P. (2001). Writing our own scripts: How bisexual men and their heterosexual wives maintain their marriages after disclosure. In B. Beemyn & E. Steinman, (Eds.), *Bisexuality in the lives of men: Facts and fiction* (pp. 157-189). New York: Harrington Park Press.

Buxton, A. P. (2004) Works in progress: How bisexual wives and their heterosexual husbands maintain their marriages after disclosure. In R.C. Fox, (Ed.), *Current Research on Bisexuality* (pp. 57-82). New York: Harrington Park Press.

Buxton, A. P. (2004) Paths and pitfalls: How heterosexual spouses cope after their spouses come out. *Journal of couple and relationship therapy, 1(2/3),* 95-109.

Buxton, A. P. (2005). A family matter: When a spouse comes out as gay, lesbian, or bisexual. *Journal of GLBT Family Studies, 1(2),* 49-70.

Deabill, G. (1987). *An investigation of sexual behaviors in mixed sexual orientation couples: Gay husbands and straight wives.* Unpublished doctoral dissertation, Institute for the Advanced Study of Human Sexuality, San Francisco.

Fox, R. C. (1995). Bisexual identities. In S.R. D'Augelli & C.J. Patterson (Eds.), *Lesbian, gay, and bisexual identities over the life span: Psychological perspectives* (pp. 48-86). New York: Oxford University Press.

Fox, R. C. (Ed.). (2004) *Current Research on Bisexuality.* New York: Harrington Park Press.

Gochros, J. S. (1989). *When husbands come out of the closet.* New York: Harrington Park Press.

Gray, C. G. (2001). *My husband is gay: A woman's guide to surviving the crisis.* Santa Cruz, CA: Crossing Press.

Hatterer, L. J. (1970). *Changing homosexuality in the male: Treatment for men troubled by homosexuality.* New York: Dell Publishing.

Hatterer, M. (1974). Problems of women married to homosexual men. *American Journal of Psychiatry, 131(3),* 275-278.

Hays, D., & Samuels, A. (1988). Heterosexual women's perceptions of their marriages to homosexual or bisexual men. *Journal of Homosexuality, 17(3/4),* 81-100.

Imielinsky, K. (1969). Homosexuality in males with particular attention to marriage. *Psychotherapy and psychosomantics, 17,* 126-132.

King, J. L. (2004). *On the down low: A journey into the lives of "straight" Black men who sleep with men.* New York: Broadway Books.

Klein, F. (1978) *The bisexual option: A concept of one-hundred percent intimacy.* New York: Arbor House.

Klein, F., Sepekoff B., & Wolf, T. J. (1985). Sexual orientation: A multivariable, dynamic process. *Journal of Homosexuality 11(1/2),* 35-40

Klein, F., & Schwartz, T. (2001). *Bisexual and gay husbands: Their stories, their words.* Binghamton, NY: Harrington Park Press.

Kohn, B., & Matusow, A. (1980). *Barry and Alice: Portrait of a bisexual marriage.* Engelwood Cliffs, NJ: Prentice Hall, Inc.

Malone, J. (1980). *Straight Women/Gay Men: A Special Relationship.* New York: Dial Press.

Nahas, R., & Turley, M. (1979). *The new couple: Women and gay men*. New York: Seaview Books.

Whitehead, S. L. (1997). *The truth shall set you free: A memoir*. San Francisco: Harper.

Whitney, C. (1990). *Uncommon Lives: Gay men and straight women*. New York: Plume Books.

Wolf, T. J. (1985). Marriages of bisexual men. *Journal of Homosexuality* 11(1/2), 135-118.

Therapy with Clients Who Are Bisexual and Polyamorous

Geri Weitzman

doi:10.1300/J159v06n01_08

[Haworth co-indexing entry note]: "Therapy with Clients Who Are Bisexual and Polyamorous."
Weitzman, Geri. Co-published simultaneously in *Journal of Bisexuality* (Harrington Park Press, an imprint of
The Haworth Press, Inc.) Vol. 6, No. 1/2, 2006, pp. 137-164; and: *Affirmative Psychotherapy with Bisexual
Women and Bisexual Men* (ed: Ronald C. Fox) Harrington Park Press, an imprint of The Haworth Press, Inc.,
2006, pp. 137-164. Single or multiple copies of this article are available for a fee from The Haworth Document Delivery Service [1-800-HAWORTH, 9:00 a.m. - 5:00 p.m. (EST). E-mail address: docdelivery@
haworthpress.com].

SUMMARY. Polyamorous partners offer each other the freedom to pursue romantic bonds with other people, in addition to being romantically close within their own relationship. Given the prevalence of polyamory in the bisexual community, it is important that psychotherapists are aware of issues particular to people who are bisexual and polyamorous and who seek mental health services. The author will also present findings from her research on bisexuality and polyamory and will discuss implications for how therapists can be of support to polyamorous members of the bisexual community. *[Article copies available for a fee from The Haworth Document Delivery Service: 1-800 HAWORTH. E-mail address: <docdelivery@haworthpress.com> Website: <http://www.HaworthPress.com> © 2006 by The Haworth Press, Inc. All rights reserved.]*

KEYWORDS. Polyamory, polyamorous, open relationships, open marriage, non-monogamy, bisexuality, bisexual, counseling, therapy, psychotherapy

INTRODUCTION TO POLYAMORY

What Is Polyamory?

Polyamory is a lifestyle in which a person may pursue simultaneous romantic relationships, with the blessing and consent of each of their partners. This is in contrast to monogamy, where relationship partners agree to romantic exclusivity. This is also in contrast to infidelity, where someone takes on additional lovers without their partner's consent. Polyamorous people commit to honesty, negotiation, and clear communication about each of the relationships in their life (Hymer & Rubin, 1982).

In a recent study of 217 bisexual adults, 33% were involved in a polyamorous relationship at the time of the study (Page, 2004). Fifty-four percent of the 217 respondents stated that the polyamorous lifestyle is their ideal relationship pattern. Some choose polyamory simply because they like having the freedom to date anyone they choose (Sumpter, 1991). Others find the lifestyle suits them because it lets them express their sexuality with lovers from more than one gender group. Counselors who work with bisexual clients should be aware that some of these clients will be polyamorous, and should learn how best to serve those clients.

The author will describe polyamory, and will give an overview of the poly-specific concerns that are most likely to come up in the therapeutic setting, with ideas about how the counselor can help their clients to work through these concerns. It should be noted that most polyamorous people seek out therapy for reasons that have nothing to do with polyamory. They are happily polyamorous, and are seeking therapy for the usual concerns like depression and anxiety. Occasionally issues having to do with polyamory itself *are* the focus of the therapy. It is these latter concerns that the discussion here will address. Many of these ideas will also apply to therapy with straight and gay polyamorous clients.

Benefits of Polyamory

Why might two partners allow one other to take on additional lovers? In part, this has to do with simple preference–just as people vary in sexual orientation, so too do they vary in preference for intimacies with one vs. multiple partners. Polyamorously inclined people enjoy developing each of the connections in their life as deeply as it feels right to (Blasband & Peplau, 1985), rather than having the intimacy level of one relationship limit the depth of the others. When both partners share the preference for nonexclusivity, there is a mutual commitment towards working through feelings of jealousy in such a way that does not involve restricting one another's sexual behaviors.

Polyamory offers several benefits. New aspects of self sometimes emerge as one relates closely to additional people (Ramey, 1975). Polyamorous partners are not as likely to feel as pressured to meet all of each other's relationship needs as monogamous partners do (Knapp, 1976; Rust, 1996). There is an emphasis on differentiation and boundary setting, and on meeting each partner's emotional and sexual needs (Kassoff, 1989). Polyamorous partners who practice communicating their needs and boundaries learn to manage jealousy in ways that don't involve restricting their partners' choices (Knapp, 1976). This leads to enhanced trust (Keener, 2004) and security (Ramy, 1975).

Dixon (1985) found that polyamorous people felt less possessive of their partners, and less competitive with other people who their partners might consider to be attractive. Some polyamorous people experience *compersion*, which means feeling joy that one's partner is sharing closeness with another person (Keener, 2004; Polyamory Society, 1997). Keener's (2004) study participants noted an absence of worry as to whether their partners might be cheating, since the permission to take other lovers was granted freely. About 1/3 of ostensibly monogamous partnerships are touched by affairs (Spring, 1997), and polyamory is an ethical solution to the very common phenomenon of extramarital desires.

Benefits to polyamory exist on the community level also. Polyamorous households of three or more adults have more physical, financial, and emotional resources to share than does the average two adult household. More people are available to split the childcare duties, house-cleaning, and rent (Makanjuola, 1987). Even non-cohabitating polyamorous lovers often form extensive kinship-bond networks (Keener, 2004), supporting one another's households with favors like pet-sitting and airport-rides.

Types of Polyamory

There are several types of polyamory. In an *open relationship*, two people give each other permission to pursue additional relationships. Typically the original partners consider themselves to be *primary partners*, with the highest level of commitment between them (Labriola, 1999). The other relationships in their lives are considered *secondary*. This is in contrast to *non-hierarchical polyamory*, in which no one relationship is prioritized above the rest (alt.polyamory FAQ, 1997). A third type of polyamory is the *poly-family*, involving three or more adults in a relationship all together (D. Corbett, personal communication, 3/17/99, as cited in Weitzman, 1999). If the poly-family partners agree not to date anyone outside of their menage, then the poly-family is termed *polyfidelitous* (Labriola, 1999; Rust, 1996). Finally, there is *swinging*, in which couples exchange partners for brief sexual encounters but do not form deep emotionally bonded relationships with these lovers. Bisexual-identified people are less likely to pursue swinging than other forms of polyamory (Rust, 1996).

How Prevalent Is Polyamory?

Page (2004) found that 33% of her bisexual sample of 217 participants were involved in a polyamorous relationship, and 54% considered this type of relationship ideal. West (1996) reported that 20% of her lesbian respondents were polyamorous, while Blumstein and Schwartz (1983) found that 28% of the lesbian couples in their sample were. Blumstein and Schwartz found that 65% of the gay male couples in their study were polyamorous, and that 15-28% of their heterosexual couples had "an understanding that allows nonmonogamy under some circumstances" (p. 312).

A HISTORY OF THE MENTAL HEALTH FIELD'S RESPONSE TO POLYAMORY

The mental health field has come to value diversity in recent years, in such areas as culture, religion and sexual orientation. This standard has not yet encompassed polyamory. Despite the demographic prevalence of polyamory, therapists are under-educated about the lives and needs of polyamorous people. Most graduate psychology textbooks, curricula, and internships do not include mention of it.

Monogamy is often upheld as a relationship standard by the therapy field, and polyamory is often pathologized. Knapp (1975) found that 33% of the therapists in his sample thought that people in open relationships had personality disorders or neurotic tendencies, and that 9-17% would try to influence a return to a monogamous lifestyle. Knapp's respondents were more likely to pathologize clients who were in open relationships than clients who had secret extramarital affairs. Hymer and Rubin (1982) found that 24% of therapists surveyed felt that polyamorous people feared commitment and 15% guessed that the clients' marriages must not be fulfilling. Likewise, Rubin and Adams (1978, cited in Hymer and Rubin, 1982) found that among polyamorous people who had pursued therapy, 27% found that their therapists weren't supportive of their lifestyles. Page (2004) similarly reported that many of her bisexual research participants had trouble finding therapists who were affirming of their bisexuality and polyamory. Weber (2002) found that 38% of a sample polyamorous people who had at some point participated in therapy had chosen not to mention the fact of their polyamory to their therapists, and 10% of those who did reveal it experienced a negative response. Even when therapists who hadn't heard of polyamory were open-minded enough to learn more about it, the client had to use some of their paid session time to educate the therapist.

The polyamorous community is notably supported by one famous mental health professional, Dr. Albert Ellis, who in the 1940s wrote a book titled *The Case For Sexual Liberty,* which affirmed the phenomenon of open marriage. Ellis (1965) couldn't find a publisher for his book until the more liberal 1960s. In this book he speaks about the frequency of non-monogamy in many cultures and affirms that "if any sexual desire, expression, thought, or activity is not morally wrong in itself, then it can never justifiably be termed sexually 'wrong' or 'sinful,' merely because it is a sexual act, and as such reprehensible to some theological and superstitious set of beliefs" (p.7).

Some therapists now advertise as being knowledgeable and supportive about polyamory on forums such as the Poly Friendly Professionals List (Decker, 1999). These therapists are mostly located in major US cities, however. And even in the regions that list a number of polyamory-aware therapists, it can be hard to find one who takes one's insurance plan. Many polyamorous people who possess health insurance end up paying for their therapy out of pocket. Polyamory-aware psychiatrists are even harder to find.

In contrast to the studies on therapists' beliefs about polyamory, many studies provide evidence for the sound psychological functioning of polyamorous people and the viability of polyamorous relationships. Watson (1981, cited in Rubin, 1982) administered the California Psychological Inventory (Gough, 1957) to 38 polyamorous people, and they scored within a normal range. Kurdek and Schmitt (1986) administered the Symptom Checklist 90 (Derogatis, 1983) to 98 gay polyamorous men and 34 gay monogamous men, and no differences in psychological symptom reporting were found.

Polyamorous couples in the Netherlands were found to have normal levels of marriage satisfaction and self-esteem (Buunk, 1980, as cited in Rubin, 1982). Two thirds of Knapp's (1976) respondents found that marital satisfaction in their primary relationships increased as they became involved in a polyamorous lifestyle. Rubin (1982) compared monogamous and polyamorous couples' scores on the Dyadic Adjustment Scale (Spanier, 1976), and the two groups scored similarly in marital adjustment and happiness. Rubin and Adams (1986) followed up on the same couples four years later, and found no difference between polyamorous and monogamous couples in terms of the longevity of their relationships. Rubin and Adams noted that among the polyamorous relationships that ended, the breakups weren't about the polyamory. Ramey (1975) similarly found that polyamorous couples tended to end relationships for similar reasons as monogamous folks, including unequal attraction and a decrease in the number of common interests.

In the gay community, marital satisfaction, relationship longevity, depth of intimacy, and frequency of sex were also found to be comparable between polyamorous and monogamous couples (Blasband & Peplau, 1985; Kurdek & Schmitt, 1986; McWhirter & Mattison, 1984; Peplau, 1981). Likewise, West (1996) found that 88% of her polyamorous lesbian study sample reported considerable happiness in their relationships, and 80% would be willing to choose this relationship style again. Dixon (1985) found that 76% of bisexual swingers in her sample reported their sexual satisfaction in their marriages to be good or excellent. These studies should lay to rest any concerns about the mental health of polyamorous people and the strength of their relationships.

BISEXUALITY AND POLYAMORY

What do we know about bi-poly individuals specifically? In 2003, this author conducted the first large-scale exploratory study on the identity development of bisexual and polyamorous people (Weitzman, in press). Findings from this research will be briefly summarized below, and some more recently analyzed portions of the data will be discussed as well.

From August 2003 to February 2004, 2169 people responded to a 54-question Web-based survey that included both multiple choice and essay questions about the experiences of bi-poly people (Weitzman, in press). The mean age of participants was 34. Sixty-six percent of the participants were female, 86% were Caucasian, and 83% were from the United States. Forty-nine percent identified themselves as being mostly attracted to members of another gender (Kinsey 1 and 2), 30% were attracted equally to members of their own gender and to members of another gender (Kinsey 3), and 16% said that they were attracted more to members of their own gender than to members of another gender (Kinsey 4 and 5).

Of the participants in this study, 54% had identified as monogamous at an earlier time in their lives, while 36% said that they had never preferred monogamy at any point in their lives. Most of the respondents lived with a single partner (57%) or alone (35%), and most of the rest of the participants lived with multiple romantic partners in a group household (7.5%). More than half of the respondents were not out to their parents as being bisexual (52%) or polyamorous (59%); over two-thirds weren't out to their extended families as being bisexual (71%) or polyamorous (79%).

There is an old stereotype that all bisexual people feel the need to simultaneously date members of more than one gender group (Sumpter, 1991). Contradicting this stereotype, Weitzman (in press) found that 70% of the responding participants felt that it did not matter to them whether their lovers were of the same or different gender from one another at any given time. Further along these lines, 50% of the responding participants stated that their preference for polyamory did not stem from a desire to simultaneously date members of more than one gender group; 34% said that a desire to date people from more than one gender group was just one among several factors in their choice of polyamory; and only 12% identified the desire to simultaneously date people from more than one gender group as the main motivating factor in their choice of polyamory. In summary, many polyamorous bisexuals simply do not regard gender as a primary factor when choosing their intimate partners, although there is a significant minority for whom it *is* important to be intimate with people from more than one gender group.

Another old stereotype is that bisexual and polyamorous people are at high risk for catching and spreading sexually transmitted diseases (Sumpter, 1991; West, 1996). Weitzman (in press) asked participants to state whether they had ever been diagnosed with a sexually transmitted disease, and if so whether this diagnosis occurred before or after they entered their first polyamorous relationship. Seventy-five percent stated that they had never been diagnosed with herpes, genital warts, HPV, trichomoniasis, gonorrhea, HIV, chlamydia, or syphilis. In comparing this finding with The Alan Guttmacher Institute's (1993) finding that one in four Americans will contract a sexually transmitted disease in their lifetime, it would appear that bisexual and polyamorous people are no more at risk for STDs than is the general population. In fact, for some of the STDs, such as HIV, herpes and trichomoniasis, the rate of occurrence in the bi-poly study sample was found to be significantly lower than the national adult prevalence rate for those diseases within the mainstream. Further, among the study participants who had been diagnosed with an STD, two-thirds noted that their diagnoses had occurred within the context of earlier monogamous relationships–prior to their beginning a polyamorous lifestyle.

As noted, this study is the first to specifically examine the experiences of bi-poly people. Hence, some of the questions were open-ended ones that called for participants' narratives. The aim was to bring forth a wide range of participants' experiences, rather than attempt to reduce those experiences into median aggregate trends. One such question was, "Do you know of any experiences which are unique to people who are both bisexual and polyamorous, that people who are straight/gay and polyamorous do not experience?" What follows are findings that have not been previously analyzed or reported.

A number of respondents listed specific benefits to being part of the bi-poly community. One is the opening of more relationship doors–there is a freedom in not needing to eliminate potential partner choices on the basis of their gender. There is also more freedom to speak openly about the full range of one's attractions and fantasies–both to one's existing partner and to new people who strike one's fancy. One respondent noted, "Some straight or gay men might be bothered that their partner wants to sleep with a woman–a bi man won't." Similarly, some straight and gay people feel uncomfortable when someone who isn't compatible with their own orientation develops a crush on them, and that is less likely to occur if a bi-poly person is the object of one's affections.

Another benefit is the ability to form relationship triads (quads, and so forth) of any gender combination. Many respondents described mixed-gender, multi-partner lovemaking as a transcendent experience, using such terms as "experiencing the power of yin and yang together." One respondent wrote: "Lying in love with friends of both sexes, sharing love between them . . . I found myself glad that I am what I am, so I could enjoy it to the fullest." Others noted that there is an ease that comes when all combinations are possible and it doesn't matter who touches whom during group lovemaking.

Some bisexual polyamorous people revel in the differences between the genders, while others revel in surpassing gender limitations. Statements from the former group include: "I enjoy getting to know the differences in how each gender makes love," "I can express different sides of myself with people of different genders," "I have the chance to learn from both sexes about the needs and desires of both sexes in love," and "I use different relationship strategies depending on the gender of the person that I am dating." In contrast, non-gender-emphasizing bi-poly people feel that: "There are not really masculine and feminine traits, but human traits," and "I can view any individual for the possibilities that they provide, rather than the limitations that they present."

Bisexuality can help to bridge the gap when one partner prefers polyamory and another prefers monogamy. If the polyamory-preferring partner is bisexual, then the compromise of *gender monogamy* is available. In *gender monogamy*, it is agreed that the polyamory-preferring partner won't date anyone else of the monogamy-preferring partner's gender. For instance, a straight female woman might give her bisexual male partner permission to experiment with other men, but not with other women.

Polyamory also allows bisexual people to be more visible as such. When a man is seen with his male partner, others assume that he is gay.

When a man is seen with his female partner, others assume that he is straight. However, if a man is known to have both a male partner and a female partner, fewer misassumptions will be made.

A number of trends were observed which, while not unique to the bi-poly community, are reportedly more prevalent therein. Respondents experienced a higher level of communication around relationship needs and boundaries in the bi-poly community than they did within the mainstream. The culture of the bi-poly community is one in which there is a lot of emphasis on processing and stating one's desires up front. Also reported was a strong sense of extended community–a wide kinship network of primary and secondary partnerships, within which exists a powerful support group.

Respondents also noted that within the bi-poly community there is a higher degree of acceptance for people's differences than there is within the mainstream. This includes acceptance for different body types and for different forms of sexual/gender expression, such as transgender preference and participation in BDSM. In fact, approximately 51% of the study respondents reported an interest in BDSM, which is substantial in comparison to the 5-10% prevalence of BDSM interest in the general population (The Kinsey Institute, 2001).

There are some negative experiences common to bi-poly people as well. One is the feeling of being doubly stigmatized, since *both* bisexual and polyamorous people are misperceived as "loose," "confused" and "unable to choose" by the mainstream. Some bi-poly people feel guilt at reinforcing the myth that "all bisexual people are polyamorous." In fact, only 54% of the bisexual people in Page's (2004) study reported a preference for polyamory.

Some bi-poly people simultaneously encounter prejudice from their gay friends about their other-gender partners and prejudice from their straight friends about their same-gender partners. This can be isolating. Another commonly encountered misperception is that the same-sex relationship is the less important one in the MMF or FFM triad. As one respondent noted, "People assume that the two women aren't romantic and that the primary interest is around the male–even if the women were together first."

Legal and biological gender inequities can also create imbalances in the bi-poly relationship. For instance, in a MMF triad, in most countries and states/provinces, there can only be a legal marriage between the woman and one of the men, not between the two men. This can cause resentment within the triad. There might also be resentment when the triad decides to have a baby and there comes the need to choose which of the men will impregnate the woman first.

COUNSELING POLYAMOROUS CLIENTS

Why Do Polyamorous Folks Seek Psychotherapy?

Most polyamorous people who seek therapy do so for reasons unrelated to polyamory. They are people who happen to be in polyamorous relationships, who wish to talk about the usual therapy concerns–anxiety, anger management, and so forth. The therapist's job is to simply welcome the client's diversity, and to assume that the client's polyamory is working well for them unless there's specific reason to think otherwise. Sometimes polyamorous people are happy with their lifestyle but seek guidance on how to manage it more smoothly. The therapist's role here is to assist them in articulating their needs, and to help partners negotiate their relationship agreements and process their experiences. Very occasionally, the therapist will encounter polyamorous clients who do not have the skills to manage polyamory in a healthy way, and for whom the attempt brings more pain than joy to their lives. It is reasonable to assess this, and to ask these clients to give serious thought to whether the benefits of polyamory outweigh their pain. Later in this paper, some signs of badly mismanaged polyamory will be identified.

Milestones in Polyamory, and Associated Growth Tasks

Coming out to oneself. There are many milestones along the path of polyamorous identity development. The first is the process of coming out to oneself about one's interest in a polyamorous lifestyle–similar to the coming out process that is experienced by bisexual, lesbian, transgender and gay people. There is a recognition that one's identity is changing along with one's romantic preferences, and that one's evolution is taking a different path from what the mainstream of society expects. There is often a search for a community of other polyamorous people, where similar ideals and compatible dating partners may be found.

The therapist can help the client to process their feelings about their changing identity. The client may be feeling excitement at the new pathways that are opening in their life, and the therapist may be among the first to hear and validate this joy. It is also possible that the client may feel shame at being different from what society expects. The therapist can help to normalize their orientation, by offering statistics about how prevalent polyamory is, and by suggesting books and Websites about polyamory.

Sometimes people who realize that they are polyamorous do so before they have ever met other polyamorous people. They may not know the word polyamory, or realize that there is a large polyamorous subculture. The therapist can help the newly identified poly client to locate resources such as local polyamory social groups or online mailing lists. Some people will embrace this; others may not yet feel ready to seek out this community. The therapist can help such clients to grow in that readiness, if desired.

Coming out to a partner. In an ideal world, when the newly identified polyamorous person was ready to start dating, they would seek lovers who were also polyamorous. But some people realize that they are polyamorously inclined when they are already involved in a monogamous relationship. So, a second milestone that some polyamorous folks experience is the stage of disclosing their preference for polyamory to their current partner.

Some people anticipate that their partner will be open-minded and not condemn their preference of polyamory, even if the desire is not a shared one. Others fear that their partner will be very angry with them for wanting to explore this–perhaps even to the point of leaving. As society often equates monogamy with emotional commitment, the partner may not understand how the poly-identified person could both love them and wish to share intimacy with someone else. So, the disclosure of one's preference for polyamory can itself be a risk. A therapist can help the newly poly-identified client to decide whether and how to share this information with their partner. Some people choose not to risk their partner's anger, turning away from their preferred lifestyle instead. Therapists can help clients to cope with the sense of grief and loss that this choice brings.

When the poly-identified person does disclose their preference to their partner, their next task is to cope with the response of their partner. This may involve anger, insecurity or blame. This is often a good time for couples therapy, to help the couple process their feelings and choose which next steps to take. Some partners are adamant that they will never embrace this lifestyle, and do not wish to hear about it any further. The poly-identified person must then make the wrenching choice between their preferred lifestyle and the partner whom they love dearly. The therapist can assist the client in processing whether to remain monogamous within the current relationship or whether to leave the relationship to pursue a polyamorous lifestyle.

Some partners are willing to learn more about polyamory even if they aren't sure that they could ever feel comfortable living that way. They are able to validate the poly-identified partner's desires, and they may agree to read some books on polyamory or talk to more people who are polyamorous, to get a broader sense of what polyamory is. They might not give the polyamorous person permission to date outside the relationship, but at least the polyamorous identity, interest, and fantasies need not be hidden from them.

Sometimes, the monogamously inclined partner will consider offering limited permissions to the polyamorously inclined partner. The polyamorous partner may be allowed to have liaisons when out of town on a business trip, or online sex with people who live far away. There may be a "don't ask, don't tell" rule that allows them to date someone else if they do so discreetly. If they are bisexual, a gender-monogamy agreement may be made. The therapist can help the couple to see if any such limited compromises are possible, and to negotiate the terms of such.

Partners' interests in polyamory. Sometimes the partner also becomes interested in pursuing a polyamorous lifestyle. Here begins the third milestone–negotiating the parameters of an open relationship. This phase is important whenever a new polyamorous relationship is forged, even for partners who all have prior experience with polyamory. Each person brings different desires, boundaries, and expectations to the relationship, and the therapist can help the clients to speak openly of their needs and cooperate in finding compromises.

A myriad of different choices must be made for each polyamorous relationship. The first is how slowly to take the process, based on each partner's comfort levels. Sometimes going slowly means that permission is only given at first to cuddle and kiss with others, rather than launching right into the full sexual spectrum. Sometimes there are limits on how often a new lover can be seen, such as once a month. Sometimes there is an agreement to first pursue a threesome, so that nobody feels left out. The therapist can help the partners to consider where their comfort levels lie as their exploration into polyamory progresses. They can also encourage the partners to agree in advance on what they would do if one partner wanted to resume monogamy after having tried polyamory.

The therapist can also help the couple to consider what type of relationship to have. Will there be a swinging relationship, where two couples meet every now and then to swap partners for a night? Will there be a primary-secondary model, in which the original couple retains primary partnership, or will it be a non-hierarchical arrangement, in which no distinctions are made as to which partner comes first? Is there a desire to ultimately have a poly-family, in which a few partners form a household all together?

Third, are new lovers subject to the approval of the existing partners? If so, the therapist can help the couple decide what is proper grounds for a veto. Some couples agree that vetoing must only occur when there is reason to believe that a new lover poses a specific threat to the relationship, and that mere insecurities ("She's so pretty! What if my partner thinks that she's better looking than I am?") aren't adequate reason to veto.

Specific categories of people are sometimes declared off-limits for dating, such as best friends or exes. Some gay people ask their bisexual primary partners to date only members of the same gender, so that heterosexual privilege does not enter their lives. Some people of color prefer that their partners only date those who are experienced with racial-ethnic minority group membership. The therapist can help the partners to discuss their experiences with prejudice and privilege as they navigate these decisions.

Fourth is the issue of scheduling. One's capacity to love may be infinite, but the number of open evenings in a week is not. How many nights in a week, how many weekends in a month, how many vacations is it okay for one's partner to take with their secondary? People vary widely in their time needs. The primary partners should feel secure in the amount of attention that they are giving to one another. Some primary partners schedule plentiful "date time" together before making plans with other lovers. It is also important to give secondary lovers a clear sense of how much time *they* can regularly expect. Two nights a week? One day per month? A second day per month if the time is spent in platonic activities while watching the kids?

How much will the partners socialize with each other's lovers? Do they wish to meet each other's lovers? Should a prospective lover be "brought home to meet the family" before intimacy is allowed to occur? Will the partners socialize frequently with each other's lovers, to grow familiarity and trust all around? It is often helpful for partners to be on friendly terms with each other's lovers, because a reserve of goodwill can be a lifesaving lubricant in the negotiation wheel at times when, say, one's primary partner's 45th birthday and one's secondary partner's med school graduation coincide.

Many partners have rules around sex. Foremost is the question of safer sex boundaries. Is latex to be used with all lovers? For penetrative sex only, or for oral sex as well? What kinds of STD tests are required of new lovers, and how often? What restrictions will be placed on sex if anyone does have an STD? What birth control methods will be used, and what will happen if a secondary lover becomes pregnant by (or inseminates) one of the primary partners? Sex can be hard for people to discuss, and the therapist can help the partners to work through any shame they may feel in discussing sex and STDs. The partners may also wish advice on how to assert their safer sex boundaries.

Sacredness of sexuality also comes into play. Some primary couples reserve specific sexual acts for themselves, such as body fluid monogamy (non-latex sex), penetrative sex or BDSM play. Some couples have rules about whether their bed can be used for sex with other lovers–for some people a bed is sacred space, whereas for others it's simply useful furniture. Some people will gallantly sleep on the couch when their primary partner is entertaining a lover in the bedroom overnight, whereas others don't wish to be anywhere in the vicinity when their primary partner is making love to another.

Further along physical privacy lines–some people love to hear the juicy details of their partners' soirees with a lover, while others have a strong desire Not To Know. And then there's the issue of public displays of affection. Is it okay to share a kiss with one's secondary lover in the presence of one's primary partner? There are no wrong or right answers to these questions–caring negotiation and compromise are key.

Another issue is the balancing of primary and secondary needs. Does a secondary lover have any rights in the relationship? Supposing that Wednesday nights are one's standing date night with one's secondary lover, but one's primary partner has a really bad day at work one Wednesday and needs care. Will the secondary lover be granted a different date night that week, to make up for the lost one? Likewise, if the secondary lover is sick and needs some caring for on a Tuesday, can they request this?

Secondary lovers sometimes set their own boundaries upon the relationship. Take the case of Yoshiko, Keisha, and Randall. Yoshiko and Keisha are primary partners, and Randall is Keisha's secondary lover. Randall has been without a primary partner for over a year, and he really wants to meet someone to settle down and have a family with. Keisha may ask of him that he look for partners within the polyamory community, so that their secondary relationship can continue once he finds a primary partner of his own. But Randall may be "poly-fluid" (able to be either polyamorous or monogamous), and he may wish to look for primary partners within a wider dating field. Keisha may have to accept the fact that she and Randall will no longer be lovers if he meets a prospective life partner who prefers monogamy. These are important parameters to discuss early on.

Secondary partners have needs of their own, especially when they do not have a primary partner themselves. Some enjoy living in an independent, bachelor style. Others feel lonely without a primary of their own, and wish that they could have more of their lover's time. The counselor can help the primary-less secondary partner to cope with some of these feelings, and to build emotionally sustaining community ties.

How "out" to be. A fourth milestone is deciding how "out" to be about one's polyamory to the non-polyamorous people in one's life. Many polyamorous people have been shunned for their lifestyle choices–by family, friends, workplace supervisors, teachers, and clergy. People have lost jobs and had their custody of their children challenged because they were polyamorous. The decision about whether to come out to any given person is based on many factors, such as the person's open-mindedness, their ability to keep the information private, the beliefs and laws of the community, and the risk factors involved in being out.

Some people prefer to be out, while others are more private. Partners may have different perceptions of the risks involved in being out. The therapist can help them to understand each other's needs, and to negotiate their boundaries of disclosure. The therapist can also help them to decide how and when they wish to come out to the people in their lives, and help them to cope with any rejection that they may receive.

When the partners are not out, some difficult decisions can arise. If Keisha's office has a picnic where partners are welcome, does she bring Yoshiko or Randall? At Keisha's graduation party, will Randall be introduced to the family as a lover or as a "friend"? If three partners raise a child together, do they tell the child not to mention the third parent to their teacher? If so, how do they help their child to reconcile the pride that the child feels in their family with the shame that this secrecy implies? The therapist can help the poly family to navigate the intense emotions that these situations can bring.

Including additional partners. The fifth milestone is the inclusion of additional partners in the primary bond. Not all polyamorous couples take this step–some are happy to remain primary only to each other, above all other partners. But sometimes three or four or more people fall in love together and form a family unit in which each of the dyadic relationships is equal in status. This type of bond brings new challenges and new decisions to make.

The family needs to decide whether to be a polyfidelitous family unit, or whether the partners may take other lovers. They also need to decide whether to move in together. It can be a challenge to find a big house in a neighborhood that doesn't have difficult zoning laws about how many unrelated adults can reside in a single unit. Next are issues about dividing the space. Will all of the adults sleep in one bed, and can a large enough bed be found? Who sleeps next to whom? How are privacy needs met? Or is there a preference for different combinations of partners and bedrooms on different nights? The therapist can help the partners negotiate this such that all partners' needs are met.

How will finances be handled? Will incomes be pooled, or kept separate? Are purchases made individually or by consensus? Do all adults pay equal shares of the expenses, or are shares proportionate to income, bedroom size, or chores contribution? Do partners with kids pay more household expenses? Are only the biological parents considered to be the child's parents, or all of the household adults? In case of a breakup, who will the children live with? How will financial and property resources be divided? It is vital for these agreements to be formalized prior to cohabitation.

While the partners considers themselves to be a family unit, the law does not. Hospitals may decline poly household members the right to visit their non-legal spouse or their non-biological/non-legally adopted child in intensive care. Health insurance companies won't insure one's second spouse, and some even ask same-sex domestic partners to state that they are monogamous in order to qualify for inclusion within family insurance plans (Barillas, 1997; Bricker, 2003). Third parents have no legally recognized child visitation rights in the event of a breakup, no matter how many years they have devoted to co-raising the child from infancy. A poly-friendly lawyer can assist the family in drawing up legal contracts regarding shared property and child-care authority.

Smaller issues also arise. On a car trip, which partner gets the front seat? If two partners want Indian food but the third wants Ethiopian for dinner, how do individual needs get balanced with group needs? Does one partner always defer to other people's wishes? Does another partner routinely take up more emotional space in a given situation? The therapist can help the partners to navigate some of the family-of-origin role issues that underlie these decisions, and to learn compromise and consensus skills.

When Might a Client Be Mismanaging Polyamory?

Most polyamorous people value their partners' safety and happiness, and work hard to consider everyone's feelings and needs. This can sometimes be a challenging balancing act, however. Here are some signs of "mismanaged polyamory" that the therapist can keep an eye out for, and (if noticed) help the client to navigate past.

A common pitfall is to get so caught up in New Relationship Energy that one forgets to pay romantic attention to one's existing partners. Sometimes this involves over-scheduling. Yoshiko may feel resentful if Keisha goes out with Randall 5 nights in one week. The therapist can help the partners to set more appropriate boundaries.

Sometimes quality of time, rather than quantity, is the issue. One often lives with one's primary partner and sees one's secondary partner outside of the home. This can create an imbalance of "carefree dates" with the secondary partner vs. after-work house-chores time with the primary partner. It is important that the primary partners also take a good number of date nights together, to enjoy fun or romance. One should also remember to do sweet little things regularly for one's primary partner–that suggestive little e-mail at lunchtime, a flower bought on the way home. The therapist can help the primary couple discover new ways of courting so as to increase their romantic energy.

A related pitfall is taking more lovers than one has time for. If one already has primary and secondary partners, then one needs to consider how much ongoing attention one can realistically offer the thrilling new person whom one met at the sci-fi convention. Yoshiko and Randall may not mind if Keisha sees Elizabeth once every month, but both may balk if Keisha wants to give Elizabeth one date night a week. Ideally, Keisha would talk about this with Elizabeth, so that Elizabeth didn't get hurt. "I'd love to go out with you once in a while–but, given my time commitments, I probably could only see you once a month." Therapists can help partners to agree on time boundaries.

Another common pitfall is to rush too quickly into polyamory. The reality of polyamory is more complicated than the theory. One may feel overwhelmed by the emotions that come up the first time that one's partner merely flirts with someone else. It is important to keep a firm finger on the pulse of one's comfort levels with each gradual step–the first attraction, the first kiss, the first time sleeping together, the first night away from home, the first long weekend trip together. Polyamory should be embarked on as a very slow process, and it is okay to pause at one stage before going further. A truism in the poly community is that one should go as slow as the most cautious partner is ready to go. Rushing the process will only lead to pain and feeling overwhelmed. Going slowly will help the partners to build trust, and this can help ready one to try subsequent stages. The therapist can help the partners to draw up a list of stages, and to periodically discuss how ready they feel to go to the next stage. The slower partner can be helped to examine his or her fears about going further. The faster partner can be helped to cope with their impatience at the pace and their regrets over missed opportunities.

Another common pitfall is the mistaken belief, "I shouldn't feel jealousy." Jealousy is normal to feel, and can be used as a touchstone for examining one's inner needs. Does one need a bit of extra snuggling? Reassurance of one's attractiveness? A thinking-of-you call when one's partner is out with their secondary? Therapists can teach partners how to express and soothe jealousy in constructive ways.

For example, Yoshiko may feel uncomfortable after seeing Keisha hold hands with Randall at a party. If Yoshiko isn't versed in assertiveness skills, she might hold her feelings in until they burst out in more dramatic fashion than she intended–"You've been with her all day, and haven't touched base with me once! Don't you care about me?" A more constructive way to express this would be to say calmly, "Hey, I'm feeling a bit lonesome right now. Would it be okay with you two if I borrowed Keisha back for 15 minutes of snuggle time? I promise I'll send her back right after that." Note the use of feelings and I-statements, and a reasonable request. Therapists can help partners to learn good communication skills such as these. They can also validate that feelings and needs are vital to share. Many people worry that they will be a burden to their partner if they ask for more time, attention, or reassurance. But most partners are happy to be asked, and prefer this to being resented by a partner whose needs haven't been met.

Another poly pitfall is the overuse of veto power. Is one partner vetoing each prospective lover that the other brings home? The therapist can help the partner to look at the root causes of their insecurity, and to figure out what reassurances are needed.

Triangulation is another potential pitfall. If Keisha has an issue with something that Yoshiko did, does she talk to Yoshiko directly, or does she only vent to Randall? Of even greater concern is the instance in which someone takes on a secondary relationship to compensate for the fact that their needs are not getting met in their primary relationship. When there is deep dissatisfaction in the primary relationship, then the primary partners need to give their relationship attention, through joint efforts to increase communication, intimacy and trust. The therapist can assist in this process.

A related trouble spot is when someone compares their primary relationship unfavorably to their newer secondary one, while failing to take into account that the demands on each relationship are different. Secondary relationships are often full of numinous spark, but they are spared the trials of having to live in close quarters with another person. Primary relationships are longer-standing. The relationship is valued for its depth, its trust, and its supportiveness, but it is not quite as shiny as it once was. The blush of first romance has often faded to friendly companionability. People who are new to polyamory sometimes note this contrast and wonder if their secondary partner might not be a better match for them. The therapist can help the partners to remember that the New Relationship Energy between secondaries will likely lessen over time, transforming into a relationship that is valued for its old dearness more so than for its luster–just like the primary relationship has. It is also important for the therapist to help the primary partners to rekindle sparks in their relationships on a regular basis, as mentioned earlier.

Other poly relationship dangers involve codependent habits. Some people have trouble saying "no," and fall into the habit of saying "yes" to whichever partner is in front of them. Suppose Yoshiko is adamant that Keisha not have unprotected oral sex with Randall, so as to reduce the risk of STDs. But Randall really wants to share oral sex with Keisha, and he mentions this frequently in bed. Keisha will need to say no to one of them, if a compromise cannot be found. She may feel tempted to have unprotected oral sex with Randall and not tell Yoshiko. Dishonesty is a sign that something is going seriously awry. The therapist can help Keisha to assert instead–to say no to Randall, or to negotiate different boundaries with Yoshiko. The therapist can also assist in finding creative compromises. If Randall agreed to be tested for STDs and to take no other partners for the time being, would Yoshiko allow Keisha and him to share unprotected oral sex then?

Sometimes a client has already been dishonest. A common scenario is this one: A new client comes in, who is in an ostensibly monogamous marriage–but the client has in fact been having an affair on the side. Recently, the client heard of polyamory, and the lifestyle appeals to them greatly. They want to know if the therapist can help them to convince their monogamous partner to enter into a polyamorous agreement, so that they don't have to give up the lover with whom they have been unfaithful.

The therapist may experience strong feelings about the client's deceit. They can express compassion for the client's desire to be close with both of their lovers, as well as for their grief at not having heard of the possibility of polyamory prior to entering into a monogamous relationship. The client must be told, however, that the odds are very much against their partner being willing to enter into polyamory after the affair has been revealed. The partner likely will feel deeply betrayed upon hearing of the affair, and if they don't break up with the client, they will likely want them to sever ties with the illicit lover. The client will have a steep road towards regaining their partner's trust. While there have been cases in which a betrayed partner does come to empathize with the client's desire for polyamory, and even rarer ones in which the partner agrees (after much trust-rebuilding) to try polyamory, this is not usually the outcome. The therapist can help the client to weigh their options, and to learn how to live honestly rather than deceptively.

Ending Polyamorous Relationships

Polyamorous relationships end for a number of reasons. Most often, they end for the same reasons that monogamous relationships end (Ramey, 1975; Rubin and Adams, 1986)–differing needs, falling out of love, and so forth. The partners may need extra support during this time, as they may feel shame that they weren't able to make the relationship work. Often a polyamorous person has been a "representative for polyamory" among their monogamous friends, and they may fear that their more skeptical friends will take the ending of their relationship as evidence that polyamory isn't a viable lifestyle. Of course, when a monogamous relationship ends, it is not typically interpreted as evidence that monogamy is not a viable lifestyle. Likewise, the ending of a polyamorous union does not signify that polyamory is unviable. The therapist can help the client to see through this double standard, and express it to their friends. The therapist can also help the client decide whether they would like to remain polyamorous in future relationships.

Polyamorous ex-partners are not limited to the usual options of "stay together or break up." There are times when primary partners realize that they no longer wish to focus the largest part of their energy on one another, but they still would like to remain emotionally and sexually a part of one another's lives. People in this situation sometimes take the middle ground approach of "de-intensifying" the relationship, wherein they transition from primary to secondary status in each other's lives. They still spend time together and value their long-standing bond, but their commitment to one another is less.

Sometimes a troubled primary couple decides to stay together, but to become monogamous once again. The therapist can help the couple to work through this decision, to grieve for any secondary relationships that ended due to this decision, and to feel okay with their choice to resume a monogamous lifestyle. The secondary lovers may also need support, as it can hurt deeply to be shut out of the primary partners' relationship sphere.

COUNSELOR CONSIDERATIONS

Therapists should consider how the setting and the structure of counseling will best accommodate the polyamorous individuals and families for whom they want to provide mental health services. Logistically, it is important that the office waiting area have enough chairs for the family to wait in prior to their session. Also, the members of a poly-family might all want to share the same large couch during therapy, just as a monogamous couple might want to sit close together during their session.

Length of session is also something to consider. Fifty minutes may be too short for a poly-family of three or more, since each partner needs a chance to weigh in on the issues. A longer session can also help the poly-family attend twice a month rather than weekly, to accommodate the partners' varying work schedules. Also, the partners might be coming to the session from work, rather than arriving together, and they may need to take some time at the beginning of the session to check in on how they all are doing.

Even with longer session times, there still may not be time in each session to give enough attention to all of the intra-family dynamics that may be at play. Sometimes an issue will involve the whole family; at other times, the issue is more a factor for a subset of the family. The therapist might be open to the possibility of different configurations of the poly-family being present at different sessions, as feels appropriate to each situation.

Where is the counselor's focus during sessions? Are one partner's needs getting more airtime than the others'? Do one partner's concerns fade into the background during each session? Is there a pull to take sides? Who does the counselor typically sit facing?

Ads and forms should be as welcoming as possible to polyamorous clientele. Polyamory can be listed among one's specialties. Poly-friendly language on intake forms encourages clients to disclose their orientations. "Name/s of partner/s" instead of "Name of spouse," is one possibility. Another is, "Check any of these identities that apply to you: Bisexual_ Lesbian _ Gay _ Transgender _ Heterosexual_ Polyamorous _ Leather _ Other _." A client who does not feel such a welcome may conceal their polyamorous orientation (Weber, 2002), decreasing the therapeutic effectiveness and rapport.

The counselor who sees polyamorous clients is often unique among her peers. Relatively few counselors have heard of polyamory, and fewer still have worked with polyamorous clients. Some colleagues will be eager to learn more. The poly-affirming counselor has the opportunity to be a leader among her peers, educating other therapists about how to work with poly clientele. Other colleagues may express prejudice against the concept of polyamory, and they may even express prejudice against the counselor who affirms the validity of the polyamorous lifestyle. Also, consultation groups in which the other professionals are polyamory-aware are hard to find.

In the Appendix, some resources are listed that can help polyamorous professionals network with one another. Also listed are some resources that provide further education about polyamory. It is vital for the poly-friendly therapist to take on as much education as possible about polyamory. This will not likely come from one's grad school or from continuing education courses, but rather from books, online forums, and including polyamorous people in one's own social networks. Consultations with other poly-friendly counselors can also augment the therapist's ability to serve their poly clientele.

Some poly-friendly counselors are polyamorous themselves. It is important for the polyamorous therapist to give careful consideration to small community issues as she pursues her own social life. Counselors may choose to discuss with their poly clients the possibility that they will run into each other at a poly event, and discuss how to navigate that possibility in a way that feels comfortable to both parties.

CONCLUSION

Information about the lifestyles and counseling needs of the polyamorous community has been presented here. Some readers may be interested in learning more, and may feel eager to welcome polyamorous clients to their practice. Other readers may feel conflicted about how polyamory fits in with religious admonishments towards monogamy, or with mainstream social mores. Some therapists worry that if polyamory became widely accepted, then their own monogamous partners may take an interest in it.

It is vitally important for counselors to examine their own attitudes towards polyamory and face any fears about it that they might have, before they begin to work with polyamorous clientele. Polyamorous clients will pick up on subtle cues of disapproval, and those will impact the quality of their counseling experience. There is no shame in referring a client on to a more experienced counselor, if one does not yet feel ready to support polyamorous clients in their lifestyle choices.

Therapists who work extensively with the bisexual community should be aware that they will almost certainly encounter some clients who live a polyamorous lifestyle, given the significant proportion of bisexual individuals in this population who prefer polyamory (Page, 2004). It is doubly important for counselors to work through their feelings about polyamory–perhaps via their own psychotherapy–and to pursue relevant training so as to be able to offer informed, affirming psychotherapy services to their bisexual polyamorous clientele.

REFERENCES

Alt.Polyamory Usenet Newsgroup (1997). *Alt.Polyamory Frequently Asked Questions (FAQ)*. Retrieved April 8, 2004, from http://www.faqs.org/faqs/polyamory/faq/

Barillas, C. (1997, April 29). Tucson passes benefits law for gay city workers. *The Data Lounge*. Retrieved April 8, 2004, from http://www.datalounge.com/datalounge/news/record.html?record=1994

Blasband, D., & Peplau, L. A. (1985). Sexual exclusivity versus openness in gay male couples. *Journal of Sexual Behavior, 14*(5). 395-412.

Bricker, L. (2003, March 21). Town insurance plans to cover domestic partners. *The Rockingham News*. Retrieved April 8, 2004, from *www.seacoastonline.com/2003news/rock/03212003/news/19004.htm*

Blumstein, P., & Schwartz, P. (1983). *American couples*. New York: Morrow.

Cloud, J. (1999). Henry & Mary & Janet & . . . *Time Magazine, 154*(20), 90-91.

Decker, J. (1999). *Poly Friendly Professionals*. Retrieved June 13, 2004, from http://www.polychromatic.com/pfp/

Derogatis, L. R. (1983). *SCLR-90-R administration, scoring, and procedures manual-II*. Towson, MD: Clinical Psychometric Research.

Dixon, J. K. (1985). Sexuality and relationship changes in married females following the commencement of bisexual activity. In F. Klein and T. J. Wolf (Eds.), *Two lives to lead: Bisexuality in men and women* (pp. 115-133). New York: Harrington Park.

Ellis, A. (1965). *The Case for Sexual Liberty* (Vol. I). Aurora, NY: Seymour Press.

Gough, H. G. (1957) *California Psychological Inventory.* Consulting Psychologists Press.

Hymer, S. M., & Rubin, A. M. (1982). Alternative lifestyle clients: Therapists' attitudes and clinical experiences. *Small Group Behavior, 13*(4), 532-541.

Kassoff, E. (1989). Nonmonogamy in the lesbian community. *Women & Therapy, 8*(1-2), 167-182.

Keener, M. C. (2004). *A Phenomenology of Polyamorous Persons.* Unpublished Master's Thesis, The University of Utah, Salt Lake City. Retrieved April 8, 2004, from *http://www.xmission.com/~mkeener/draft_224.pdf*

Knapp, J. J. (1975). Some non-monogamous marriage styles and related attitudes and practices of marriage counselors. *The Family Coordinator, 24*(4), 505-514.

Knapp, J. J. (1976). An exploratory study of seventeen sexually open marriages. *The Journal of Sex Research, 12*(3), 206-219.

Kurdek, L.A., & Schmitt, J. P. (1986). Relationship quality of gay men in closed or open relationships. *Journal of Homosexuality, 12*(2), 85-99.

Labriola, K. (1999). Models of open relationships. In M. Munson & J. Stelboum, (Eds.), *The lesbian polyamory reader: Open relationships, non-monogamy, and casual sex* (pp. 217-225). Binghamton, NY: Harrington Park Press.

Labriola, K. (1996). *Unmasking the green-eyed monster: Managing jealousy in open relationships.* Retrieved April 8, 2004, from *http://www.cat-and-dragon.com/stef/Poly/Labriola/jealousy.html*

Makanjuola, R. O. A. (1987). The Nigerian psychiatric patient and his family. *International Journal of Family Psychiatry, 8*(4), 363-373.

McWhirter, D. P., & Mattison, A. M. (1984). *The male couple: How relationships develop.* Englewood Cliffs, NJ: Prentice Hall.

Page, E. H., (2004). Mental health services experiences of bisexual women and bisexual men: An empirical study. *The Journal of Bisexuality. 3*, 3/4, 137-160.

Peplau, L. A. (1981) Research on homosexual couples: An overview. *Journal of Homosexuality, 8*(2), 3-8.

Polyamory Society. (1997). *Polyamory Society Compersion Index.* Retrieved April 8, 2004, from http://www.polyamorysociety.org/compersion.html

Ramey, J. W. (1975). Intimate groups and networks: Frequent consequence of sexually open marriage. *The Family Coordinator, 24*(4), 515-530.

Rubin, A. M. (1982). Sexually open versus sexually exclusive marriage: A comparison of dyadic adjustment. *Alternative Lifestyles, 5*(2), 101-106.

Rubin, A. M., & Adams, J. R. (1986). Outcomes of sexually open marriages. *The Journal of Sex Research, 22*(3), 311-319.

Rust, P. C. (1996). Monogamy and polyamory: Relationship issues for bisexuals. In B. A. Firestein (Ed.), *Bisexuality: The psychology and politics of an invisible minority* (pp. 127-148). Thousand Oaks, CA: Sage.

Spanier, G. B. (1976). Measuring dyadic adjustment: New scales for assessing the quality of marriage and similar dyads. *Journal of Marriage and the Family, 38*, 15-28.

Spring, J. A. (1997). *After the affair: Healing the pain and rebuilding trust when a partner has been unfaithful.* New York: Perennial Currents.

Sumpter, S. F. (1991). Myths/realities of bisexuality. In L. Hutchins & L. Kaahumanu, (Eds.), *Bi any other name: Bisexual people speak out* (pp. 12-13). Boston: Alyson.

SwingerDater.com (November 20th, 2003). *A Brief History of swinging: Having a firsthand knowledge.* Retrieved June 13th, 2004, from http://www.swingdater. com/c/thread/id/8.html

The Kinsey Institute (June 27th, 2001). *Frequently Asked Sexuality Questions to The Kinsey Institute.* Retrieved May 20, 2005, from *http://www.indiana.edu/~kinsey/ resources/FAQ.html#bdsm*

Weber, A. (2002). Who are we? And other interesting impressions. *Loving More Magazine, 30,* 4-6.

Weitzman, G. (1999, March). *What psychology professionals should know about polyamory: The lifestyles and mental health concerns of polyamorous individuals.* Paper presented at the 8th Annual Diversity Conference, Albany, NY. Retrieved April 8, 2004, from *http://www.polyamory.org/~joe/polypaper.htm*

Weitzman, G. (in press). Counseling bisexuals in polyamorous relationships. In B. A. Firestein (Ed.), *Becoming visible: Counseling bisexuals across the lifespan.* New York: Columbia University Press.

West, C. (1996). *Lesbian polyfidelity.* San Francisco: Bootlegger.

APPENDIX
POLYAMORY RESOURCES

Psychotherapy and Polyamory

1. What Psychology Professionals Should Know About Polyamory: The Lifestyles and Mental Health Concerns of Polyamorous Individuals By Geri D. Weitzman, Ph.D., *http://www.polyamory.org/~joe/ polypaper.htm*
2. The Psych-Polyamory Mailing List–For poly-friendly mental health practitioners. To subscribe, send a blank e-mail to *psych-polyamory-subscribe@yahoogroups.com*
3. The Poly-Friendly Professionals Directory: *http://www.polychromatic. com/pfp/*

Books on Polyamory

1. Dossie Easton & Catherine A. Liszt. (1998). *The ethical slut: A guide to infinite sexual possibilities.* San Francisco: Greenery Press.
2. Deborah M. Anapol (1997). *Polyamory: The new love without limits: Secrets of sustainable intimate relationships.* San Rafael, CA: Intinet Resource Center.
3. Celeste West. (1996). *Lesbian polyfidelity.* San Francisco: Bootlegger Publishing.

4.   Marcia Munson and Judith P. Stelboum (Eds). (1999). *The lesbian polyamory reader*. New York: Haworth Press.
5.   Ryam Nearing (1992). *Loving more: The polyfidelity primer*. Boulder, CO: Loving More.

Websites on Polyamory

1.   *http://www.polyamory.org*–A Website of useful Poly 101 info
2.   *http://www.lovemore.com*–Another Website of useful Poly 101 info
3.   *http://www.openweave.org/NCPoly/PolyTerms.html*–Polyamory terms and concepts
4.   *http://www.faqs.org/faqs/polyamory/faq/*–Frequently asked questions on polyamory
5.   *http://www.faqs.org/faqs/polyamory/faq-supplement/*–Poly Pitfalls
6.   *http://www.ourlittlequad.com*–Our Little Quad: Polyamory for the Practical
7.   *http://www.cat-and-dragon.com/stef/Poly/Labriola/jealousy.html*–Coping with jealousy.

Polyamory Mailing Lists

1.   The Loving More poly discussion lists–*http://www.techmesa.com/cgi-bin/lyris.pl*
2.   poly@polyamory.org–A national poly list. *http://poly.polyamory.org/mailman/listinfo/poly*
3.   Usenet Newsgroup *alt.polyamory (see http://www.polyamory.org above)*
4.   Yahoo group PolyMono–for monogamous people with polyamorously inclined partners. Send a blank e-mail to *PolyMono-subscribe@yahoogroups.com*
5.   Yahoo group CPNPolyMono–for poly folks who have monogamously inclined partners. Send a blank e-mail to *cpnpolymono-subscribe@yahoogroups.com*

Developing Successful Sexual Health and Support Services for Bisexual People: Lessons Learned from the BiHealth Program

Julie Ebin
Aimee Van Wagenen

doi:10.1300/J159v06n01_09

[Haworth co-indexing entry note]: "Developing Successful Sexual Health and Support Services for Bisexual People: Lessons Learned from the BiHealth Program." Ebin, Julie, and Aimee Van Wagenen. Co-published simultaneously in *Journal of Bisexuality* (Harrington Park Press, an imprint of The Haworth Press, Inc.) Vol. 6, No. 1/2, 2006, pp. 165-189; and: *Affirmative Psychotherapy with Bisexual Women and Bisexual Men* (ed: Ronald C. Fox) Harrington Park Press, an imprint of The Haworth Press, Inc., 2006, pp. 165-189. Single or multiple copies of this article are available for a fee from The Haworth Document Delivery Service [1-800-HAWORTH, 9:00 a.m. - 5:00 p.m. (EST). E-mail address: docdelivery@haworthpress.com].

SUMMARY. In the last decade and a half in the Boston metropolitan area, community-based approaches have developed to meet the range of mental and general health support needs of bisexual people. We will chronicle some of this history and describe the web of programs and services available in Boston, focusing in particular on the BiHealth program at Fenway Community Health. We believe that BiHealth has been successful at serving bisexual people because of its unique approach to addressing bisexual behavior and identity. This approach is to carefully distinguish and take into consideration sexual behavior, on the one hand, and sexual identity, on the other, and to address them separately or in tandem, as appropriate. This approach includes recognizing and addressing different sub-groups of bisexual people, including self-identified bisexual people, non-identified bisexual people, and bi-curious people in particular. Here we describe the unique broad-based approaches to medical and mental health that BiHealth offers and we consider the importance of linkages to community, grassroots activism, and resources in addressing both bisexual behavior and identity. In conclusion, we offer lessons learned that we hope others will find useful in developing programs in other places for self-identified bisexual, non-identified bisexual and/or bi-curious people. *[Article copies available for a fee from The Haworth Document Delivery Service: 1-800-HAWORTH. E-mail address: <docdelivery@haworthpress.com> Website: <http://www. HaworthPress.com> © 2006 by The Haworth Press, Inc. All rights reserved.]*

KEYWORDS. Bisexuality, bisexual women, bisexual men, bisexual identity, polyamory, sexual behavior, sexual health, HIV/AIDS, HIV prevention, HIV education, HIV outreach, peer education, Boston area

AN INTRODUCTION TO BIHEALTH

Self-identified bisexual people, people who have sexual experiences and/or relationships with people of more than one gender and do not identify as bisexual ("non-identified bisexual people"), and people who are attracted to and may be considering sexual experiences with people of more than one gender ("bi-curious people"), are all people potentially at risk for HIV and STD infection (Boulton, Hart, & Fitzpatrick, 1992; Earl, 1990; Goldbaum, Perdue, & Wolitski, 1998; Rila, 1996; Stokes, Taywaditep, Vanable, & McKirnan, 1996; Ziemba-Davis, Sanders, & Reinisch, 1996). People who fall into these three groups also have distinct medical and mental health needs. While many prevention educators, medical and mental health providers are coming to recognize and respond to the needs of clients who fit into these groups, bisexual people collectively face sexual and mental health risks and are still not sufficiently reached.

Traditional approaches to health for bisexual people in any of these groups often target either sexual health or mental health, identity or behavior alone, as with HIV-prevention programs that target gay-focused audiences or heterosexual audiences alone, or as with coming out therapy groups that only can address the needs of people who identify as bisexual or who are willing to engage with others in questioning their sexual identity (Gómez, Garcia, Kegebein, Shade, & Hernandez, 1996; Lawrence & Queen, 2001). Neither of these approaches alone adequately addresses the diverse needs of bisexual people, nor are they avenues for bisexuals to obtain relevant information and support particularly suited to–or even aware of–their distinct needs.

Although the focus of the BiHealth program is on sexual health, these concerns are addressed through a variety of BiHealth's networks to other programs. Currently, BiHealth's services include a volunteer outreach crew called "The Safer Sex Education Team," safer sex education trainings for that volunteer team, two support groups: one for bi and bi-curious men and one for polyamory peer support. There was previously a queer women's polyamory peer support group which has since spun off from BiHealth. It also includes HIV/STD risk reduction counseling, phone counseling for bi and bi-curious individuals, provider education on bi-inclusivity in the provision of services, and design and production of educational materials and brochures around safer sex and bisexuality.

In addition, BiHealth addresses the medical and mental health needs of bisexual people by being of and for the community. It connects to several community-based organizations and, as such, supports and contributes to a wide community net of support, mental health, HIV prevention, and primary care services. For example, referral to mental health services is a crucial part of our offerings to clients. When clients make use of BiHealth services, we are able to refer them to the other mental health services available at Fenway Community Health Center, the larger organization of which BiHealth is a part, and to other alternatives through Fenway's therapy referral resources. Below we will outline the program's evolution and will go on to discuss many of BiHealth's specific services and connections to community, as well as the lessons we've learned working with BiHealth. Central amongst these lessons are the importance of welcoming the diversity of sexual orientations, gender identities and stages of identity development amongst our volunteers and clients and the importance of addressing sexual identity and sexual behavior distinctly, when appropriate, and in tandem, when appropriate.

NOTES ON TERMINOLOGY

For the purposes of the discussion that follows, we have come up with some working terminology to describe the people that we group under the larger umbrella term *bisexual*. There is extraordinary diversity among bisexual people regarding their sexual behavior and relationships, sexual orientation self-identification, and the processes by which they come to choose whether or not to self-identify as bisexual (Fox, 1996; Lever, Rogers, Carson, Kanouse, & Hertz, 1992; McKirnan, Stokes, Doll, & Burzette, 1995; Rust, 1992, 2000). To try and capture just a slice of this diversity, we talk in this essay about three groups of bisexual people that we find particularly important for addressing the lessons we have learned from BiHealth.

The first of these groups is defined in terms of identity–we call this group "self-identified bisexual people." People in this group may or may not have sex or relationships with people of more than one gender; presumably most of them have sexual attraction to people of more than one gender, although sometimes people make choices around sexual identity for reasons other than attraction.

The second group is defined in relation to both identity and behavior–we call this group "non-identified bisexual people." People in this group do have sex and/or intimate relationships with people of more than one gender, but for any number of reasons, do not identify as bisexual; attraction to people of more than one gender may or may not be present for non-identified bisexual people. Sometimes people refer to this group as "behaviorally bisexual." We have avoided this term here because it can exoticize and misrepresent bisexuality and bisexual people by equating bisexuality with sexual practice. We find a double standard follows the term "behaviorally bisexual" in that one would generally not talk about "behaviorally heterosexual" or "behaviorally gay" people.

The third group of people is defined in relation to attraction–we call this group "bi-curious people." Bi-curious people are attracted to and may be considering sexual experiences or relationships with people of more than one gender. They may also be considering the adoption of a bisexual identity, but for any number of reasons, this is not always the case. We have encountered bi-curious people that we here include in the universe of bisexual people who prefer not to categorize their sexuality by adopting the identity label "bisexual."

Our terminology is problematic in many ways. One is that these are not discrete categories. Some people use the term "bi-curious" as an identity label for themselves. Some people respond to the term in advertising, for example, but have in fact had sexual relationships with, and not simply attractions to, people of more than one gender. We maintain the bi-curious grouping despite the inability to completely distinguish it from the other two groupings because it captures an important group of people not captured in the other two. Similarly, people may be attracted to people of more than one gender and not have had intimate relationships or sexual experiences with people of multiple (or any) genders, yet may identify as bisexual, bi-curious, or not identify themselves.

Another difficulty with these terms is that the labels are sometimes only valid descriptions for limited periods of time. People sometimes transition between the groups or out of them all together. Language can seem to present reality and identity as fixed and unchanging and this does not capture the range of experiences of bisexual people (nor of straight, gay, or lesbian people, for that matter). In using this terminology, we recognize the incompleteness of the categories. The terms we use highlight some experiences and leave others out, yet we use these groupings for our purposes here because we feel they reflect a reality for many of the people who we encounter in our work with BiHealth.

PLAYING SAFE WITH BOTH TEAMS: THE ORIGIN OF BIHEALTH

The roots of the BiHealth program are in a 1999 conference called "Playing Safe with Both Teams: Bisexuality and HIV Prevention" (BiHealth, 1999). This one-day conference for HIV service providers and other health professionals was organized by Marshall Miller (who later became the program director for BiHealth) and was co-sponsored by Fenway Community Health's Living Well program and the Bisexual Resource Center. Miller sought to increase visibility, awareness, and knowledge among service providers about their self-identified bisexual clients and non-identified bisexual clients. Alongside health service providers, bisexual community members, groups, and activists participated in the conference, learning–but primarily teaching–about HIV prevention and bisexuality from their points of view.

The conference was novel and at BiHealth we know of no other conference of this kind having taken place to date. It was also a great success, with a turnout of over 100 people. Most importantly (at least for this story) the Massachusetts Department of Public Health took notice. This eventually resulted in the creation of and funding for the BiHealth program at Fenway Community Health.

The BiHealth program began with a series of community meetings in which people brainstormed about the health issues facing the bisexual community and about how best to address them. As with the Playing Safe with Both Teams conference, folks at BiHealth looked to integrate and connect community members into the program. Community need, combined with funding, support, and encouragement from the Department of Public Health, drove forward the program's HIV prevention outreach and education efforts.

BiHealth created the Safer Sex Educator Team, an outreach program staffed almost entirely by volunteers, and found early and sustained success in recruiting and maintaining a volunteer corps of peer outreach educators. This includes people who are themselves members of or who identify with the gay, lesbian, bisexual and transgender (GLBT) community, people who are themselves curious or questioning, and people who care about and are interested in issues of bisexuality, HIV prevention and health. BiHealth brings these folks in for a training on safer sex and issues of bisexuality. Some don't go on to participate in the formal outreach program, but they do leave having learned something about safer sex, different kinds of STDs, or sexual identity and behavior, and many go on to be informal educators to their friends and acquaintances. Others, like the authors of this essay, do go on to participate and to become a part of the Educator Team. Julie Ebin started volunteering with BiHealth as an educator and outreacher and now serves as the Program Manager for BiHealth. Aimee Van Wagenen also started as an outreacher and is now a team leader–a type of mentor-volunteer–with the Safer Sex Educator Team, BiHealth's outreach program.

A LESSON LEARNED:
SEPARATING ATTRACTION, BEHAVIOR, AND IDENTITY

A very crucial but simple lesson that we have learned from BiHealth has profound effects when incorporated into practice. This lesson is the necessity of separating attraction, behavior, and identity in our language and understanding of bisexual people's sexual orientation. BiHealth taught both of us this lesson early, when we first encountered the program during out respective trainings to become safer sex educators.

Julie looks back to her first training. She describes first learning about distinguishing attraction, behavior and identity in her thinking and her personal philosophy:

> Marshall Miller, the facilitator, started off by explaining a framework that he'd found helpful for thinking about sexual orientation, including the differences between attraction, behavior or experience, and identity. Attraction was obvious–as Marshall put it, "who you get your tingles from." Behavior was also fairly obvious: who someone has kissed, or had sex with, or been in a relationship with, etc. His explanation of identity clarified an idea that I had not thought of on its own before: the words you use to describe yourself. These three areas, he said, are all components of a person's sexual orientation. The interesting point for me, however, was that these three components might all be in alignment or they might not. So a woman might have attractions that have been roughly 30% to men, 70% to women, but her sexual experiences and relationships may have been solely with men. She might or might not identify as bisexual. She might even identify as lesbian. I had never thought of attraction, behavior, and identity as distinct and possibly even separate.

In training volunteers to become part of our team, BiHealth draws upon the work of bisexual activist-educators in teaching about the distinction between attraction, behavior and identity. Trainees are introduced to scales developed by Bobbi Keppel and Alan Hamilton (1988) that map these three different components. The Sexual and Affectional Orientation and Identity Scales (SAOIS), expand on the Klein Sexual Orientation Grid (Klein, 1993). The scales bring the complexity of these three interrelated concepts home graphically and allow for the expansion of the concept "attraction" into different types of attractions or preferences–sexual, emotional, social and lifestyle (Keppel & Hamilton, 1998).

Of course, these scales do not provide perfect models. One drawback in particular is that they do not do justice to transgender identity in relation to many of these categories because they do not take into account the possibility of gender change of the subject. With the inclusion of diverse participants at BiHealth trainings and programs, however, the limitations of the models are exposed, acknowledged and discussed in fruitful dialogue. For example, Julie recalls a dialogue initiated by a participant in her first training who identified as an intersex person–someone who is born with *a reproductive or sexual anatomy that doesn't fit the typical definitions of female or male* and is usually "assigned" to one gender at birth. This participant spoke of his experience as an intersex person who had originally been assigned as female. He spoke about how he had always been primarily attracted to women and continued to be, so that when he had identified as a woman he would have been on the "homosexual" side of the scale, but now that he identified as a man he would be on the "heterosexual" side of the scale. The label of "heterosexual," however, didn't really capture the truth of his sexual and gender identity. His experience adds a further complexity to the concepts of the SAOIS scales, but the basic lesson still applies–for many people, the dimensions of attraction, relationships or behavior, and identity vary from one another.

At BiHealth, distinguishing between sexual attraction, behavior, and identity is a central principle guiding the development, design, and practice of HIV prevention services. As simple as this lesson is, it is a surprisingly important lesson to learn and to keep learning. People very commonly blur the two distinct concepts of behavior and identity. We often hear people use and understand common sexual identity terms (gay, lesbian, straight) as words that describe the gender of a person and the corresponding gender of his or her sexual partner(s). In this common usage, sexual identity is employed as a shorthand for sexual acts (and for relationships)–"gay" refers to two men having anal or oral sex and "straight" refers to sexual behavior between a man and a woman. In fact, in the previous examples, all of the people involved could identify as bisexual. This shorthand is used in everyday conversation and, too often, by those of us providing health services both in conversations with each other and ones with clients. But sexual behavior and sexual identity are not terms of equivalence; one cannot stand in for the other. Very often, sexual identity is a poor predictor for past, current, or future sexual behavior.

Being aware of the principle of separating behavior and identity is essential in doing HIV prevention targeting the universe of people (Goldbaum et al., 1998; Gómez et al., 1996; Lawrence & Queen, 2001; Rila, 1996; Stokes et al., 1996). Based on our experience at BiHealth, we also think this is a principle that that should be central to all HIV prevention, sexual health, and support services. This is because while one program may focus its services on bisexual people, another may focus its services on gay/lesbian people, and a third may focus services on straight people, all three programs will encounter clients who engage in same-gender sexual behavior, clients who engage in different-gender sexual behavior, as well as clients who engage in both. These clients who engage in both same-gender and different-gender sexual behavior, regardless of which (if any) programs they access, are all part of the universe of bisexual people, yet they may present themselves in different ways. They may think of themselves as bi-curious, but they may not. They may think of themselves as confused about their sexual identity, but they may not. They may identify as bisexual consistently or intermittently. They may remain as non-identified bisexual people.

The lesson here is that services for gay and lesbian people and services for straight people are also services for people who are bisexual. Our work with BiHealth has proved that the inverse is true too–services for bisexual people are also services for people who are straight and gay and lesbian. The HIV prevention services BiHealth offers are inclusive and applicable to people of diverse sexual identities and behaviors. In some ways, this is simply out of a practical necessity. Because bisexual behavior encompasses a diversity of sexual pairings (male-male sex, female-female sex, male-female sex, trans-male sex, trans-trans sex, and trans-female sex), BiHealth's HIV prevention curriculum includes the kinds of sex that most everyone (gay, lesbian, straight, bisexual, and/or transgender) has, including sex seldom spoken of or seen as taboo, such as women having anal sex or at times mention of sex involving BDSM (bondage/discipline, domination/submission, and/or sado-masochism).

Furthermore, because BiHealth doesn't always provide services in exclusively or even predominately bisexual-identified spaces (these spaces are few and far between), the diversity of clients that BiHealth encounters demands an inclusive approach to providing HIV prevention services. Similarly, because mental health and support services rarely are able to cater to exclusively or predominantly bisexually identified individuals, it is important to be open to and to provide support for same- and other-gender attractions and relationships regardless of the stipulated or assumed identity of the program's or practice's clients.

COMMUNITY, SEXUAL IDENTITY, AND SEXUAL HEALTH

Does this discussion on separating behavior, identity, and attraction mean that we think sexual health and support services should forget about sexual identity and only deal with clients in terms of their sexual behavior? For several reasons, we think that sexual identity has a central place in support services that help clients as they experience deep struggles around their sexual identities. Dealing with clients only in terms of behavior would not meet their emotional, mental health, social or political needs.

We think there are other reasons not to abandon sexual identity in providing sexual health and support services, even when the services are for HIV prevention, where it is sexual behavior and not identified sexual orientation that directly puts people at risk for contracting HIV (Goldbaum et al., 1998; Gómez et al., 1996). Because sexual identity is a major way that people understand, organize, and make meaningful their sexual lives and relationships, HIV prevention programs must be attentive to sexual identity. This is true for providers of other mental health, primary care, and support services as well. Programs and their staff must be "culturally competent," and sexual identity issues are a key part of the culture for any given group, particularly for sexual minorities–and even more so for bisexual people, whether bisexually self-identified or non-identified.

Further, sexual identity can place people in relationship to community and to a sense of community (Donaldson, 1995; Fox, 1996; Hutchins, 1996; Rust, 1992, 1996; Udis-Kessler, 1992). This is important because community context can play a significant role in promoting HIV prevention attitudes and behaviors. We can think of a number of ways that sexual identity places people in relationship to community. It places people in relation to a *geographic community* in spaces where they live, work, eat, go dancing, and have sex. Sexual identity places people in relation to *community resources* by providing ways to get news and buy books, to access health services, and to find networks for socializing and organizing. Sexual identity also places people in a *community of consumption* in providing outlets for purchasing goods and services, and in offering types of products and brands that people buy. In an abstract way, sexual identity can also connect people to a sense of *community identity*. This is important for HIV prevention because if people identify and connect with a community, research shows that they are more likely to practice safer sex (Boulton & Fitzpatrick, 1993).

Attention to bisexual identity and community has practical implications for providing HIV prevention services. Since bisexual people often feel marginalized, validating their identity by talking about bisexuality and safer sex together may be more useful in getting them to learn about safer sex than by talking about behaviors alone. Using the word "bisexuality" in the context of safer sex helps to send the message that bisexual people can find here the relevant information that they need, and can help bring people in to learn about safer sex who might not otherwise feel that a "gay and lesbian safer sex" demonstration or a "reproductive health" demonstration would serve their needs.

At BiHealth, we feel HIV prevention should be sensitive to and inclusive of sexual identity concerns. It should include and connect people in relation to community–this can mean doing outreach in those geographic spaces of community. It can mean advertising in, connecting people to, and becoming a part of community resources and networks, and it can even mean connecting with and connecting people to a community of consumption! For example, BiHealth has trained workers from local sexuality boutiques in safer sex. BiHealth also sometimes refers clients to sex toy stores and bookstores (when they ask where they can buy the free supplies that we offer), as well as to other community spaces and resources that also happen to be places of consumption (like bars, bookstores, health services). We feel that HIV prevention that is sensitive to and inclusive of identity concerns can foster community in the abstract sense: learning about safer sex within a bisexual context can help bisexually identified, bi-curious, and/or questioning people to feel part of a community, and thus also make them more likely to practice safer sex and to feel like they have more emotional support.

FROM THEORY TO PRACTICE: IDENTITY, BEHAVIOR, AND BIHEALTH'S SERVICES

The Bi and Bi-Curious Men's Support Group

One of the key BiHealth services that targets by identity and identity-related concerns is the Bi and Bi-Curious Men's Group. Men with bi and bi-curious identity issues here have their own space to discuss and get support for these concerns, as well as for their behaviors and for safer sex. This group draws a different population of men who have sex with men than those who we would draw by just targeting by behavior, by gay identity, or through the gay community alone. This is therefore effective at reaching a population underserved by resources that target in those other ways.

The group is a space where the theoretical notion that the distinction between behavior and identity matters is born out. Identity and behavior are discussed and/or addressed, sometimes separately and sometimes together. This support group, co-sponsored by the Bisexual Resource Center, meets monthly and typically draws about 5-10 bi- and bi-curious-identified men of diverse racial, age, and class backgrounds for a facilitated discussion around the men's experiences of sexuality, sex, relationships and dating, identity, safer sex, and some of the broader life transitions that they are facing.

One rather simple way that BiHealth works with the need to address concerns of behavior and concerns of identity with the Men's Group is in the terminology we use in advertising and postings to recruit members to the group. Using the term *bi-curious* in advertising and postings in place of, and sometimes in addition to, the more fixed identity term *bisexual* draws men to the group who do not (and may never) adopt the identity and label of bisexual for themselves. This one term, bi-curious, taken from the language of adult services and personal ads, is inclusive of individuals across a range of sexual behavior and identification.

Marshall Miller, the former program director and jack-of-all-trades, served as facilitator or back-up facilitator of the Men's Group for a number of years. He talked to Aimee about the success of using the term bi-curious:

> When advertising, using the term *bi-curious* is a great way to get people in the door. For many men, the process of questioning their sexual orientation begins with fantasizing about other men–it's not an identity at that point, just a desire. The best term they have to describe this desire is bi-curious, a term that you see all over personal ads and adult Internet sites. They go looking for 'bi-curious' and they find our ad for the support group and give us a call. That one word has been amazingly effective at getting people to come in and receive HIV prevention education who otherwise might never come through our doors. (Personal communication, October 17, 2003)

Ads and postings for the Men's Group have appeared in many outlets at different times: in a variety of Web and e-mail postings directed to gay/lesbian/bisexual/transgender (GLBT) groups; on the Fenway Community Health, Bisexual Resource Center and other community calendars; in the local gay newspapers; and in the "Adult Services" classified section of a local free weekly paper. Posting to a range of outlets as well as to outlets beyond the established GLBT community is also essential in attracting a diversity of men to the group.

By using the term *bi-curious*, and by advertising in a broad range of outlets, the Men's Group succeeds in attracting men with a diversity of sexual identifications, relationship and behavioral experiences. The group includes men who are bisexually identified and happy with how they identify, but who come to the group in search of community and connection in Boston–a new residence for many of the men in this category. The Men's Group also draws men, some currently or formerly gay-identified, who have some experience and connection with the GLBT community, but who are undergoing some identity struggles, or who are looking to take the next step in reckoning with their identities, in talking with the friends and partners, or in further coming out. Lastly, the Men's Group includes men who have just begun to think about what their sexual desire means for them. For most of the men in this last category, the Men's Group is their very first step into the GLBT community and into any gay or bisexual-identified space.

The Men's Group connects men to the bisexual community by introducing them to a sense of community, to bisexual-specific community resources (like the Bisexual Resource Center), and to GLBT community resources. The goal of the group is not to get the men to join the community, to adopt a bisexual or gay identity, or to come out as bisexual or gay, though this is a goal for some members of the group. For many men, the group helps them in their process of figuring out who they are. It gives them an opportunity to meet other men who share an attraction to people of more than one gender, and it gives them language and comfort in talking to friends and partners about their identity, their desires, and safer sex. Many men leave the group feeling less isolated and better about themselves. This boost in self-esteem in turn can lead to greater honesty in the men's lives–with themselves and with their intimate partners. Marshall Miller comments, "For some men, the group is about fostering the courage to tell more people in their lives about their attractions, whether it's their friends, family, or especially their partners" (Personal communication, October 17, 2003).

For BiHealth, the group is an opportunity to introduce or reinforce safer sex and related negotiation skills for male-male and male-female sexual practices. Some groups of men for whom this is particularly important are: men who may be new to sexual relationships with people of one gender or another; men who do not identify as gay and so may not seek out or feel comfortable with the support that the gay community provides for men who have sex with other men; and men who are in primary relationships with a female partner and having sex with other men sometimes with and sometimes without her knowledge and consent.

Also important for BiHealth is that the Men's Group links men to a bisexual and broader GLBT community. In attending a meeting, some men set foot into a GLBT health center for the first time. They get information about and referrals to GLBT organizations and resources. Marshall Miller indicates that:

> The biggest referral is to bisexual community groups. They realize the Bisexual Resource Center exists and might attend a social event or two. Some will become activists and educators themselves, and members of the Bisexual Resource Center board of directors. Powerful social change can happen through community building, and the Bi-Curious Men's group is one of the front doors to the community. (Personal communication, October 17, 2003)

Phone Counseling

Advertising about the Bi and Bi-Curious Men's Group has several benefits in addition to letting men of all sexual orientations know about the Men's Group. For one, it puts bisexuality as a concept on the public radar screen in both straight and gay contexts. A second, more practical one, is that a few times per month someone will call the contact number from BiHealth's ad for the Men's Group looking for support around bisexual identity questions. Occasionally phone calls come from folks who have been referred to the group from elsewhere in the health center or from those who have found contact information on BiHealth's Website. More often, however, people have found the number from ads and postings for the Men's Group.

In this way, the ads for the group act as a gateway for phone counseling. Even though many folks only call with concerns about whether the Men's Group is for them or not, BiHealth staff are often able to talk with them about a host of other issues and, importantly, to connect them to resources. Staff talk with people about sexual identity and attraction, safer sex, support services, and the kinds of resources available to them. They are able to explain what the Bi Men's Group is like in more detail, and also to tell folks about the mixed-gender support and social groups at the Bisexual Resource Center (BRC). Sometimes women call as well, through word of mouth, our website, or the link on the BRC's Website. Usually people just want to talk to a human and be reassured that the groups are appropriate, safe places for whatever issue they are concerned about. Occasionally they are not ready for the group or cannot make it to an evening group and are looking for something more one-on-one.

Julie, who often takes these calls, usually tries to engage callers in conversation about safer sex concerns (this is BiHealth's primary mission), and then refers them to any appropriate support services. These include not only the groups mentioned earlier, but also other support groups: two peer-run polyamory groups-one a mixed gender support group at Fenway and the other a BiHealth spin off social group for queer women that meets at a local cafe–as well as a women's coming out group at the Women's Center in Cambridge. Other Fenway referrals include: individual and group mental health counseling; LGBT-competent primary care; HIV counseling and testing services; HIV-related groups including one for newly diagnosed folks and one for partners of HIV+ people; the Violence Recovery Project, as well as the GLBT Helpline and Peer Listening Line (two hotlines). Lastly, staff can refer callers to outside support services and information resources. The most common are bisexuality resources such as the Bisexual Resource Center and its Website that links to book, movie, music, conference and calendar listings; these include listings for its social organization, Biversity. Also popular are polyamory resources such as the local groups PolyBoston and Family Tree.

After a phone counseling call, if the caller feels comfortable leaving an address, we will send them out a packet of bisexuality and safer sex resources, including: pamphlets from the Bisexual Resource Center; BiHealth's own pamphlet entitled "Safer Sex for Bisexuals and Their Partners" (Miller et al., 2001); a flyer for HIV testing at Fenway; other bisexuality, safer sex and/or community resource information; and, depending on their interest, various safer sex supplies, including condoms, lube, dental dams, and/or Reality condoms. If they do not feel comfortable leaving an address we will offer to put together a packet for them to pick up. At certain periods the program has been able to buy bulk copies of the Bisexual Resource Guide to give out–with the added bonus of being able to support sales of the book.

Because so many of the calls come from people who are not part of the bi or even the gay community, often the phone calls are people's first contact with a bisexual-positive resource. Even though the "Safer Sex for Bisexuals and Their Partners" brochure and the Bisexual Resource Center's brochures and calendar are available via the World Wide Web, many of the men do not know about these resources, do not have access to the Internet, or worry that by accessing the information through the Internet that their sexual attractions might be found out by family members or, if on public computers, others nearby. Thus phone counseling and the resource distribution follow up has been a great way to get people the services that they might not otherwise know about, know where to seek out, or have access to.

Outreach and Volunteer Trainings

HIV and STD prevention outreach remains a big part of BiHealth's program focus. The Safer Sex Educator Team, staffed for the most part by volunteer educators, docs outreach primarily in bars and clubs, handing out safer sex supplies and engaging people in conversations about safer sex. The volunteer model has made BiHealth's Safer Sex Educator Team one of the most successful outreach programs in Massachusetts and it continues to receive financial support from the Massachusetts Department of Public Health. Over the course of the Safer Sex Educator Team's history, the Department of Public Health shifted funding priorities and asked BiHealth to focus its services on men who have sex with men–a group that includes gay men as well as bisexual men–who epidemiologically speaking are a population with the highest rates of new HIV infections in the US (Centers for Disease Control and Prevention, 2003). Despite this shift, we have not changed our attention to and concern with addressing sexual identity and behavior, separately when appropriate and in tandem, when appropriate. Although this program shift has meant less of a specific focus on bisexual identity, it has proven that BiHealth's bisexually inclusive approaches to outreach and prevention are also good approaches for engaging a wide variety of people at risk.

One of BiHealth's successful strategies is to continue to recruit safer sex educators in an inclusive way. Diversity at BiHealth means welcoming people of many sexual and gender orientations; importantly, it also means welcoming people at many stages of sexual and gender identity development. Below Julie remembers the diversity of her initial training's participants–diversity here is discussed in terms of sexual orientation, but also gender identity, occupational background and orientation towards monogamy and sexual expression in relationships:

> The woman next to me identified as lesbian, but she was about to start a job as an HIV testing counselor and wanted to be able to better understand and serve her bisexual clients. There was someone affiliated with the leather and BDSM communities who was out to her boss. There were a few people there who said that they

were polyamorous–a term that our trainer and facilitator, Marshall Miller, needed to define for me and others on a giant notepad on the wall as literally "having many loves" or "practicing open and honest non-monogamy." There were several bisexual activists who were closely affiliated with the Bisexual Resource Center.

There was someone who was a sex activist who had expertise in sex with, as she put it, "people of size." There was someone who explained that he was an intersex person which was a state and identity that I had never heard of before. There were two men who either were currently or had previously been married to women but now were exploring their feelings toward men. There was an EMT worker who wanted to understand and help his friends who identified as lesbian but had sex with men.

The Safer Sex Educator Team is a group made up of diverse sexual and gender identities, and we have found this diversity to be effective not only in helping our volunteers learn from each other, but also in doing outreach. Sometimes a gay man is comfortable talking with another man about condoms and lube. Sometimes, however, he is more comfortable talking with a woman about these topics either because he knows that he doesn't have to worry about sexual tension with her, or for a variety of other reasons.

Another approach is that BiHealth continues to train our volunteers to not make assumptions about identity and behavior and to be inclusive in the use of terms and anatomy. For example, trainings encourage volunteers to do outreach about safer sex by talking about specific sexual behaviors, the particular body parts involved, and the kinds of safer sex aids that they can use, rather that about safer sex in more general terms. This approach doesn't make assumptions about identity and behavior, and it is inclusive of all gender identifications–everyone can practice safer sex regardless of whatever kind of sex they are engaging in (or are wanting to engage in), and regardless of whether they are bisexual, transgender, gay, lesbian, a non-gay-or-bisexual-identified man who has sex with men, bi-curious, questioning, intersex, pansexual, same-gender-loving, or even straight.

BiHealth is able to continue to affect a broad audience through its trainings, which are opportunities to help potential volunteers increase their knowledge about safer sex, HIV and STDs, as well as to give them an opportunity to talk with others about sex, sexuality, diverse sexual and gender identities, and sexual risk-taking, including reflecting on their own orientations and sexual risk-taking behavior. It is a safer sex intervention as well as a kind of sexual activism. In a culture that often has a puritanical attitude and approach to sexuality, this is a supportive and new opportunity for many. The volunteer trainings are similar today to the trainings that Julie and Aimee attended, although BiHealth continues to update them and include innovation.

Sexual Diversity Panel

One early development of the Safer Sex Educator Team trainings that has become a fixture is the Sexual Diversity Panel. This panel powerfully exposes volunteers-to-be to a range of sexual orientations, behaviors, attitudes towards safer sex, and (mis)attempts at safer sex. The panel functions to ensure that diversity in sexual orientation and gender identity is represented in trainings, but it also brings a diversity of experiences around sexual risk-taking behavior, sexual practices and preferences, and philosophies about relationships. Five to six people speak at this Diversity Panel for about five minutes each about their sexual identities and past experiences with safer and unsafe sex.

The panel in the past has included transgendered people; people who identify as bisexual, pansexual, omnisexual, gay; people who identified as polyamorous and people who had long term polyamorous relationships; people who identified as kinky and people affiliated with BDSM; people who attend sex parties, people who engage in anonymous sex and people who engage in sex in public spaces; people who have HIV and people who have other STDs; and people who have been sex workers.

Sexual Diversity Panelists open up their lives to training participants in discussing their identifications and sexual behaviors. The talk about behaviors they are proud of and behaviors they regret and provide context for some of their less than safer sex decisions and invite questions. The panel challenges training participants' assumptions regarding identity, sexuality, behavior and appearance. It also challenges our volunteers to recognize that even those who present themselves as "in the know" about sexual identity and safer sex don't always live up in practice to the ways they present themselves.

Safer Sex Education in the Field: An Example

The lessons that we have learned at BiHealth and that we try to teach to our volunteers–that behavior and identity are separate, if intertwined, elements of clients' sexual and intimate lives and cannot be conflated and that assumptions based on appearance regarding sexual and gender identity and behavior will often be wrong–get put into practice in the doing of outreach in the field. Below, Aimee talks about the lessons that she took from her training from the Sexual Diversity Panel and elsewhere and about checking assumptions in her outreach practice:

> As conversations with clients develop and they divulge aspects of their sexual lives, my assumptions are constantly challenged and continuously proven wrong. The Diversity Panel helped me to always assume that my assumptions are very likely wrong–at least about one (and often more) of the characteristics of the client I'm speaking with–his or her gender, anatomy, sexual identity, or the gender of his or her past, present, and future sexual partners. For me and for my work doing outreach, this recognition means that I do not know what safer sex practices to promote and to educate any one client about. In practice, this means opening conversations with clients by talking about barriers and STD risks in the abstract and by talking with every client about different kinds of sex–oral, anal, and vaginal. As clients ask questions (or when I ask questions of them) and disclose elements of their sexual lives, I then move away from abstraction to talk about what they want to know about safer sex for themselves and their partners.

In trying to practice the distinction between behavior and identity in outreach, we have found that a demonstration of the Reality condom (or female condom) is a great conversation starter, particularly with male-appearing clients (an assumption, for certain!). While most people have seen and are familiar with the male condom, many people have never seen a female condom. Because of this unfamiliarity with the female condom, many people are interested in seeing, touching, and watching a quick demonstration of how to use one–that is, we don't tend to have to twist people's arms to get them to take a minute for our demonstration. In doing a demonstration, we can explain how the condom is used for vaginal sex and how it used for anal sex. In doing so, we may still make incorrect assumptions. A man we are speaking with may not have sex with women and so the vaginal sex demonstration may not be relevant. Or a man we are speaking with may have exclusively vaginal sex with women and so the anal sex demonstration may be irrelevant. He may have exclusively oral sex so that neither demonstration is relevant, or we may be mistaken in assuming that he has a penis or that the sex that he has involves a penis. But the demonstration doesn't tend to alienate anyone because clients tend to be interested in seeing how the female condom works and it often leads clients to ask questions about how they might personally use it or about other kinds of barriers that they can use.

Importantly, demonstrating the Reality condom with a male client allows us to talk about both male-male sex and male-female sex. This can and often does serve as a signal to a client that because we have recognized that he may be having sex with men, women or both that he can be comfortable in talking to us about whatever kind of sex he is having (or hoping to have!). It can be a signal to them that we are open to talking with them about whatever kind of sex they are having–oral, anal, and/or vaginal–and that we are not labeling or judging them for it. Educators can use this inclusive approach with all of their supply demonstrations, as many of the supplies, e.g., lube, dental dams, and condoms, are relevant to different kinds of sex involving varied gender pairings.

CONCLUSION

The lessons that we've learned from BiHealth are lessons that we think may be helpful to others designing or implementing sexual risk reduction, support, and mental health service programs for self-identified bisexual, non-identified bisexual, or bi-curious clients. In our experience, they're also fruitful lessons in providing services to just about anybody. We don't imagine that the lessons we've learned can be a roadmap to providing sexual risk reduction, support, and mental health services everywhere, but we do think there are several practical principles of benefit to many programs.

Fundamental among these is to put into practice the distinction between behavior, identity, and attraction in providing services to clients. This means not making assumptions about sexual behaviors/relationships or attractions based on what you know about your clients' identities and not making assumptions about your clients' identities or attractions based on what you know about their sexual behavior/relationships. This includes not giving clients a label, but rather letting them choose one or not for themselves. It also means remembering that even if your practice or programs aren't specifically for bisexuals, you're likely to encounter bisexually identified, bi-curious, and non-identified bisexual clients.

Another important and related principle is to present as options inclusive language and materials that encompass both identity issues and sexual behaviors. Some examples include: mentioning the terms bisexual and bi-curious in discussing identity as an alternative to gay or lesbian; using the same labels in advertising and outreach; having bisexual-specific materials in your office (such as our brochure "Safer Sex for Bisexuals and their Partners"); and having non-specific bi-inclusive materials for those who may not identify as bisexual (such as our brochure "Safer Sex," which is inclusive of safer sex with people of more than one gender but not bisexual-specific).

A second lesson that we encourage people to take away from our program is the importance of connecting clients to a sense of community. Crucial to this is providing both bisexual identity-focused space as well as having space that is bi-friendly but welcoming of people of all sexual orientations and identities. The first is important because there are very few places where the unique issues related to bisexuality can be addressed among peers–in particular people who have similar experiences and/or feelings–and the validation that that provides. On the other hand, having an approach like that of BiHealth's current incarnation–one that is welcoming of bisexual people yet also includes people of a wide variety of sexual orientations and gender identities–is important both for bisexual acceptance and integration into broader BGLT and mainstream communities, as well as for creating inclusive space for non-bisexual folks. Whether fostering bisexual-specific space or bi-welcoming space, sexual health and other support services must be sensitive and inclusive of bisexual identity concerns in reinforcing and connecting clients to community. The connection to community validates bisexuality and improves bisexual health–sexual, mental, and emotional.

Another lesson that we've learned is that practicing the distinction between identity and behavior with clients requires intervention and education with program staff and volunteers. BiHealth's volunteer trainings introduce this distinction to some and reinforce it for others. BiHealth also recruits staff and volunteers from a diversity of sexual and gender orientations at a diversity of stages in gender and identity development. This practice powerfully reinforces messages to all of us about the need to practice the distinction between behavior and identity and creates a working environment where holding assumptions in check is an everyday necessity. Recruiting from a diversity of sexual and gender orientations also means the program connects to, supports, and grows from a number of communities.

The connection of our programs or service provision to community is the final lesson learned. BiHealth's connection to community resources, groups, and activism provides the program, its staff and volunteers, with the strength and resiliency that comes from grassroots efforts. It also allows us the ability to provide pathways to community to our clients. When we're able to both be part of and to connect clients to community spaces and resources, we're able to begin the work of social change necessary to validate all aspects and states of bisexuality: as an identity, as having fantasies about or attractions to people of more than one gender, as a range of sexual experiences and relationships, or as a wide variety of combinations of these three areas that make up people's individual experiences of bisexuality.

REFERENCES

BiHealth Program at Fenway Community Health. (1999, June 21). *Playing safe with both teams: Bisexuality and HIV prevention.* (Conference transcript). Retrieved April 20, 2005 from http://biresource.org/bothteams/index.html

Boulton, M., & Fitzpatrick, R. (1993). The public and personal meanings of bisexuality in the context of AIDS. *Advances in Medical Sociology, 3,* 77-100.

Boulton, M., Hart, G., & Fitzpatrick, R. (1992). The sexual behaviour of bisexual men in relation to HIV transmission. *AIDS Care, 4*(2), 165-175.

Centers for Disease Control and Prevention. (2003). *HIV/AIDS Surveillance Report* (Vol. 14). Retrieved January 10, 2005 from http://www.cdc.gov/hiv/stats/ hasr1402.htm.

Donaldson, S. (1995). The bisexual movement's beginnings in the 70s: A personal retrospective. In N. Tucker (Ed.), *Bisexual politics: Theories, queeries, and visions* (pp. 31-46). New York: Harrington Park Press.

Earl, W. L. (1990). Married men and same sex activity: A field study on HIV risk among men who do not identify as gay or bisexual. *Journal of Sex and Marital Therapy, 16*(4), 251-257.

Fox, R. C. (1996). Bisexuality in perspective: A review of theory and research. In B. A. Firestein (Ed.), *Bisexuality: The psychology and politics of an invisible minority* (pp. 3-50). Newbury Park, CA: Sage Publications.

Goldbaum, G., Perdue, T., & Wolitski, R. (1998). Differences in risk behavior and sources of AIDS information among gay, bisexual, and straight-identified men who have sex with men. *AIDS & Behavior, 2*(1), 13-21.

Gómez, C. A., Garcia, D. R., Kegebein, V. J., Shade, S. B., & Hernandez, S. R. (1996). Sexual identity versus sexual behavior: Implications for HIV prevention strategies for women who have sex with women. *Women's Health: Research on Gender, Behavior, and Policy, 2*(1/2), 91-110.

Hutchins, L. (1996). Bisexuality: Politics and community. In B. A. Firestein (Ed.), *Bisexuality: The psychology and politics of an invisible minority* (pp. 240-259). Newbury Park, CA: Sage Publications.

Keppel, B., & Hamilton, A. (1998). *Using the Klein Scale to teach about sexual orientation.* Boston: Bisexual Resource Center. Retrieved January 10, 2005 from: http://www.biresource.org/pamphlets/klein_graph.html.

Klein, F. (1993). *The bisexual option* (2nd ed.). New York: Haworth Press.

Lawrence, R. M., & Queen, C. (2001). Bisexuals help create the standards for safer sex: San Francisco, 1981-1987. *Journal of Bisexuality, 1*(1), 145-162.

Lever, J., Rogers, W. H., Carson, S., Kanouse, D. E., & Hertz, R. (1992). Behavior patterns and sexual identity of bisexual males. *Journal of Sex Research, 29*(2), 141-167.

McKirnan, D. J., Stokes, J. P., Doll, L., & Burzette, R. G. (1995). Bisexually active men: Social characteristics and sexual behavior. *Journal of Sex Research, 32*(1), 65-76.

Miller, M., Chvany, P., Cohen, D., Hamilton, A., Mohns, E., Ruthstrom, E., Sheehy, L., & Solot, D. (2001). Safer sex for bisexuals and their partners. *BiHealth Program at Fenway Community Health.* Retrieved April 20, 2005 from *http://www.fenwayhealth. org/services/wellness/bihealth.htm*

Rila, M. (1996). Bisexual women and the AIDS crisis. In B. A. Firestein (Ed.), *Bisexuality: The psychology and politics of an invisible minority* (pp. 169-184). Newbury Park, CA: Sage Publications.

Rust, P. (1992). The politics of sexual identity: Sexual attraction and behavior among lesbian and bisexual women. *Social Problems, 39*(4), 366-386.

Rust, P. C. (1996). Finding a sexual identity and community: Therapeutic implications and cultural assumptions in scientific models of coming out. In E. D. Rothblum, & L. A. Bond (Eds.), *Preventing heterosexism and homophobia* (pp. 87-123). Thousand Oaks, CA: Sage.

Rust, P. C. R. (2000). Review of statistical findings about bisexual behavior, feelings, and identities. In *Bisexuality in the United States: A Social Science Reader* (pp. 129-184). New York: Columbia University Press.

Stokes, J. P., Taywaditep, K., Vanable, P., & McKirnan, D. J. (1996). Bisexual men, sexual behavior, & HIV/AIDS. In B. A. Firestein (Ed.), *Bisexuality: The psychology & politics of an invisible minority* (pp. 149-168). Thousand Oaks, CA: Sage.

Udis-Kessler, A. (1995). Identity/politics: A history of the bisexual movement. In N. Tucker (Ed.), *Bisexual politics: Theories, queeries, and visions* (pp. 17-30). New York: Harrington Park Press.

Ziemba-Davis, M., Sanders, S. S., & Reinisch, J. M. (1996). Lesbians' sexual interactions with men: Behavioral bisexuality & risk for sexually transmitted disease (STD) & Human Immunodeficiency Virus (HIV). *Women's Health: Research on Gender, Behavior, & Policy, 2*(1/2), 61-74.

SELECTED ONLINE RESOURCES

BiHealth Program at Fenway Community Health, Boston
    http://www.fenwayhealth.org/services/wellness/bihealth.htm
Bisexual Resource Center, Boston
    www.biresource.org
Biversity Boston
    http://www.biresource.org/biversity
Boston Bisexual Women's Network
    http://biresource.org/bbwn

Family Tree
  ftree.contra.org
FC Female Condom (or Reality Condom) Product Information
  http://www.mayerlabs.com/consumer/products/fcfemalecondom.asp
PolyBoston
  polyboston.org

Index

Affirmative psychotherapy. *See also*
    Psychotherapy
  about, 53-55
  with African American bisexuals,
    74-75
  for bisexual transgender people, 53
  with bisexual women and bisexual
    men, 6-9
African American bisexuals. *See also*
    Bisexual people
  about, 67-69
  deconstruction of hegemonic forms
    of femininity and masculinity
    and, 74
  hegemonic identity systems and,
    69-72
  labeling and, 67-68
  promoting well-being through
    integrative therapy for, 76-79
  providing affirmative therapy for,
    74-75
  social capital and, 69
  well-being and, 69
American Psychological Association,
    5-6
Authenticity, jargon of, 70,72

Bi and Bi-Curious Men's Group, at
    Fenway Community Health,
    176-179
Bi-curious people, defined, 169-170
BiHealth program (Fenway
    Community Health)
  about, 167-169
  Bi and Bi-Curious Men's Group,
    176-179

example of safer sex education in
    field of, 183-185
origins of, 170-171
phone counseling and, 179-181
prevention outreach and, 181
Safer Sex Educator Team of,
    181-183
separating attraction, behavior, and
    identity in language at,
    171-174
Sexual Diversity Panel, 183
sexual identity and support services
    at, 174-176
terms used to identify bisexuals at,
    169-170
training volunteers and, 172-173
volunteer training and, 181-182
Biphobia, acknowledging, 23
Bisexual-heterosexual couples. *See*
    Mixed-orientation couples
Bisexual identity
  assumptions made on basis of, 56
  coming out and, 31-33
  multiple identities and, 70
Bisexuality
  affirmative approaches to, 3-4
  cultural diversity and, 37-40
  defined, 30-31
  invisibility and, 56
  negative attitudes toward, 4,42
  pathologizing, 73-74
  perspectives of, 29-30
  polyamory and, 144-148
  relationships and, 33-35
  shifts in perspective in psychology
    and, 3-6
  types of, 56

BOOK ORDER FORM!

Order a copy of this book with this form or online at:
http://www.HaworthPress.com/store/product.asp?sku= 5835

Affirmative Psychotherapy
with Bisexual Women and Bisexual Men

—— in softbound at $19.95 ISBN-13: 978-1-56023-299-5 / ISBN-10: 1-56023-299-4.
—— in hardbound at $37.95 ISBN-13: 978-1-56023-298-8 / ISBN-10: 1-56023-298-6.

COST OF BOOKS _____

POSTAGE & HANDLING _____
US: $4.00 for first book & $1.50
for each additional book
Outside US: $5.00 for first book
& $2.00 for each additional book.

SUBTOTAL _____

In Canada: add 7% GST. _____

STATE TAX _____
CA, IL, IN, MN, NJ, NY, OH, PA & SD residents
please add appropriate local sales tax.

FINAL TOTAL _____
If paying in Canadian funds, convert
using the current exchange rate,
UNESCO coupons welcome.

❑ BILL ME LATER:
Bill-me option is good on US/Canada/
Mexico orders only; not good to jobbers,
wholesalers, or subscription agencies.

❑ Signature _____

❑ Payment Enclosed: $_____

❑ PLEASE CHARGE TO MY CREDIT CARD:

❑ Visa ❑ MasterCard ❑ AmEx ❑ Discover
❑ Diner's Club ❑ Eurocard ❑ JCB

Account #_____

Exp Date_____

Signature_____
(Prices in US dollars and subject to change without notice.)

PLEASE PRINT ALL INFORMATION OR ATTACH YOUR BUSINESS CARD
Name
Address
City   State/Province   Zip/Postal Code
Country
Tel   Fax
E-Mail

May we use your e-mail address for confirmations and other types of information? ❑Yes ❑No We appreciate receiving
your e-mail address. Haworth would like to e-mail special discount offers to you, as a preferred customer.
We will never share, rent, or exchange your e-mail address. We regard such actions as an invasion of your privacy.

Order from your **local bookstore** or directly from
The Haworth Press, Inc. 10 Alice Street, Binghamton, New York 13904-1580 • USA
Call our toll-free number (1-800-429-6784) / Outside US/Canada: (607) 722-5857
Fax: 1-800-895-0582 / Outside US/Canada: (607) 771-0012
E-mail your order to us: orders@HaworthPress.com

For orders outside US and Canada, you may wish to order through your local
sales representative, distributor, or bookseller.
For information, see http://HaworthPress.com/distributors

(Discounts are available for individual orders in US and Canada only, not booksellers/distributors.)

Please photocopy this form for your personal use.
www.HaworthPress.com

BOF06